WHILE I RUN THIS RACE

Book design and publishing services by **Combustoica**, a prose project of About Comics. www.COMBUSTOICA.com

WHILE I RUN THIS RACE

A Memoir

Pocahontas Gertler

*To Gene,
my beloved husband, my hero, my very best
friend.*

*To my amazing blended family.
You fill my heart with joy and have
taught me so much about the power
of unconditional love and acceptance.*

*In memory of
Mario & Joshua*

Guide My Feet While I Run This Race
(African American Spiritual)

Guide my feet while I run this race.
Guide my feet while I run this race.
Guide my feet while I run this race,
for I don't want to run this race in vain!

Hold my hand while I run this race.
Hold my hand while I run this race.
Hold my hand while I run this race,
for I don't want to run this race in vain!

Stand by me while I run this race.
Stand by me while I run this race.
Stand by me while I run this race,
for I don't want to run this race in vain!

I'm your child while I run this race.
I'm your child while I run this race.
I'm your child while I run this race,
for I don't want to run this race in vain!

Search my heart while I run this race.
Search my heart while I run this race.
Search my heart while I run this race,
for I don't want to run this race in vain!

Guide my feet while I run this race.
Guide my feet while I run this race.
Guide my feet while I run this race,
for I don't want to run this race in vain!

WHILE I RUN THIS RACE

Who among us has ever truly unraveled the great mystery of life? Wise men and fools have all had their turn at it with treatises, sermons, fables, metaphors, similes and more in an effort to capture the essence of what life is and how to live it with purpose, meaning, fulfillment and success. Life has been described as many things, including a journey, a test, an adventure, a puzzle, a three ring circus and even as a box of chocolates by Forrest Gump.

I leave it to minds much greater and much more intellectual, philosophical and spiritual than mine to wrestle with these complex comparisons and similarities and to debate their accuracy. Through the years and sometimes from day to day, one description seems more appealing to me than some of the others. A race is often cited as a metaphor for life. Today, that imagery resonates deeply with me, perhaps because I know that I am approaching the finish line, at least I am much closer to it than I used to be.

The African American spiritual, "Guide My Feet While I Run This Race" has always served to remind me to seek the guidance of the Creator in all things so that indeed I do not run this race in vain. It has been said that life is a marathon, not a sprint. I have had to learn to pace myself, to persist and to endure; to develop strategies, to keep going, to avoid false starts, to stay the course, to always do my personal best and to keep my eyes on the prize.

It is also said that the race is not to the swift but to those who endure to the end. Though the wording is not exact, the thought has a Biblical basis and any number of passages in the Scriptures encourage us to endure, to remain faithful to God that we might win the race; that we might capture the victor's cup or be awarded the crown in triumph and humility.

Even as children, we learn the moral of Aesop's fable of the tortoise and the hare. We are told not to give up, not to quit because the slow and steady pace wins in the end.

I have run this race for more than seven decades and although I'm not as fast as I once was, I am still plodding along. I have competed against many adversaries including poverty, ignorance, illness, abuse, persecution, sexism, bigotry, intolerance and racism.

Clearing each hurdle and defeating each opponent served to make me stronger and more determined to keep on running toward peace, justice, harmony, wholeness, unity and love for all humanity. My life is my marathon, my fervent prayer of gratitude to the Creator.

May He continue to "guide my feet while I run this race".

PREFACE

I write this not as a word for word, true and accurate account of my life but rather as snapshots that capture the essence of some of the pivotal people and events as I remember them more than three quarters of a century later. Thus I will allow myself the latitude of changing some names and places to protect both the innocent and the guilty while keeping my story authentic and relating it with integrity and with far more truth than fiction.

Terminology and ethnic designations that would have been considered proper and acceptable in the historical context of the day may well be deemed politically incorrect or even insulting and demeaning in modern times. I use these terms as they applied to the time period in which they were commonly used.

African Americans were referred to as colored people and as Negroes in polite society, as opposed to the demeaning terminology and ethnic slurs often hurled by racists or used by others steeped in ignorance and bigotry. Native Americans were generally referred to as Indians or by tribal affiliation but there were those who freely used epithets like savages, heathens or redskins when addressing or alluding to American Indian people. Native people were sometimes categorized as "colored" especially those who intermarried with Negroes.

Recollections of my very earliest experiences were obviously conveyed to me by others but my own memories soon intersected the telling and retelling of the second-hand stories and the combined interpretations became a very personal part of my own psyche and saga.

I write, therefore, for my own enjoyment and satisfaction with the hope that someday, my descendants and others may read and discover some new and interesting insight or information about their predecessor, Pocahontas Little Dove Gertler. Could it be that some sin confessed or some blunder made might serve to deter others from a similar fate? Perhaps some bit of wit or wisdom, perchance some act of courage or kindness related here, might help to guide and inspire or engage and amuse those who come after.

The relating of more recent events will doubtless be less flawed by lapses of memory or by faulty recall. It is my hope that with age has come deeper insights revealing the crux of many lessons learned and evidence of growth achieved through the varied experiences along life's journey.

The good, the bad, the beautiful, the ugly and the mundane have all served to make me who I am. In the words of an old gospel song, "I wouldn't take nothin' for my journey now".

INTRODUCTION

The voices of the dead were silent as my grandmother and I walked along the path just outside Laurel Grove Cemetery. The grass was freshly mowed and offensive weeds and brush were neatly sheared. Clearly, the white folks had the means, the resources and the will to provide a fitting resting place for their dead, contrary to those who operated the segregated cemetery located in the part of town designated for non-whites. Its unkempt, overgrown plots strewn with weeds and with mostly unmarked graves were a study in contrast to the pristine setting of the white cemetery.

The black wrought iron gates marking the entrance to Laurel Grove Cemetery were closed and locked but we could see inside quite clearly through the bars. In thoughtful observation, with a far away look in her eyes, my grandmother murmured, "Even in death, they separate themselves from us .colored people. Their stately mansions and imposing monuments cannot buy them entrance into God's kingdom where the first shall be last and the humble shall be exalted."

A squirrel skittered across a marble gravestone and a bird sang sweetly in a tree overhanging a granite angel perched protectively on a monument, keeping quiet vigil over what appeared to be the grave of a small child. I wondered if one of the first words that child had learned to say was "nigger". At a very tender age, white children were taught to demean us and at eight years of age, I had already experienced the sting of their scorn. Still, I felt compassion for the little one buried beneath the earth and I prayed for the happy repose of its soul.

The green, velvety grass was lush beneath our feet as we made our way slowly around the perimeter of the graveyard, pausing to examine the exquisite plants and flowers so sculptured and groomed that they hardly looked real. Grandmother said they were not like the wild things that grew on her reservation where the Great Creator allowed their natural beauty to unfold. Here at this all white cemetery bordering the ghetto, the live green plants and colorful flowers were as close to nature as we could get within the confines of the city. I wondered if Paradise looked anything like this little piece of heaven on earth where azaleas, rhododendron and other shrubs and flowers in a splendiferous profusion of hues spread their scent on the warm, gentle breezes. The soft winds caressed my cheeks with the delicacy of the wings of a cherub. The sun was low in the almost cloudless western sky and a few wispy, bronzy pink clouds scattered overhead like celestial feathers getting ready to cover the earth with a downy blanket of soft twilight.

There were no woods or parks nearby to enjoy in the dirt and cement jungle of the colored part of Savannah where we lived; just urban squalor, noise and the dreary gray shacks and tenement houses that dotted the landscape for miles around. Only the white people were allowed to enjoy the lovely city parks.

Grandmother and I would often steal away in the cool of the late afternoon and early evening to enjoy the quiet and serenity among the dead. Most Indians avoided the places of the dead but Grandmother said that the living were more likely to harm or endanger you than were the dead. She had no fear of enjoying the beauty and solitude of nature in the cemetery. There were no guards visible so no one harassed the short, chubby old Indian woman and her petite, brown granddaughter.

Grandmother stared at the places where the dead white people lay in quiet repose and she no longer felt threatened by those who had chased her people off their land and confiscated it. The people were dead and gone who had stolen her name and forcefully dragged her off to the Indian boarding school, far away from her family, attempting to mold her into a little imitation white person. There was no reason to fear them as they could no longer hurt her.

"We must forgive them," she said. "They didn't know any better. They were weak and greedy and were not enlightened by the Creator. Maybe now, they know the truth in the Spirit World."

"All whites are not bad," she continued. "Some have been friends and allies of Indian people. Others are simply misguided and misled and do not know the Red Road. They are taught to believe that they are better than we are. They are taught that our beliefs are heathen and that our names are pagan. Some learn better and become true messengers of peace and brotherhood. Others cling to their evil beliefs and never learn the truth. We must not carry hate in our hearts for them but rather pity them and forgive them because all creatures are our brothers. It is the law of the Great Creator to forgive our enemies. It is The Great Law of Peace."

Then, Grandmother turned her sun bronzed face to me. Her eyes were creased at the corners with the lines of aging but twinkled when she smiled. There was a sound of pure love in her voice. "You are my namesake, Pocahontas!" she said. "The whites renamed me, calling me Viola but Pocahontas is my original name, meaning 'playful one'. You are Pocahontas Little Dove, playful and tenderhearted. Wherever you walk, you leave footprints of kindness and love. Never lose your tender heart and your playful spirit. You are a child of peace."

My grandmother had always seemed to be in tune with my highly sensitive nature. She frequently reminded my parents that I must be handled more gently and did not require the harsher discipline that some children appeared to need.

Through the years, Grandmother Viola and I took many walks around the white cemetery after she came to live with us in Savannah. She told me many stories about her Cherokee Indian people and about the Tuscarora Indian relatives on my grandfather's side of the family. She also taught me to do simple beading and to knit and crochet. I never did become very skilled at these as I was far more prone to read books or to write stories and poems. Together, Grandmother and I made dolls from grass and from corn husks. I loved grooming the corn silk hair of my husk dolls and I created elaborate hair styles for my grass dolls, braiding and styling the grass roots.

I quickly learned to play the string games with which Indian children entertained themselves. Grandmother and I sang songs together and I loved listening to her stories. She was proud to be an American Indian and wanted me to proudly acknowledge both the Negro and the Indian parts of my heritage. I treasured our special times together as I began to learn and to embrace the totality of my blended heritage.

One summer, I traveled on the train with Grandmother to North Carolina to bury her sister. I saw Cherokee and Tuscarora relatives, many of whom I had never met, as they gathered for the funeral. The raven haired women looked so much like my mother that it was almost as though someone had duplicated them using the magic of a mysterious copying machine. Cherokee and Tuscarora societies are matrilineal, that is, the child's primary identity is through the mother's blood line. I am my mother's daughter.

Surrounded by such love and acceptance, I felt unadulterated joy while being embraced in this warm cocoon by so many aunts, uncles and cousins. The older women sat on the floor with their legs folded under them and pulled me onto their soft, cushioned laps. As they cooed and cuddled me, it felt to me like the warm embrace of Mother Earth made flesh.

"You are one of us," they repeated. "Always remember, you have our blood. You are Indian. You are Cherokee. You are Tuscarora."

Not too many years would pass before Grandmother would be laid to rest beside her beloved sister. When she went to the Spirit World, I knew that a part of Grandmother would always be with me to guide and inspire me through difficult times, to comfort and cheer me in sorrow, to celebrate with me in times of joy and to remind me to dance and laugh and sing. Above all, Grandmother still reminds me to revere Mother Earth, to love the Creator and to love my neighbor as myself.

Many moons have passed since Grandmother and her beloved relatives crossed over to the Spirit World but I have always remembered, I am one of them. I have their blood. I am Indian. I am Cherokee. I am Tuscarora. I am African American.

BUT YOU DON'T LOOK INDIAN

"But you don't look Indian!" exclaimed the stooped, silver haired octogenarian as she peered curiously up at me over her tea cup. Indeed I do not look Indian according to the old stereotype of the Indian of the Plains with light skin, a Roman nose and distinctive regalia. The Shabbat evening service had just ended at the synagogue. Members of the congregation stood at oneg cheerfully greeting each other with the words, "Shabbat shalom", literally meaning Sabbath peace, as they partook of the blessed wine and the bread called challah. This was not the time or the place to go into an explanation of my heritage, and the dear woman's hearing impairment probably would not have permitted her to absorb what seemed a foreign concept.

A Black Indian! It must have been a bit curious and confusing for this devout Jewish woman of eastern European ancestry. It certainly was not the first time that this response had come from various sources upon hearing my name and certainly not surprising considering my dark skin color and African American appearance. Both heritages make me who I am and with integrity, I choose to honor both, Black and Indian. To honor one does not in any way diminish the other. Society labels us by appearance even if that means denying entire parts of ourselves. I clearly stood out in this gathering of predominantly white skinned, Jewish Americans.

My husband, Gene, is Jewish by birth. We have been members of the synagogue since the summer of 1998 when we retired and relocated to Prescott, Arizona from our home in southern New Jersey. Newcomers and some old timers are still not quite comfortable with who we are, how we came to be here and just where we fit into the scheme of things.

After I joined the synagogue women's group called Sisterhood, I was invited to give an informal talk which allowed me to include information about segments of my journey as an African American/Native American woman. This talk barely scratched the surface of the story that began for me on a winter night under rainy, cold, dark mid-January skies in the year 1933. The journey began with a slap on my small, brown rear and I took my first breath and emitted lusty cries in the maternity wing of the ghetto's Charity Hospital in Savannah, Georgia.

I, Pocahontas Little Dove, rested my head upon the breast of Mother Earth on the wintry Friday evening of January 13, 1933, my arrival going largely unnoticed except by my family and those closest to us. It was the time of the Wolf Moon, so named by the Cherokee Indians because of the wolves who foraged for food under the light of the pale January moon.

According to the plan of Uneqwa (the Great Creator), the timing of my birth seemed appropriate considering my lineage and maternal heritage. Since most Indian cultures are matrilineal, the child's primary identity is through the mother's blood line. My maternal grandmother was born of the Wolf Clan of the Eastern Band Cherokee Nation of North Carolina, hence, my birth under the Wolf Moon seemed especially significant. My maternal grandfather was born of the Bear Clan of the Tuscarora Indian Nation. The bear and the wolf are powerful totems and I use them in the decor of our home and in the jewelry that I wear to remind me of who I am and to surround me and mine with an aura of good medicine, well being, strength and healing.

My father's African American lineage cannot be easily traced because most of the African ancestors were brought to this country on slave ships. Heritages and names were lost through the dehumanizing system of slavery, most never to be found or reclaimed. Researchers continue to uncover significant documentation of the intermarriages and resulting offspring of Black and Indian unions.

Many people are puzzled when they hear the terms Black Indian or African-Native American, and are unaware that we exist. There are millions of Americans with varying degrees of Black and Indian blood, many of whom are simply classified as Black or African-American by our Census Bureau. In recent years, options have been placed on the census forms allowing citizens to check more than one box and officially claim more of who we are. Current research has uncovered more and more scientific and historical evidence regarding the long standing alliances between African Americans and Native Americans and their descendants.

America has not yet come to terms with accepting the reality that people with any degree of African blood would want to acknowledge other parts of themselves, despite the largely accepted one-drop rule. Are we not entitled, as are people of other racial and ethnic groups, to claim all of who we are?

Thus began the journey that would take me on a path known only to God. My destiny would be revealed as I traversed the proverbial road of life over places both rough and smooth, with detours, hills, valleys, plateaus, arid deserts and glorious mountaintops.

After the allotted time, my mother and I were discharged from the hospital to embark upon a voyage to an uncertain fate in uncertain times. As we traveled to our humble home, my parents, Maggie Sea Flower Walls and Samuel David Harden, must have felt somewhat like the Biblical Mary and Joseph taking their babe into an unknown and insecure world, relying upon the grace of God and the kindness of strangers to sustain them.

DREAMS DEFERRED

My mahogany limbs were thin and jerked in my mother's arms when I was startled by even the slightest unanticipated sound or movement. My mother, Maggie, held me tenderly against her full bronze breast, wondering if she had received adequate nutrition during the pregnancy to produce milk rich enough to nourish me, this fragile child who seemed so highly sensitive to everything around her. Having lost a boy child who did not survive premature birth, Maggie felt especially protective of the small dark bundle in her arms. She gazed upon me with wonder in her eyes, a wonder mixed with fear and worry.

Poverty, hunger and cold were no strangers to my parents but little did they know that these three scourges would become almost daily companions for many years to come. Hunger pangs punctuated many a sleepless night and the bitter cold was painful to bear with too few frayed quilts and blankets for warmth in the unheated, uninsulated, dilapidated houses that we called home. The immediate goal was to survive, one day at a time, with bright hope for a better tomorrow.

Survive we did, even as the family grew. The ill-fitting, hand-me-down shoes and clothing were not always age appropriate or flattering but they kept us warm. The generosity and kindness of neighbors and the charity of the soup kitchen got us through.

Mother was especially cordial and polite to the women servers at the soup kitchen and they in turn would reach to the bottom of the soup kettles and give us more substantial and less watery portions. We children were taught to be polite, clean and well groomed so that the servers would be favorably impressed and give us extra large helpings. Sometimes, my mother brought a quart jar or two which the servers filled with left-over soup for us to take home. This provided us with another meal and Mother added water to the soup in order to stretch it a little farther.

My father's pride kept him from standing in line at the soup kitchen but my mother was pragmatic enough to know that her children needed nourishment. She was protective and resourceful and did not intend to let us starve if she could do anything to prevent it.

The Great Depression took a heavy toll on the poor in Savannah, Georgia. Maggie's husband, my father Samuel, was unemployed and doing odd jobs in an effort to keep the rent payments current on our shabby shack of a wood-frame house on Maple Street.

Samuel was tall, handsome, muscular and ebony-skinned. Times were tough for any Negro man in 1933, but he was an optimist and a hard worker. His love for Maggie Sea Flower and her love for him fueled their resolve to build a good life for their family no matter what befell them. They made a striking couple and a strong team with hopes and dreams for a better future. They did not know that what they were up against would kill their dreams as it killed the dreams of so many of their contemporaries. Their dreams too would be deferred, as the poet Langston Hughes described, and wither like a raisin in the sun.

Some remnants of the dream survived and were passed on to me, my siblings and to our generation to be reshaped in a giant step toward realization. We would fulfill parts of the dream, dream bigger dreams, transform them into visions and pass them on to our descendants, refusing to let the dreams die.

MAMA CRIED

There were a number of Indian women who, like my mother, became an integral part of our community with their Negro husbands. The race police didn't seem to mind since we were all "colored people", as long as the Indian women didn't look too white. Their offspring, in various shades of brown, were plentiful and infused the ghetto with hybrid vigor.

The whole color scenario was a complicated affair and added to that complex hierarchy was the hair texture nightmare. Every Negro was familiar with the saying: "If you're white, you're alright; if you're brown, stick around; if you're black, get back." It was considered good fortune if one's skin were light enough to pass the brown paper bag test. That could be tricky considering the tanning capacity of the hot Georgia sun. One might pass the test in winter and fail it miserably in the summer.

I was much darker than a paper bag, though not as dark as Samuel, and Maggie knew that the darker one's complexion was, the more difficult life would be because of the prejudice and discrimination of the times. She loved her dark brown baby girl, but she wished that I had been born with lighter skin so that life might spare me some of the insults and hurts that were sure to come, not only from white people, but from people of color who had become infused with self-hatred, internalizing the racism and the color coded standards set by whites. Those Negroes who were described by locals as "light, bright and damned near white" were treated with favor when it came to employment, housing and other opportunities, especially if they managed to speak articulately and without a Negro dialect.

Wishing that my silky, black hair would remain curly and not start to kink made Maggie feel guilty but the guilt was assuaged because she was merely wishing for whatever would make my life more tolerable. The "good hair-bad hair" classification pitted even family members against one another. Poverty, dark skin and "bad" hair were a triple threat. Maggie hoped that perhaps I would be gifted with extreme intelligence or blessed with other talents to compensate for the lack of exceptional physical features. I would need to be outstanding in some respect in order to surmount the circumstances of birth, race and economics.

Lost in these troubling thoughts, Maggie gently wiped away her tears which had fallen on my face as she imagined that by some magic, her tears could wash away some of the pigment or at least dilute it to the light color of a brown paper bag.

I opened my dark brown eyes and my plump little lips made a sucking noise followed by soft cooing sounds like those of a mourning dove. Pocahontas Little Dove was the name Maggie had chosen for me, partly because of those sounds and more importantly to honor her own Cherokee mother, Pocahontas.

The name Pocahontas Little Dove would later become associated with my peaceful nature as a child, always striving for conflict resolution; and associated later still with the Dove of Peace. Ultimately, it would become associated with my dedication and involvement in causes relating to peace and social justice. I, the dark child with the uncommon name, was destined to lead an uncommon life.

Many years would pass before I grew to understand the depth and breadth of the damaging and negative effects of racism. The painful struggle to build a healthy self-esteem, the journey toward self-acceptance and a sense of self-worth took time, effort, insight and daring. I finally learned enough to know that it was not I who was flawed but rather that the yardstick by which society measured me was defective. That darned measuring rod was so warped and bent that it would never be capable of measuring my true worth and value.

Perhaps by some methods of measuring success, mine has been a rather ordinary life, unmarked by heroism, fame or great acquisitions of wealth, power and achievement. Yet, the success of a life well lived may not be measured in those terms. Perhaps it is the adherence to the sacred principles of service and giving that are far more important. Believing that trouble lasts only for a season, I have tried never to let temporary setbacks deter me from fulfilling my destiny, however humble. Once, when asked if she ever became discouraged when she could not successfully feed all the world's hungry, Mother Teresa replied, "I do not pray for success, I ask for faithfulness." I too have endeavored to be faithful.

Striving to maintain faithfulness and trust, I have followed my own star and sung my own special song. I have listened to the voice within, marched to the different drummer in my own heart, slain personal demons and societal dragons and tried to touch the lives of others with kind and gentle hands. I have survived for lo these many decades despite roadblocks, detours and obstacles deliberately or inadvertently placed in my path. In my resolve and commitment to live with integrity, I have been blessed with a measure of both faithfulness and success. Sometimes, I have paid a great price for that resolve and commitment but if I had to choose all over again, I would gladly pay whatever the cost, not to die with the music still in me.

JESUS, SANTA CLAUS AND OTHER MYSTERIES

Many moons waxed and waned and before long, a few Wolf Moons had passed. I could remember at least parts of the preceding years. The earlier details were filled in with the stories that I heard repeated by parents, grandparents, aunts, uncles, cousins and friends of the family. Many of these friends were called aunts, uncles and cousins and were embraced as part of the extended family in our close knit community.

I distinctly remember the crib in which I slept as a toddler. I can picture the chipped, vivid blue paint. I wonder now if it might have been lead-based paint. Well, that would perhaps help to explain any limitations in my mental acuity. It was during those days that I came down with an agonizing case of mumps. My mother wrapped my cheeks with a cloth soaked in camphorated oil, bringing it under my chin and tying the cloth on top of my head like a bunny rabbit's ears. I remember feeling quite ill but I was not a complainer, I'm told. After all, I was the eldest child and early on I understood that I must be a role model for my sister, Bunny, who was eighteen months younger.

Bunny was a beautiful baby. Everyone marveled at her beauty! She had light skin like my mother's and she did not cry often as they said I did when I was a baby. I had often heard the stories of how dark and ugly I was at birth, compared to Bunny when she was born. Contrary to her happy disposition, I was colicky and fretful. As I grew older, I sometimes worried that my mother would no longer love me now that she had a beautiful light skinned child with a more placid disposition. My strategy for winning and holding my mother's love was to be extra good and extra helpful. If I caused no trouble and became indispensable to her, I reasoned with my childish mind that she might love me and keep me.

I was almost four years old when my sister Gloria was born on Christmas Eve. Mother went to the hospital in the middle of the night and when Bunny and I awoke the next morning, we were told that Santa Claus had brought us a beautiful baby sister. Now that there were two of them, I would have to try even harder to behave perfectly and to make up for being born ugly.

Santa Claus brought some toys and goodies too, so that helped to ease my worry. I got an organ grinder bank and the monkey tipped his hat and the man beat a drum and clapped the cymbals each time I dropped a coin in the slot. That was fascinating to me and the relatives gave me several pennies to put in my new bank.

While I played with my bank, Bunny set about filling my new flute with sand. I got a mouth full of sand when I tried to play it and she laughed. I couldn't smack her because I was supposed to be a good role model. Feeling frustrated and upset, I cried instead. In an effort to comfort me, my father told me that they had saved my best gift for last. I had asked Santa for a doll and I was praying this would be it. I tore hungrily into the wrapping and pulled out a box and opened it. Inside was the ugliest doll I had ever seen! It had huge red lips and its skin was as black as coal. It wore a brilliantly patterned, gaudy, sack-like dress that hung from its pot-bellied frame. Its frizzy, kinky hair was tied in sections with a different colored ribbon on each tuft and it looked like Topsy in "Uncle Tom's Cabin". Enraged, I heaved the ugly doll across the room, breaking off its foot as it struck the wall.

The family reacted with shock as they had never seen me throw such a fit before. I was sure that Santa Claus brought me that doll because he thought it looked like me, black and ugly. He must have thought that this was the kind of doll I deserved. I had prayed for a beautiful, white doll with straight, blond hair. Maybe Jesus didn't love me after all, I thought, and Santa had brought that ugly doll as unmistakable proof. Already, racism had brainwashed me, created self-hatred and inflicted the insidious wounds of internalized racism upon my young mind.

Through my tears, I tried to explain my upset to my father and aunts. I think my father understood, but my young aunts laughed, adding insult to injury.

When my mother and the new baby came home from the hospital a few days later, I was still withdrawn and sad. When I saw the beautiful new baby, I knew I had better snap out of it and start helping to take care of her and I soon became my old indispensable self. I repressed my secret hurt and hid it deep in my heart.

Something changed for me that day and my role became that of keeping other people happy. I continued to play games where I pretended that my dad's sister Aunt Dahlia was my little girl and that I was her mother. I was very nurturing and combed her hair and play-acted taking her to Sunday School. We said Bible verses and sang "Yes, Jesus Loves Me" but I wondered if he really did.

I still enjoyed rocking in my very own small, cane rocking chair and when Aunt Dahlia took me to the real Sunday School at the Methodist Church, I wore my black patent leather Mary Jane shoes and carried my black patent leather Lucy Locket purse. I saw Jesus all white and blond in the stained glass windows of the sanctuary, and many thoughts swirled around in my little head as the congregants belted out yet another chorus of "Whiter than snow, Lord, whiter than snow. Wash me and I shall be whiter than snow".

My innocent, susceptible, young mind was already being bombarded with the myths and subliminal messages that white was right and better. The repetitious lies methodically brainwashed the most vulnerable and perpetuated racism in older folks, passing it down from generation to generation.

Children of whatever race, in times past and in times present, are molded and told whom to emulate, with whom to associate, whom to avoid and how to treat those who are different. They learn which standards of beauty are valued and acceptable and which are devalued and held in disdain. It is taught consciously and unconsciously by word and deed, by example and attitude, by media and by society's institutions and systemic values, and it is absorbed as easily as oxygen is in breathing. Volumes are filled with revisionist history portraying which cultures and heroes should be emulated, honored and imitated and which cultures and heroes should be trivialized, ridiculed or omitted.

Religion was a double-edged sword. It was used sometimes to reinforce the idea of white superiority with images of a white God/Jesus, white angels, white saints and an abundance of white symbols representing the ideas of good and purity. On the other hand, we were taught that God/Jesus loved everyone and that God created all. That made the concept of brotherhood and equality confusing for the mind of a dark skinned child who could see inequality all around and who had difficulty finding enough positive reinforcement to counter the resounding message that dark or black was bad or dirty.

Religion was an integral part of our upbringing and a mixture of traditions from both sides of the family made for early ecumenical exposure and opportunities for inclusiveness in some respects but for exclusion in others. The contradictions left many questions in my mind that I did not yet have the language to ask.

The spiritual aspects of holidays were emphasized by my parents so our material expectations were not high. We had very little money so we were pleasantly surprised whenever we got anything at all. My parents did the best that they could to make the holidays special with candy treats and whatever else they could afford. Sometimes, there were Christmas presents or new Easter dresses and Easter baskets for us kids but limited finances kept us focused on the sacred rather than on the secular. We were taught all the Bible stories about Jesus' birth, life, death and resurrection.

A CHILD WITH AN OLD SOUL

During the good periods when Dad found work and we had sufficient food and clothing, life had its warm, fuzzy moments. Dad would sing, teach us songs, tell us stories and bounce us on his knee. He would toss us high into the air and play flying angel.

I felt so secure knowing that his strong arms would catch me every single time.

The ancients would say that I appeared to possess an old soul, seeming much wiser than my tender years. I was a keen observer who watched and listened and learned.

As each new sibling expanded our family, I assumed more and more duties and responsibilities in caring for my younger sisters and brothers and for the upkeep of our clean but shabby home. My mother always stressed that cleanliness was next to godliness and that was reinforced throughout my childhood.

By the age of six or seven, I had learned to stand on a wooden Coca-Cola crate at the old wood stove and cook meals as well as any woman could. Starting the fire in the wood stove was a bit risky though and once when I lit the kerosene soaked wood, it flared up singeing the right side of my hair almost to the roots. My guardian angel must surely have been keeping watch over me because the only harm I suffered was a not-yet-fashionable asymmetrical hair style for a while until it grew in. I learned to fix baby formula, bathe and diaper the babies and care for them efficiently. It never occurred to me that these responsibilities were unusual for one so young, acting in the role of a miniature adult.

My mother went to work to supplement the family income and her hours were brutally long and hard. Her former experience as a one-room schoolhouse teacher in rural Georgia did not qualify her for anything other than menial domestic work in the homes of white people in segregated Savannah. Mother said that many of the Jewish people were generally more respectful and nicer to her than were the other white people for whom she worked.

Working from dawn to dusk kept her exhausted. She walked regally, nevertheless, with her spine straight and her head held high despite the daily humiliations to which she was subjected. She was underpaid, overworked and exploited, as were the other women of color.

Having received a good, basic high school education at the boarding school where she excelled academically, my mother was certainly capable of doing other kinds of work had the opportunities been available to her. She was intelligent, sensitive and reached out as a contributor to the community. Members of the community recognized, respected and appreciated her astuteness. She had learned the ancient healing arts from her Cherokee mother, a medicine woman, and these healing skills were greatly valued since few in the community could afford conventional medical care. Who knows what my mother might have become, had she been permitted to realize her potential! Mother nursed the sick, visited the lonely and the elderly, read to the illiterate and wrote letters for them and taught us to do the same as we grew up.

My mother was a beautiful woman and she carried herself with modesty and grace. She dressed for work as neatly and as tastefully as her limited wardrobe would allow. She was never provocative in dress or manner as she wanted to discourage the advances and sexual harassment of her male employers. Feelings of entitlement sometimes led these men to feel that they had the right to disregard the boundaries of women of color and to behave crassly and without common decency. Often it came down to a choice between maintaining one's job or protecting one's personal safety and principles. We heard whispered reports from neighbor women of rapes by white employers whose wives were sometimes complicit with the evil misdeeds of their husbands, either too afraid or too uncaring to intervene. From time to time, fair-skinned children were born to the women of color. Everyone knew about the abuses but no one talked about the white fathers except in whispers.

It was terribly frustrating to be relegated to the demeaning way of life in the ghetto with no visible way out and little control over one's destiny or even over one's own body. Mothers worried about how to protect their young daughters from rape or from being otherwise abused. The lines began to show in my mother's pretty face as she worried about the family finances, the work load that I carried at home and the safety of all her children while she was away at work. Quietly spiritual, she relied heavily upon her faith in the Great Creator to sustain her through those difficult times.

I learned to do the mending, the cooking and cleaning, the ironing and whatever other tasks needed attention. The most difficult chore was washing clothes on a washboard in galvanized tubs outdoors. I heated water on the stove but it cooled quickly making doing the laundry a very frigid chore in winter. In the sweltering heat of summer, I placed the laundry tubs beneath a Chinaberry tree in the back yard and took advantage of its cooling shade.

Since I had already missed one year of school in order to babysit my younger siblings, my mother was greatly concerned about my education. She began home schooling me at night after work and on weekends. We used makeshift materials. Grocery bags from the store were converted into writing paper. Books for reading lessons consisted of the Bible, Sears-and-Roebuck catalogs and odds and ends suitable for my mother's creative and innovative teaching were retrieved from other people's discards. Food cans, cereal boxes and the like provided supplementary reading and arithmetic material.

OFF TO SCHOOL

Eventually, I enjoyed a brief but happy stint in kindergarten at the neighborhood Episcopal Church. I looked forward daily to seeing the smiling, familiar brown faces of the friendly teachers and children who looked like me. When my mother and I went to kindergarten the very first day, we were taken to a brightly decorated room where small chairs formed a circle in the center. Children and teachers were gaily marching around the room waving small American flags and singing "Three Cheers For The Red, White and Blue". I remember wondering why they were singing about "three chairs" when I saw at least twenty or more chairs in the room!

Mother left me there assuring me that she would return. I don't recall feeling too anxious or uncomfortable. I'm told I was always very adaptable. In actuality, I think I learned early on to put on a happy face, to put up a brave front and never let them see me sweat.

Having missed almost a year of regular school, I was quite excited when my mother told me that I was about to be transferred to St. Mary's Parochial School to enter first grade. I was totally unprepared for the sight of yardstick-wielding nuns in black and dark brown Franciscan habits tied at the waist with thick ropes of white cord. Falling from the waist, the white cords had three carefully tied knots in them. I learned that the knots stood for poverty, chastity and obedience, the vows that the nuns had taken. Giant wooden Rosary beads hung from their waists also. Their black shoes and stockings were sometimes visible beneath their long skirts when the nuns walked briskly or occasionally sat down.

I could see only the white faces and hands of the nuns and I wondered for years whether or not they had hair or if perhaps they shaved their heads. In the sixth grade, I finally saw a tendril of reddish brown hair which had inadvertently escaped from under the veil of our nun. Another nun must have informed her of it for after morning recess, it was safely tucked out of sight beneath her veil. My curiosity had been satisfied and discovering that the nuns had hair humanized them a bit more for us kids who had seen the hair but dared not give any indication that we had caught a glimpse of the forbidden.

That first day of school was unnerving. "What is your name, child?" asked the nun. "Pocahontas? Saints preserve us! That's a heathen name! We'll have to give you a good Christian name. Evelyn! Yes, Evelyn suits you just fine." The young nun with the Irish brogue gave a sigh of relief followed by a satisfied smile at my instantaneous new identity. With that swift, magical shift toward my redemption, she proceeded to enroll me in her first grade class.

The other nuns all agreed that the name Pocahontas was a heathen name and such savage ways must be abandoned for the salvation of our souls. There was no St. Pocahontas after all or any Christian derivative thereof. It was common practice for the nuns to change the names of children without parental consent, and thus, Pocahontas became Evelyn until in adulthood I legally reclaimed my birth name. My neighborhood friend, Frank, instantly became Francis. My friend, Toletha, instantly became Theresa. It all reminded me of Cinderella and the Fairy Godmother's magic wand. Poof! What power!

The segregated public schools in the ghetto were so poor and inadequate that a parochial school education was the best choice available to us, though that too was segregated. We did not underestimate the advantages of a good, Catholic education so parents and children cheerfully accepted and agreed to abide by the culturally insensitive rules in order to become enrolled. We considered it part of the cost of an education and kept our objections to ourselves. Tuition was nominal and the basic educational foundation was sound.

Religious indoctrination was primary and daily lessons from the Baltimore Catechism preceded reading, writing and arithmetic. As we progressed through the grades, history and geography were added and Latin skills beyond the liturgical Latin used in the Mass were honed. We learned Catholic hymns in both English and Latin, folk songs many of which were Irish, minuets, waltzes and Irish dances. We memorized the Gettysburg Address, The Preamble to the Constitution, The American Creed, The Charge of the Light Brigade and other great historical and literary works. We acted in plays and short musicals written by the nuns.

I later realized that the system of values instilled in us served us well in most cases. I also recognized that we got a pretty solid introduction to a liberal arts education, especially considering that we were disadvantaged children. We were fortunate in ways that I would come to recognize and appreciate more and more as I encountered a diversity of people not so exposed. Over the years, I have felt at a distinct advantage in many ways. On the other hand, I have had to deal with some ambivalent feelings regarding the cultural insensitivity and corporal punishment to which we were subjected. I feel that some of the harsh methods created issues of confused identity and low self-esteem which were sometimes a struggle and difficult to overcome.

When I entered first grade at St. Mary's Parochial School, writing on lined paper was a new experience for me and my letters, though accurate and neat, sometimes wavered on the page. We had not been able to afford the luxury of lined paper at home. The brown paper grocery bags had been unlined and for some reason, my mother had not drawn lines on them. Nevertheless, I quickly acquired the skill of writing on the lines at school and soon got awards for good penmanship via the Palmer Penmanship Method.

Our first grade class was very large with seventy-five eager little souls crammed into one small room. These were less than ideal conditions and I am sure that some of the rigid regimentation imposed was necessary in order to maintain discipline.

Having been home schooled, I already knew most of the first grade curriculum and I quickly became one of the teacher's aides, along with my friends, Joseph and Francis. I showed unusual maturity and skill in teaching other first grade students and the nun had mixed feelings about losing me when she skipped Joseph, Francis and me to the second grade after a few weeks.

SQUEEZING LIFE'S LEMONS

Those first few months at St. Mary's Parochial School were both exhilarating and frightening. I was a keen observer and it did not take long for me to realize that survival skills would be needed, not so much in defense against the other children. That was the easy part. Surviving the nuns was the real challenge. They were terrifying!

Surely, the nuns had good intentions, but many of them seemed terribly misguided and lacking in substantial knowledge of early childhood education and child psychology. The abusive methods of corporal punishment would make modern day educators cringe.

Eventually, I would be able to shed most of the negative memories of discipline and teaching methods bordering on medieval torture and truly appreciate the many positive life lessons learned during those pivotal years. Foundations for a lasting spirituality were laid. Granted, they needed a lot of reworking over time but ultimately blended with my traditional Indian spirituality, my father's deep Methodist faith and my own eventual, responsible search for truth and meaning in a more mature and integrated way.

An enduring system of values and a work ethic that served me well in the years that followed were established. At home and at school, these lessons were being absorbed and reinforced, along with a discipline that would prove invaluable to a child of color negotiating the tides and swirls of the river of life.

Before St. Mary's Parochial School, the Methodist Church Sunday School had supplied a fairly happy and comfortable place of learning outside the home. I had already gained a reputation there as an award-winning Bible student and could recite poems and Bible passages, as was customary on Easter and other occasions, better than most in my Sunday School and Vacation Bible School classes.

Even adult Methodist church services were enjoyable, except for the long, often dull sermons. The cacophony of Southern style preaching was a bit disquieting at times, especially the parts about hellfire and damnation, but the less scary drama could be captivating and intriguing. I had an ear for music and a decent voice so I enthusiastically joined in the congregational singing.

As I listened to the selections sung by the choir, I speculated that I might someday become a choir soloist. After all, I felt rather empowered, confident and capable in some respects as a child. The adults in my life had made me feel very special with their extremely high expectations of me. They admired my talent, intelligence, my sense of style and the flair I had for making hand-me-down clothes look good.

The price of this self-image was steep and required a tremendous amount of work and energy in order to continue to win the kind of approval and recognition that I so craved. There was always a lingering shadow of doubt and fear of letting people down, of not being good enough, of feeling like an imposter, of being found out. The ever present need for perfection and pleasing people kept me trying to keep my balance on an emotional tightrope. What if I failed? What if I were not as smart as they thought I was?

I was already becoming a budding workaholic and people pleaser without the maturity to name the conditions psychologically or to understand the serious implications. Needless to say, my young mind lacked the skills and insights to work through these issues in a healthful way. Instead, I sometimes developed coping strategies that increased rather than reduced the stress. With no viable support system and my intense desire not to displease the nuns, my parents and others, the tension became almost unbearable at times. It was rather like walking on a frozen pond and not knowing where the thin places were.

The habit-clad nuns at St. Mary's School smacked you with a ruler or a cane if you made a mistake or sometimes even if you hesitated too long in giving a correct answer! Their faces were so pale and stern-looking, peeking out from the black and white habits that enveloped them, giving them the appearance of giant penguins. My fear was so palpable at times I could taste it. No one seemed to notice my hidden fear and I was lauded for my confidence and superior performance.

I was a disciplined child and quiet by nature so good conduct was not a problem. The expectations I placed upon myself, my intense need for recognition and approval and the expectations that I thought others had of me created immense pressure. The strangeness of these robed women and their very different church intimidated me. It took a lot of energy to hide the fears and to appear as confident as others thought I was.

I was traumatized by an experience that occurred during Mass when I was a brand new first grader. It was my first time attending Mass. The nun smacked me with a ruler when I stood up at the wrong time by mistake. "You are so stupid!" The nun hissed as she shoved me back into the pew.

I had never been called stupid before and in the presence of the other children, it embarrassed and humiliated me. The memory of this experience was to linger for a long while before it became transforming. At the time, it was excruciating, crushing my spirit and shattering my heart into a thousand pieces. It also made me very angry and my childish mind silently vowed retribution.

I was no shrinking violet but I was highly sensitive. I was precocious enough to figure out that to openly resist these nuns could be fatal, or worse. Fueled by my anger and outrage, a strategy was born. "I'll show them that I'm not stupid" I resolved. "I'll be the smartest, most well behaved student they have ever seen, then they'll have to like me. I'll show them." But they didn't like me. They liked the light skinned children with silky hair better, even if they were not as smart or as well behaved as I was. They liked them even more if they came from comparatively well-to-do families, were well dressed and were Catholic.

I reasoned that though that nun might consider me ugly and stupid, I had it within my power to be neat and well groomed, to develop my character, to radiate an inner beauty and to succeed academically. I would compensate by making the most of what I had and by changing the things that I had the capacity to change.

I was beginning to realize that life is not fair, but I had always been accustomed to doing my best, whatever the circumstances, and so I continued to excel. Gradually, I began to notice a shift in the attitude of the nuns. There was an all out effort to convert me to Catholicism but my parents would not give their consent. Word was spreading that I was a bright child and a well behaved one, not too well dressed, but neat and clean! Most of all, I was exceptional, especially for a Protestant!

The plan had apparently worked. I was being recognized in spite of the fact that I did not fit the profile of the favored among the nuns. I had become a first grade teacher's aide and the other kids liked and respected me because I helped them without making them feel dumb. Often, I could get through to them more easily than could the nun. My on-the-job training as the eldest sibling at home gave me certain skills and a maturity which paid off handsomely at school.

Joseph and Francis were very bright boys and we bonded as classroom aides and remained friends until we all graduated from ninth grade together. In the interim, I developed a tremendous crush on Joseph but he never suspected it. Neither did anyone else since this was my carefully guarded secret. I shared it with no one.

From the time that Joseph, Francis and I were skipped to the second grade, I already had my eyes on the prize. My intent was to someday become valedictorian of my class. I was following my mother's and grandmother's sage advice of squeezing life's lemons and making lemonade.

WAR AND PEACE

There was a war going on, World War II, and the nuns were very patriotic as well as religious. We saluted the flag and sang The Star Spangled Banner after morning prayers each day. On some days, we bought and sold Holy Childhood stamps to save pagan babies in Africa. They were starving and much worse off than we were so we raised as much money as we could. On other days, school was dismissed early so that we could collect scrap iron and other surplus materials to help the war effort and defeat the Japanese.

We sang patriotic songs and did a lot of flag waving. Enthusiastically and loudly we sang, "We did it before and we will do it again. We'll chase the Nipponese back to their cherry trees; yes, we did it before and we'll do it again!" Hitler Youth could not have been more passionately nationalistic than we were.

Then it was time for Baltimore Catechism lessons and we quickly switched gears to "Love thy neighbor as thyself", "Love your enemies", "Turn the other cheek" and "Thou shalt not kill". We did not realize the chilling irony of it all.

We had regular duck-and-cover air raid drills at school and at night during black-outs, we kids expected to be snatched out of our beds by invading Japanese and German soldiers. I remember reading in the Savannah Morning News that the Japanese were making lamp shades from the skins of captured American soldiers. My mind could not wrap itself around such horrors.

My active imagination struggled while other children seemed to go on enjoying the blissful naivete of childhood to which they were entitled. I worried about the innocent people in foreign lands being killed by bombs, especially the children. I fretted over the babies who were left orphaned. I worried that the United States would be bombed and I prayed for our safety and that of our military. I could not comprehend the cruelty, or determine who I should hate, or discern whose side God was on.

Upon seeing an Asian man in the corner grocery store one evening, I raced home in a panic to tell my parents that the Japanese had invaded. They finally calmed me down enough to explain that the man was the Chinese American who owned the nearby laundry.

My cousin Robert came home from U.S. Army duty in Europe and told us stories that we could not believe. He spared us any blood and gore that he might have witnessed and told only of European cities, culture, people and the enjoyable and amusing things that he had experienced. Robert said that the Europeans treated him and the other Negro soldiers well and did not show the racism that white Americans displayed. He said that white American soldiers told the European girls that the Negro soldiers had tails like monkeys. This was in an effort to dissuade the girls from dating the Negro soldiers.

Apparently, their strategy was not too effective and Robert, being handsome and single, was eligible and sought after by the fräuleins in Germany. To our dismay, he carried a picture in his wallet of himself posing with an attractive, young blond woman named Sigrid. That picture could have gotten him lynched in Georgia and my father firmly reminded Robert of that fact.

The war raged on as I coped in my own way, praying for peace in the war-torn world and for serenity in my own turbulent, unsettled heart.

TOO MUCH FOR ONE SMALL CHILD

Sister Mary Gregory, teacher of the combined second and third grade classes, seemed much less threatening than the young, thin, high-strung but beautiful Sister Mary Stigmata who taught first grade. Sister Mary Gregory was more like my own chubby Indian grandmother, short and soft spoken. Her cherubic face was kind but seemed to command respect. Her warm, dark eyes sparkled when she spoke to the children and we wanted to please her. There were not many discipline problems and harsh punishments were not meted out in her classroom. She made me feel safe and special. I loved her and sometimes drew pictures of her, secretly of course, coloring in her dark little mustache. She inspired me to want to become a nun.

So strong had this desire become that I made myself a make-believe nun's habit from one of my mother's old, discarded black dresses. I felt a sense of authority in my veil and perhaps a sense of piety. At that time, I had never seen a Negro nun but I toyed with the idea of becoming the first if there were no others. There really wasn't much play time available but I spent what time I could in my nun's habit, teaching the younger neighborhood children who eagerly lined up on the steps of our front porch after school and on Saturdays. I even had a make-shift blackboard and a ruler, but like Sister Mary Gregory, I used the ruler only for pointing. My play-school was the only pre-school available to the neighborhood children, our equivalent of a Head Start Program, and the parents were grateful for it.

My attempt to launch an adult literacy program was not as successful. Adults were embarrassed and less likely to reveal that they lacked functional literacy skills. One on one however, some of the adult residents in the neighborhood asked me to read their mail to them or to assist them in answering letters. In some cases I actually wrote the letters for them. Sometimes they told me that their glasses were lost or broken and I never let on that I knew they could not read or write. Even at that tender age, I felt that God had entrusted me with these tasks and that I would always try to give back in service to Him.

Many years later when I was a college student, I had the opportunity to teach adult migrant farm workers to read, through a program sponsored by the National Council of Churches. It was a humbling and rewarding experience to give the gift of literacy to the least of these.

During my elementary school years, I began to take religion very seriously, with daily after-school visits to the parish church on my way home from school. I prayed for my father who had started drinking too much. I prayed for my mother who worked far too hard and began having chronic health problems. The symptoms she described sounded like fibromyalgia and chronic fatigue syndrome, which had not yet been named or recognized and would not be for decades to come. I tried to help out as much as I could to help lighten her load.

I bargained with God and promised to be a saintly child if He would only help my father stay sober and find a better job. I reasoned that my mother could stay at home or at least work fewer hours and feel healthier and less grouchy if my father could support the family.

ENTREAT THEE NOT TO LEAVE ME

In spite of my prayers, my mother left my father. She took my younger siblings with her to her parents' house, leaving Bunny and me with relatives. She told us that she would return but that she needed to leave for a short while in order to try and scare my father into doing better. We were instructed not to disclose her secret. Bunny seemed to take things in stride as long as she had me. I was scared to death but dared not show it.

We went to live with our father's sister, Aunt Dahlia, and her husband and their two daughters. We were cramped and unhappy though they were kind to us and tried to cheer us up. Our father visited us each day and one day told us that he had quit drinking and that he was going to the reservation to retrieve our mother and our younger siblings. After a few days, he returned with my mother and the children and we returned to our own humble dwelling.

I tried to be super good so that my mother would not leave again. My fear of abandonment became overpowering. On some level, I struggled with a fear of abandonment for a great portion of my life.

My father's sobriety did not last and before long, my mother left again. This time, my mother appeared at school with a suitcase each for Bunny and me. She explained to the nun that she had to go away on a family emergency and that after school, we were to go to Aunt Adell and Uncle Buster's house. Bunny and I knew the real reason she was leaving and we feared she would not return this time.

The nuns excused us from our classrooms so that we could bid farewell to our mother in the corridor. We tried not to cry as she held us tightly in her embrace, kissed us and told us to study hard and to be good.

Aunt Adell had lived with us for a short while when she was a teenager. She returned as a young woman with her new husband while they looked for a place of their own. Uncle James seemed like a nice man and she adored him. We were totally unprepared for what happened a few weeks later. Aunt Adell's screams woke and startled the household one morning at daybreak. She had awakened to find a note from Uncle James saying that he was gone for good. The betrayal of trust reverberated throughout the family and shook us to the core. Aunt Adell's recovery was slow and painful. A couple of years later, she met Uncle Buster and they were married at the Methodist parsonage. It took a while for me to trust Uncle Buster and to know that he would not disappear as Uncle James had.

Aunt Adell was my mother's youngest sister and my favorite aunt. She and Uncle Buster were childless and lived in a nice, neat but modest cabin just outside of town. They saw us off to school after a good breakfast each morning and made sure that we studied and did our homework each evening. They loved us and were very good to us while our mother was away. We had plenty to eat but I was lonely for my mother and feared she would not return this time. She stayed away for several weeks which seemed like an eternity. When my mother returned, I begged her never to leave us again. She never did but I was always afraid that she would.

SEARCHING FOR MEANING AND PURPOSE

I made novenas, said the Rosary and prayed for the special intentions of my parents. I prayed for an end to the war and for the welfare of pagan babies in Africa. I prayed about my vocation and felt sure that I was destined to become a nun. I prayed that somehow my family would be delivered from the poverty in which we lived. I prayed for every wrong in the world to be righted, those known and those unbeknownst to me. I didn't ask for much for myself except when the cardboard patches in my shoes wore thin and pebbles from the street pressed through, signaling that I desperately needed a new pair of shoes.

Sometimes, on very frigid days when my fingers were numb and aching with cold, I prayed for gloves to keep my hands warm and for a new coat if that would not take away somehow from the starving children in Africa.

Martyrdom became an obsession and I internalized what I interpreted as the path to sainthood. I wanted to be worthy of sainthood and I accepted that suffering and self-denial were part of becoming a saint. The nuns had preached that in order to become holy, one must put God first, the other fellow second and self last. There was no mention of self-worth, self-concept or self-esteem. True piety, as I understood it, meant humbly acknowledging "O Lord I am not worthy that Thou should'st come to me; but speak the words of comfort, my spirit healed shall be."

Suffering was deemed noble, and in my naivete I became obsessed with it. I certainly did not go in search of more suffering than I already had and I had no intention of wearing a hair shirt or engaging in self-flagellation but my ill-fitting, hand-me-down shoes became their own torture chambers, exacting penance and creating problems that only my foot surgeon would be able to correct in later years.

I didn't know at the time that I was already suffering more than any child of my tender age ever should. I knew cold and hunger on a frequent and intimate basis. I felt the strain of watching my parents struggle to keep body and soul together as their marriage disintegrated while losing the battle to keep their children clothed and fed. They struggled to find the few dollars to keep my sister and me in Catholic school. Fifty cents per child per week for tuition added up to a dollar that was hard to spare and desperately needed in order to buy food.

Eventually, Bunny and I were told that we would have to go to public school the very next year and that felt like being sentenced to hell. Horror stories about the public schools were circulated and many were all too real. Those thoughts hung heavily on my mind all during that summer. What joy there was had gone out of childhood. There were too many serious adult issues to think about and they were much too much for one small child to sort out and process.

The nuns and priests told us that in order to find purpose and meaning in our suffering, we should offer it up to God in reparation for our sins and for the sins of the world. That made much more sense to me than suffering hopelessly and in vain. Thereafter, whenever suffering and sacrifice came into my life, I remembered those words and I made an effort to be cognizant of their purpose and meaning, practicing mindfulness and endeavoring to be open to the lessons to be learned. Sometimes, I must concede that there seemed to be no lessons and no rhyme or reason for the suffering except those known only to God.

Even today, I wrestle with the unanswerable question of why suffering afflicts the good and the innocent as well as the bad and the guilty. Some years ago, my search led me to a very comforting book by Rabbi Harold Kushner, "When Bad Things Happen To Good People". I have learned that we cannot always find satisfactory answers to explain the seeming injustices and mysteries of life. Faith can sustain us during those times with the certainty that God is ever present with us through our pain and suffering, giving us the strength and courage to endure.

My profound faith and deep trust in The Giver of Life sustain me. When doubt clouds my mind, I try to remember to hold on, knowing that it is often darkest before the dawn. I must never forget how much The Source of Strength has brought me through and I must keep faith in the blessed assurance that I will not be abandoned by the Great Mystery.

THIS CRUEL WORLD

My father used alcohol to self-medicate his inner pain and his feelings of inadequacy and loss of dignity. When there was no work and he was experiencing despair and loss of control, the drinking increased. In the beginning, there were long periods of sobriety when he had the opportunity to be a real man capable of taking care of his family. During those times, he was joyful, amusing and fun, playing and singing with us children and teaching us about life, spirituality and how to get along in a world where people of color faced injustices and difficult challenges. He was an affectionate and loving father and often told us how smart and beautiful we were, but he was becoming increasingly worried about not being able to support us and protect us from the hardships and cruelties of life.

When he began working at the shipyard and earning better money, once again there was enough food and new shoes were affordable from time to time. The family did not have to move, yet again, in search of cheaper housing.

My sister Bunny and I went out to meet my dad each evening when he came home from the shipyard, whistling and singing and swinging his lunch box as he marched down the street is his steel-toed work boots. He looked like a Black Adonis with muscles rippling against his smooth ebony skin that glistened with the sweat of hard labor. My dad was a hard worker and good at what he did. Soon, he was trained to be a welder at the shipyard, a skill usually reserved for white workers. Some of the white workers became resentful and referred to my dad as an "uppity nigger".

One day, my dad told us not to come beyond a certain point to meet him because it was too close to the poor white neighborhood that bordered ours. He said that a group of white men threatened to set their dogs on him and that one particular dog was huge and mean. After that, we did not venture too close to the boundary. Then it happened! We saw our dad approaching and one of the white men unleashed the huge, mean dog. The dog attacked and Dad's steel toed boot landed with a thud on the dog's head. The dog rolled over dead.

The men tackled Dad and though he fought valiantly, they overpowered him and brought him to his knees, holding a gun to his head. I screamed and Bunny wet herself. We were horrified and frozen with fear to the spot, expecting to see our dad killed before our very eyes. The men finally let Dad go and my mother cleaned and bandaged his wounds but he was never the same after that encounter. This homegrown, government-sanctioned terrorism forever changed him. I'm not sure that I have ever felt safe in the world since that traumatic event and I know for a fact that the inability to keep his family safe destroyed something within my dad.

It turned out that the white men were members of the Ku Klux Klan. The local Jewish storekeeper overheard them saying that they would firebomb our house that night with our family in it. Lynching was a distinct possibility and was not rare in that part of the country so such threats had to be taken seriously. The police could not be summoned. We dared not trust them. We had heard too many stories about officers who wore the police uniform by day and the KKK hoods and robes by night.

The storekeeper warned us to flee from harm and promised to let us know if and when it was safe to return. Under cover of night, my family fled. We had never owned a car so the storekeeper spirited us to safety in his vehicle. With lights out, he drove slowly and quietly to our house and my dad, my mom, and children numbering three plus one infant, squeezed into the car with a few possessions stuffed into cheap suitcases and pillow cases. Under a moonless summer sky, the car moved slowly toward West Broad Street before its headlights illuminated our way to the Greyhound Bus Terminal.

At the bus station, the storekeeper crammed some paper currency into my dad's hand and quickly drove away. We boarded the bus and went to my maternal grandparent's home just outside Qualla Indian Reservation in Cherokee, North Carolina.

The kindly storekeeper had a son, Aaron, who was just a year older than I, and the two of us had become friends while our parents engaged in the business of buying and selling. As we grew older, we sometimes talked about school and what we were learning. In fact, at one point I smuggled a small bottle of holy water into the store and baptized Aaron when the first grade nun had told us that the Jews killed Jesus and were doomed to hell for all eternity unless they repented and were baptized. I could not bear to think that my good friend would be doomed to hell. Aaron in turn had given me a Jewish medal with a Star of David on one side and a prayer for protection on the other. The night we escaped from the Klan, I clutched that medal close to me. To this very day I have never parted with it and I generally carry it on my person.

After a few weeks, the Klansmen moved on and as promised, the storekeeper got word to us that it was safe to return home. With kindness, bravery and courage this Jewish man recognized our humanity and rescued our family at great risk to the safety of his own. Once again, we managed to survive for a while longer in this cruel world.

My father's world was shattered. The encounter with the Klan brought him to the bitter realization that he was powerless to protect his wife and children and to defend his family. His broken spirit would never be repaired. His wounded soul would never heal. Like the straw that broke the camel's back, this was one too many egregious humiliations to absorb.

ALL GOD'S CHILDREN GOT SHOES

When we returned to Savannah, Dad searched for a job. He had lost the job at the shipyard because of having to leave without notice. School would begin again soon for me and my sister, Bunny. There were now four barefoot children altogether in need of shoes. Discouraged and unable to find work, Dad began to talk of going to New York City to find work. He and my mother discussed having him go first. After finding a job and getting settled, Dad planned to send for the rest of the family.

My dad's brother, Tommy, had settled in New York years earlier and had become a New York City policeman. There were no colored policeman in Savannah at that time. Uncle Tommy said that there were good jobs available to colored people in New York and that many more opportunities abounded there. As a matter of fact, Uncle Tommy's description of New York City sounded heavenly and I began to daydream about this promised land.

Dad found an interim job at a restaurant and brought delicious left-overs home for us to eat. He and Mom began saving every spare cent earned from overtime and extra jobs for the relocation to New York. Meanwhile, Bunny and I confided to a few of our closest friends that we might be moving to New York soon.

Dad tried earnestly to stay sober and to be a good provider. One day, he came home with a bolt of green and white striped cloth. I have no idea where he got it. Perhaps he bought it cheaply or one could imagine other scenarios which I would rather not think about. My mother began to sew and before long, my sisters and I had green striped dresses, my mother had green striped dresses and aprons, my brothers had green striped shirts, we had green striped curtains gracing all the windows and green striped slip covers on our broken down upholstered furniture! I think about it now and it reminds me of the leisure clothing that Maria made for the Von Trapp children from the draperies in the movie "The

Sound of Music". Even today, I am not particularly fond of striped clothing.

That same summer, Dad brought home a huge burlap bag filled with brand new shoes. We were so excited as we emptied the shoes on the floor of the living room and started to match them up and try them on. We became speechless when we discovered that the shoes were all for the same foot. They were display window shoes without mates that some white shoe store owner had given Dad. I do not know what motivated the action. Could it have been a cruel joke? Who could think that one would actually walk around with two left feet or two right feet?

We were desperate enough to give it a try. We became hysterical with laughter as we tried on the shoes and looked at each others feet which appeared deformed and strange in the ill fitting shoes. My sisters created comical dance steps and began singing "All God's Chillun Got Shoes", "Slew Foot Sue" and "His Feet Too Big For De Bed". We laughed until we cried. I seriously tried to figure out how to utilize the shoes around the house so that we could save our good shoes and make them last longer to wear out in public. Alas, the display shoes were too uncomfortable; at least one shoe of the set always was.

A SEASON IN PURGATORY

I entered Sister Mary Roxanne's split fourth and fifth grade class the following fall. Sister Mary Roxanne was another young, pretty, high strung nun who yelled a great deal and really did not seem to care for dark skinned, shabbily dressed little girls. Beatrice, Veronica and Ruth Anne sat at the front of the room in their pretty dresses with matching hair ribbons and socks and highly polished shoes. Beatrice and Veronica sometimes wore their Girl Scout uniforms to school and Sister made such a fuss over them. They lived in a better part of town and were obviously from families who could afford to have them participate in activities such as Girl Scouts.

Ruth Anne had very light skin and beautiful silky hair and Sister Mary Roxanne never yelled at her even when she gave wrong answers. She was certainly bright enough but did not have as much at stake as I had and therefore didn't work as hard or get high marks. Ruth Anne and I had been in the same class since the second grade and we liked each other even though we were not on the same socio-economic level. We were in-school-friends only, because Ruth Anne lived in a lovely brick house with a sculptured lawn in the nice colored section of town and her upwardly mobile parents would never have permitted us to take our friendship beyond school premises.

Sister Mary Roxanne seemed to want to humiliate me at every opportunity and this kept me nervous and tense. I wondered how I would endure two years in her classroom. My grades dropped slightly and I dreaded going to school each day.

I stopped at church to pray to Jesus and Mary every day after school. In spite of my prayers, the lighter skinned, well dressed girls still got the better parts in the school programs, still were assigned seats in the front of the classroom and still got the teacher's attention and approval. It was utterly depressing. I held all this inside for I felt there was no one to whom I could bare my soul except Jesus and His Blessed Mother, Mary. I sometimes wondered if they would understand since they too were white. Maybe they did not like dark people either, even though the nuns said they did.

I asked Jesus and Mary to make me white or at least light-skinned to alleviate some of my suffering. After all, Jesus could change water into wine. Surely he could perform a minor miracle and change my skin from dark to light and straighten my hair if I prayed hard enough. I checked my skin after each prayer session but my skin and hair remained the same.

My mother had told me long ago that The Great Creator loved Negroes and Indians and that actually, The Great Creator was Indian and loved everybody. Maybe there was hope after all. Maybe equality and racial justice was more than just my childhood hope and dream. I could not understand the why of racism or why I had to suffer so much. I longed for someone to rescue me. I felt hopeless, shattered and broken. Why had our parish nuns and priests told us that God answers our prayers when He was not answering mine? Perhaps I was not worthy. Perhaps I was praying incorrectly or perhaps, God just did not care.

Why were the nuns and priests favoring light-skinned children over darker ones? Were they even aware of what they were doing? God did not seem to hear my prayers, even when I was patient and prayed faithfully, making indulgences, performing acts of self-denial, making sacrifices and saying novenas and rosaries conscientiously.

STRONG IN THE BROKEN PLACES

This is not intended to be an indictment of the Roman Catholic Church or of the good nuns and priests who served our parish. It is simply another example of the insidiousness of racism and of how good people with the best of intentions unknowingly enter into complicity with and into partnership with perpetuating evil. These devoted, well meaning, religious people were simply products of American History and of their personal histories and upbringing in circumstances where racism was and is a part of the very fabric of our society.

White skin privilege was and remains a harsh fact of life. Institutionalized and systemic racism continues to oppress people of color whether consciously and intentionally or unconsciously and unintentionally. I feel fairly certain that these devoutly religious people thought they were doing the right and noble thing by Christianizing us even though their sometimes brutal methods inflicted lasting psychological damage.

Indeed, our country has made progress in the decades since my childhood but contrary to the opinions prevalent in some sectors, racism is far from over. It has morphed into different forms, sometimes more covert but just as damaging and lethal.

I would like to believe that today, unfettered by the racial legacy of the past and armed with new knowledge and insights, these very priests and nuns, like many of those who followed, would be at the forefront of the fight for equality and justice. Even in the days of my long ago childhood, many of the enlightened priests and nuns went quietly about the business of making us feel valued and worthwhile though the Civil Rights Movement still seemed light years away. When others learned better, I suspect they too did better.

When that tumultuous school year with Sister Mary Roxanne ended, resilience came from somewhere. Perhaps God's answer to my prayers was different from what I expected. Perhaps He simply gave me the strength and the courage to keep going instead of the color change that I requested. Hemingway said, "The world breaks everyone and afterwards many are strong in the broken places." I chose to be one of the many who are strong in the broken places. I looked forward to recovery time that summer with the opportunity to heal the broken places and to brace myself for the final year with Sister Mary Roxanne.

WHAT DOES NOT KILL YOU MAKES YOU STRONGER

This new outlook on things was short lived. That very evening, I learned that my mother's younger brother and his wife were moving into the tiny shack with us until he could find a job and they could get settled in a place of their own in Savannah.

Now, I loved Uncle Fred and Aunt Mag, but there were already too many people living in our run down little house with no indoor plumbing and there was not enough food even for the immediate family to eat. But, two desperate relatives were coming. They had to escape the sharecropper boss in north Georgia and had no where else to go. Seems as though sainthood for me was coming faster than I was prepared to accept it.

My mother explained that this would be a better arrangement. Aunt Mag could babysit and help with the housework so that I would be less burdened. It did not work out that way and soon, my mother was complaining that Aunt Mag sat on her lazy fat squaw behind all day and made even more work for me. The tension mounted and I grew depressed and withdrawn.

One day while scrubbing the front porch, I collapsed on the wet floor, unconscious. The doctor was called and Mom and Dad were told that my abdomen was swollen from malnutrition and that I was suffering from extreme exhaustion and would have to be admitted to a hospital. I had been giving most of my food to my younger siblings so that they would not be hungry and cry. I reluctantly revealed this when I was admitted to the charity ward of the hospital where I had been born about ten years earlier.

I worried that my mother had to make the long walk all the way to the hospital to visit me at night after work and I vowed to get well as soon as possible so as not to impose another burden upon her. I loved my mother so much and wanted to protect her. I wanted nothing more than for her to love me back just as fiercely as I loved her. I know now that she did but for many complicated reasons, she was not always able to show it in ways that I wanted and needed.

I tried to obey the doctors and nurses in the hospital and to heed their instructions to eat, rest and relax, but I kept having creepy, crawling sensations under my skin. Sometimes, I would wake up screaming, thinking that there were bugs crawling all over my body. The medical staff lovingly reassured me by pulling back the covers and examining the bed. They finally gave me medicine that made me groggy and sleepy. When I wasn't sedated, I was urged to eat.

A team of doctors and other people took me into an examining room one morning and there was much hushed talking and note-taking among them. After the two doctors completed their examination, they told me that they would be meeting with my parents later that day and that I would be allowed to go home in a couple of days.

Uncle Fred and Aunt Mag had already moved out when I returned home from the hospital and things were back to normal. Mother stayed at home for a while and meals were better than usual. My father, who was a skilled hunter and fisherman, went on more hunting and fishing trips with his friends to supplement our food supply. We dined on baked 'possum and raccoon, venison, rabbit, squirrel, turtle, catfish and a variety of wild birds. We were introduced to mangoes when my father got temporary work on a ship that made trips to Cuba. We were thrilled when upon his return, he taught us words like *amigo* and *adios*.

Between school terms, Bunny and I generally spent several summer weeks with our maternal or our paternal grandparents. Visits with the grandparents were unique and different but each was characterized by lots of love and by lots of good food. Both sets of grandparents were farmers so the experience of feeding chickens and pigs, gathering eggs and milking the cows was part of the daily routine. I always hid when it was time to slaughter an animal for food. I knew where the meat on my plate came from at mealtime but I did not want to witness the process by which it got there. Both of my grandmothers said I was tender-hearted and treated me sensitively.

Both farmhouses were very much alike, rough hewn cabins with large porches and a porch swing. The rooms were clean and sparsely furnished. There were wells with buckets on a pulley for drawing water and outhouses equipped with Sears and Roebuck catalogs to be used as toilet paper. We learned to crumple the pages in order to soften them and make them more usable. Some people used dried corn cobs but I could not bring myself to even try that.

My father's parents were cotton farmers in rural Georgia but also grew a variety of vegetables, mainly for the family's consumption. Cotton was the cash crop, their source of income. I was allowed to go to the cotton field one day. It was not my calling. I donned my overalls and sun hat after breakfast and picked fifty pounds of cotton before nightfall, breaking only for lunch. To this day, I thank God that an encore was never required of me. After that, I worked in the house and garden with my grandmother, Violetta, whom we affectionately called Big Mama.

Big Mama and Papa Richard sang hymns and read the Bible to us nightly. We said grace before each meal and recited Bible verses before supper. On Sundays, we traveled to church in a mule drawn wagon, packed with cousins and a picnic lunch of fried chicken, ham, potato salad, greens, corn bread and pound cake, pie or layer cake, enough to feed Pharaoh's army. Services at the African Methodist Episcopal Church lasted all day long with a break for lunch. Church resumed after lunch and concluded in time for the people to return home before nightfall. There were no headlights on the mule-drawn wagon.

Indian fry bread was one of the defining pleasures when we visited my mother's parents outside the Cherokee Reservation in North Carolina. They later moved to Georgia also. I remember the tall corn growing in the fields, watermelon and cantaloupe, peanuts and potatoes pulled up by the roots, collard and turnip greens, string beans, lima beans and squash. We learned early on that The Three Sisters in Indian culture are corn, beans and squash.

I remember roasting ears of corn in the fire at night while we listened to the elders tell stories of bygone days. We pulled taffy, plaited it and shared it as we listened to stories about animals who talked and exhibited human traits and characteristics. These stories taught us lessons about how to live in the world and how to treat other people. These were our "bible" lessons as this was how we learned about morality and values. Religion was not separate from the rest of Indian life but spirituality was incorporated in everything we did and experienced. It was an integral part of life. We experienced the Great Spirit in the trees and the flowers, in the wind and the rain, in the crops and in every living thing that was imbued with a spirit and had a name.

My cousins and I sometimes carried messages for my grandfather, Papa Saul, to neighbors or to nearby people with whom he did business. There were no telephones. Once, several of us took a letter to a white man who lived in a large, white house about three miles away. I suspect he had a telephone. The house was surrounded by a white picket fence and looked nothing like the cabins of the Indians and Negroes in the area.

We rang the bell that was attached to the gate and soon a frail looking, elderly white man who resembled Colonel Sanders emerged from the house. He had a severe tremor and walked with a cane. As he approached us, he stammered, "Who-whose l'lil, n-n-n-niggers is you?" My bronze cousins stepped back leaving me in front as I was carrying the letter. "We're not niggers, Sir," I said politely but proudly. "I'm a Negro and my cousins here are Indians. We're Saul Wall's grandchildren and we came to bring you this letter, Mr. Miller." I handed him the letter which he took in his pale, trembling hands, seemingly not knowing what to make of me.

He stared down at me for a few moments then asked, "Wh-where did you learn to talk all proper like that?" "From the good nuns at St. Mary's School, Sir", was my response. "W-w-well don't g-g-get uppity, gal," he said as he turned and went to sit on his porch to read the letter. We stood waiting to be dismissed or to deliver a return message. Finally, the old man said, "You young'uns best git on home. Looks like rain".

We reported to Papa word for word what had happened. Papa said Mr. Miller was a strange old bird but that we had done a good job.

We were delivering a message to another farm family when we saw a group of black men in dirty white and black striped clothing working along the side of the road with picks and shovels. Two white men on horses carried rifles or shot guns and wore sidearms. They were ruddy and mean looking as they barked orders at the sweaty, tired-looking prisoners who were chained together and could only shuffle along. I had never seen such a pathetic sight before in my life and I looked on in horror as the hair rose on the back of my neck.

"That's the Chain Gang," my cousin whispered. "Don't look at them, just keep walking." Keep walking I did, because I was too scared not to. I thought that they must be horrible people who were guilty of doing horrible things in order to merit such treatment. Still, I felt pity for them. Though wretched looking, they were human beings after all. It would be decades before I read the documentation and research and learned about the outrageous practices in our country's justice system that kept tens of thousands of Black Americans enslaved and exploited well into the twentieth century.

Black men were routinely and arbitrarily arrested on trumped up charges or for petty offenses like loitering or vagrancy, fined huge sums which they could not pay and were jailed and sold as forced, unpaid laborers in coal mines, quarries, brickyards, farm plantations, lumber camps and the like. Others were simply captured, seized and forced into involuntary servitude and forced to endure brutal treatment and abuse for years.

I wonder how many of the men my cousins and I saw on the road that day were actually innocent victims of the systemic racism that created and perpetuated these horrific practices and allowed them to continue from the aftermath of the Civil War until the beginning of World War II. That legacy, combined with the legacies of slavery, Jim Crow and other racially motivated injustices leave gaping wounds in the Black American psyche that cannot be ignored if true racial healing and harmony are ever to become a reality in our land.

A WOMAN OF VALOR

We always hated to see the summer come to a close but generally looked forward to returning to school despite the apprehension I felt this particular school year. I was not exactly thrilled but I was resigned, if not entirely ready, to face Sister Mary Roxanne for another year. I was sustained by the belief that what does not kill you makes you stronger.

When the school bell rang, the children lined up and there were whispers that there was a new fourth and fifth grade nun. I wondered if Sister Mary Roxanne had sent her even more evil sister to take over or whether the Great Spirit in His mercy had seen fit to perform a miracle and send a kinder gentler nun. The latter was true and the new nun, Sister Mary Deckler, liked me.

Enterprising one that I was, I negotiated a full work-tuition scholarship with help of the compassionate nun. I agreed to clean classrooms after school in exchange for tuition. This ended the eternal worry about tuition fees for the next four years. Not having to worry about tuition money made up for the fatigue of cleaning classrooms before going home to the many chores that awaited me there.

Sister usually had some food tucked away to give to me for a job well done. Sometimes, she gave me a holy picture or a book, a blessed medal or a set of inexpensive Rosary beads. She probably gave me many blessings and said many prayers for my intention as well.

Sister Mary Deckler was much like Sister Mary Gregory. She talked with the children about race and explained to us about ancient African civilizations. She told us about the advanced mathematics and astronomy and other sciences on the continent of Africa in earlier times and how we were descended from great people and not from savages living like animals in the jungle. She told us never to let anyone make us feel inferior because we human beings were all equal in the sight of God and that we were all children of God. Robert asked Sister why then had God cursed Negro people as the children of Ham. She gently explained that we were not cursed but that some people misinterpreted the Bible that way and wrongly used it as a basis to enslave and oppress us.

She told us also of heroic Indians, for many of the children were of mixed blood. Beyond this, she explained something about anti-Semitism and how the Jews were made scapegoats and accused of killing Christ. It was not commonly revealed in Catholic school that the Roman governor Pontius Pilate, and not the Jews, had turned Jesus over to be crucified. That was a very brave statement for a nun to make.

Sister Mary Deckler treated us children as though we were as good as anyone and assured us that we were. She liked dark skinned children and light skinned children and treated us all the same. She was even kind and loving to ugly children like Ida and slow children like Edward and she shared her lunches with hungry children like me. I thought the Blessed Mother must be something like Sister Mary Deckler. Life was worth living again. Sister Mary Deckler was truly a woman of valor.

The year of recovery with Sister Mary Deckler was wonderful and I started to regain my self-confidence and to blossom again. I thrived on the praise and encouragement that Sister Mary Deckler gave in abundance. Sister said that prayer plus work equals success, so I prayed as though everything depended on God and worked as though everything depended on me. My grades soared and learning became exciting again. Life was so much happier that year. I felt good about God and about the world and my place in it.

THE FACTS OF LIFE

There were still problems at home but school was a positive distraction. For a while, my father gave up the bottle and kept a steady job. His drinking had increased after the encounter with the Klan and he seemed never quite the same after that. During his sober periods, he continued to offer sound encouragement and guidance to his children motivating them to strive for something better.

He felt that the world was changing and that it would be better for his children and for future generations. He believed that the racism and poverty that so restricted his life would eventually give way to justice and equality for his children. He and my mother told us that the children must be educated and ready to step up to the plate making choices that would facilitate this. They said that we must be ready to take advantage of the opportunities that would be open to us.

My father and mother felt that education was the key that would open up new vistas of opportunity for their children and for all people of color. They had dreams and desires that their children would have what they themselves had not been allowed to experience; a more level playing field and the opportunity to compete and to win in the game of life.

Being more of an idealist and optimist, my father sometimes dreamed on a vast and unrealistic scale. My mother was a more pragmatic visionary and found herself having to help keep his feet on the ground, without destroying his dreams. She seemed to know that the struggle for equality would be a long and bitter one. Sometimes, she would allow herself to lighten up and soar with Dad's dreams for a while, but she never seemed to lose sight of the enormity and gravity of the business of surviving as people of color in the South. I took on this consciousness and felt driven not only to equal but to excel academically, morally, spiritually and in every way and at all times.

I planted my feet on an arduous path for one so young and perhaps demanded much too much of myself at times. Struggle was all that I had ever known and it had robbed me of my childhood. I was far too serious and had never really learned to play. Somewhere in adulthood, realizing what I had missed, I decided it was not too late to have a happy childhood and set about learning to play and see the past through a different lens. It was indeed an empowering realization that I could choose to see things from a different perspective and be a victor and a survivor rather than a victim. I realized that I could wallow in self-pity and say "Woe is me!", or I could say "So what!" and move beyond it. The latter seemed much more appealing.

Sixth, seventh and eighth grades with Sister Mary Columbina were years of growth and the experience was mostly pleasant. By the eighth grade, I had started to change in many ways and even Joseph, my friend since first grade, took notice. It was very much a platonic relationship but he actually told me that I was pretty and it felt really good to hear that. Prior to that time, I was focused on being smart, not pretty. I felt that the then-accepted standards of beauty were too far beyond my reach. Some of the other boys in the class commented on my blossoming and developed crushes that boosted my ego and added to my self-confidence.

Mrs. Gross, the school nurse, gave special classes on the facts of life to the girls twelve years old and older. The parish priest held similar classes for the boys. I knew virtually nothing about human development and sexuality. The subtle and not so subtle message that I had gotten from my mother and others was that boys and men were basically bad and not to be trusted. The reasons for this were very vague but the message was clear that a girl should avoid being alone with them or something terrible might happen. It was not lady-like and was even dangerous to allow a boy to touch you, so I was afraid to even sit next to one. I knew little about my own body and the mysteries starting to unfold were unnerving.

Fortunately, I was a little more enlightened after the sessions with Mrs. Gross but I still had many misconceptions like fearing that pregnancy could happen without one even being aware that sperm had entered one's body. The whole Immaculate Conception and virgin birth thing gave credence to that and kept me vigilant. I imagined sperm as capable of leaping tall buildings, through layers of clothing and wide spaces in a single bound. I wouldn't risk touching a boy let alone kissing one or getting close enough for one of those gymnastic sperm to come leaping into me. I was a good girl but I doubted that God would choose me for an Immaculate Conception. It was a confusing time for a naive young girl with little access to sound information.

As time passed, the picture became clearer though it was difficult sorting out truth from fiction. Some of the girls passed on credible information, but some were even more confused and misinformed than I was. It was rumored that a few of the older girls were more experienced, whatever that meant, and went to confession regularly.

Mrs. Gross was the most reliable source and was never shocked by the outrageous questions asked by the girls. She even had a question box so that those of us who were too shy or embarrassed to ask our questions orally could write them out and anonymously place them in the box and she would answer them.

This method worked to some degree and eventually, we girls learned most of what we needed to know in order to adjust somewhat to our changing bodies, practice good hygiene and avoid impure thoughts and actions. Abstinence was the only form of birth control acceptable to good Catholics and this was the only information that we were given. It was a girl's responsibility to practice self-control, because boy's were weaker and more easily tempted if girls were immodest in dress or behavior. Nevertheless, piece by piece, the puzzle began to form a picture. The picture was still distorted and unsettling and it would be a long while before it evolved into a more realistic and healthy entity.

MY SMALL WORLD

My world was very small and insular, covering a radius of a few city blocks. Exposure was very limited. There were harsh incidents of domestic violence and child abuse in the neighborhood from time to time. I experienced nightmares for a while after witnessing our neighbor brutally beat his wife with a heavy slab of wood from their fence. I tried to scream but vomited instead. Some of the neighbor men intervened, probably saving the woman's life. Poverty and hopelessness seemed to bring out the worst in some people. Yet, in others, it brought out compassion and generosity.

Sometimes, fights broke out among men engaged in illegal gambling and there were reports of people being stabbed or shot.

Once, a man who had been knifed ran past our house. He was drenched in blood and breathing heavily as he made his way quickly to the end of the block and around the corner. I do not know if everyone was affected as deeply as I was by incidents such as these but they seemed to etch themselves into my memory forever. The trauma of it made me physically ill. I could not and cannot stomach violence. There were times when I think I actually suffered periods of post-traumatic stress disorder.

My parents tried to shield us from this kind of violence but it was virtually impossible always to do so. For me to recall these brutal incidents opens up scars and post-traumatic feelings even today.

Hearing about the rape of a little neighborhood girl was terrifying to me as a child and made me fearful and vigilant. For a long time, I looked over my shoulders, traveled the streets only when necessary and obsessively checked the locks on our doors and windows, especially whenever my parents had to be away.

Crime and safety issues were factors in our neighborhood but in general, the neighbors looked out for each other and kept watch over the children. The police could not be counted upon to protect Negro citizens. They were often the perpetrators. One mounted policeman who patrolled our neighborhood was so drunk much of the time that he could hardly ride his horse. He had a beautiful brown horse with a white face, a silky mane and tail and large, intelligent brown eyes. Whenever the officer was too drunk to ride, the neighbors draped him over the horse's back with his gun still holstered, and the horse came to Miss Ruby and Mr. Leroy's house next door to us.

The horse always knew where to go. Miss Ruby was so kind and she always gave the horse a treat and served black coffee to the officer to sober him up. Sometimes, she would also give him a plump piece of golden fried chicken to eat when he came to. When he regained consciousness, the officer would thank her and Mr. Leroy and joke with us children and let us pet his horse while Miss Ruby gave us chicken legs and wings or slices of her delicious pound cake. Miss Ruby was known for feeding the hungry and she came to my family's rescue often during lean times. We never knew how she and Mr. Leroy could afford to be that generous but we were glad that they were.

It certainly was not safe to venture into the white neighborhoods for fear of being attacked, suspected or falsely accused of doing something wrong and at the very least, one could expect to be taunted, hit with rocks or spat upon. Golden haired white children might yell out names like burr head, monkey, coon, pickaninny or other ethnic slurs. Groups of them might chant, "Eenie meanie, miney moe, catch a nigger by the toe; if he hollers, let 'im go. Eenie, meanie, miney moe." I went to school, to church and to a few other safe places but stayed close to home for the most part unless accompanied by an adult.

All public places were segregated; restaurants, movie theaters, churches, swimming pools, libraries and the like and Negroes had to ride in the back of the buses and trains. Signs on restaurant doors, water fountains and rest rooms said "Colored" or "White" or "White Only". Sometimes, additional signs said "No Negroes, Indians or dogs allowed". We were not permitted to try on clothes or shoes in the stores and had to be careful not to bump into white people on the sidewalks. It was customary not to make eye contact with them and to defer to them on all matters, stepping off the sidewalk if necessary to allow them to pass. Not to do so was considered not knowing one's place and could result in dangerous confrontation or worse.

One hot summer day, when I was about five years old, my mother and I went shopping downtown. She had taught me to read so I recognized the signs above the water fountains in the store. The sign above the sparkling clean water fountain with the shiny chrome faucet and handle said "White". A dirty, rusted-out fountain in a dim corner had a sign above it that said "Colored". I knew from past experience that I was expected to drink from the dirty, rusted out fountain and that the water from it was warm and not refreshing. I stood contemplating the two water fountains as my mother browsed the merchandise under the watchful, suspicious eye of a white salesman. He appeared to be unaware of my presence since he was preoccupied with racially profiling my bronze skinned mother.

It seemed an opportune time and I gave in to the urge to take a drink of cold water from the pristine, immaculate, "White" water fountain. I stepped up on platform and turned the shiny handle. The cool, refreshing liquid slid down my parched throat like a sweet elixir, sweeter still because I had defiantly resisted the evil system of oppression in my own small, daring way. Still basking in the moment, I raised my head just in time to see a rotund, red faced, rabid looking, sweaty white woman looming toward me, screaming profanities. "Git away you lil' nigger! Git, git!" she roared. My mother jumped protectively between the woman and me and grabbed my tiny hand. The woman, seeing that my mother's skin did not match mine, said to my mother between a snarl and a smirk, "Where did you git that lil' black pickaninny?" Her eyes held an inexplicable hardness and hate. My mother just glared at her and walked away with me in tow. Mother explained to me that it is sometimes better to walk away and live to fight another day in another way. The sweet spirit of resistance stayed with me, nevertheless, and I have never lost it.

I have come to recognize the psychological depths and ramifications of racism. Virulent racism is pathological, a mental disorder which makes the perpetrators delusional. How else can one explain the insanity of scapegoating entire groups of people and trying to subjugate and exterminate them while having delusions of grandeur and superiority about one's own racial or ethnic group?

We had a few books in our house and I traded with the neighborhood kids because I loved to read. Sometimes, I found books in the trash or my parents brought home discards from their work places. A Shakespeare collection and "Gulliver's Travels" turned up one day and I was ecstatic! I read them and hungered for more.

Occasionally, I visited the small public library for Negroes. The inventory was small but large enough to create in me a lifelong passion for reading. Many of the books were in shabby condition passed down from the regular public library that was off limits to Negroes.

Reading was the key to unlocking the confines of my small, limited world. The vastness of the world beyond our neighborhood and beyond the city of Savannah began to slowly unfold. With fascination and wonder, I read voraciously, whatever I could find. I had no context or frame of reference for some of what I read but

I kept on reading nevertheless and slowly the dots began to connect.

When I was about ten years old, we acquired a small tabletop radio. That opened another window into this extensive new world that I little understood. I grew to love a variety of programs but my favorite was the Saturday afternoon opera.

"NOT FAILURE BUT LOW AIM IS CRIME"

My eighth grade class reached a milestone in the year 1946. Graduation was approaching. Most of the students had attended St. Mary's School from grades one through eight and would go on to the other Catholic parochial school for colored children, St. Benedict's School on the other side of town. The then future Supreme Court Justice, Clarence Thomas, attended St. Benedict's School with my younger brothers.

At St. Benedict's School, grades one through nine were taught allowing the students to experience just one more year of Catholic education. The Catholic high schools were for white students only. Colored children who wished to further their education had to do so in the segregated, sub-standard public school system, unless their parents could afford to send them to one of the few private schools or off to institutions of higher learning in locales outside Savannah.

The closing days at St. Mary's were filled with emotion. Children who had been together for eight years were about to be dispersed. Closing exercises had been planned and dressed rehearsals were being scheduled. Final exams were over and the valedictorian and salutatorian were soon to be announced. The rumor mill brought me news that although I had the highest grade point average for the entire eight years, there had never in the history of the school been a non-Catholic valedictorian. To be considered also was the fact that my skin coloring was much too dark to have me so prominently displayed.

When the Mother Superior finally made the announcement, I was awarded honors and Joseph was awarded salutatorian, even though he too was dark, but he was Catholic. A pretty, light-skinned Catholic girl who had actually come in third in the grade point ratings became valedictorian. I was afraid to question the infallible decision of the Mother Superior but my hurt and anger over the injustice gave me the courage to ask why I had been denied the honor since my grade point average was highest. I was told that I should be satisfied with third place honors and that Jesus and the Blessed Mother did not seek earthly glory. Like them, I was expected to accept the disappointments of life with patience and humility. It was the saintly thing to do.

That was the end of the discussion. The subliminal message had been given year after year that dark skinned people were unworthy and that little was expected of them in the way of achievement. Furthermore, the Catholic Church was the only true church and others could not really expect salvation unless they converted.

I accepted this with resignation, which seemed to be my only option. I certainly could not go to my parents. They had burdens enough and did not need to be bothered by my whining. Besides, I had begged them to allow me to convert to Catholicism, so I partially blamed them for my failure to be awarded my rightful honor and prayed that they would see the error of their heathen ways and join the True Church. The nuns had done a thorough job of brainwashing me and I had developed ambivalent feelings towards my own beloved parents as a result. I was totally unaware that I was well on my way to becoming engulfed in religious bigotry. The journey to wholeness and religious tolerance would come in time but not without struggle and enlightenment.

A MILE IN THEIR MOCCASINS

The ninth grade class at St. Benedict's School was self-contained and taught by a petite, middle aged nun named Sister Mary Gonzaga. Though small in stature, she was a strict and firm disciplinarian but the students quickly saw that she was also very fair and treated them with respect. She seemed to have no consciousness of color and she admired and praised excellence in the classroom. This was a good formula for a smooth running classroom with very few problems.

Sister Mary Gonzaga taught most of the courses. The specialist teachers were Father Hill who taught Latin and Sister Mary Miriam who taught music. I excelled academically and Father Hill was impressed with my ability to conjugate Latin verbs. In music class, the other students remarked that I sang like an opera singer. I realized much later that this was a good thing. At the time, I thought it undesirable to sound that way and I sang softly except when I was alone. Some of those alone times were on Saturday afternoons while listening to the opera on the one tiny tabletop radio that my family possessed. I yearned to become a singer of classical music.

Many things were happening at home that year. My father went to New York to work and sent money home periodically. He did not send enough however and my mother, with five children by this time, was forced to return to work full time. Again, I took on the heavy responsibility of running the household. I had always assisted with a major share of the chores but having almost total responsibility for the house and for four younger children was taxing and exhausting and almost more than I could handle.

My father was working as a longshoreman in New York but after one winter of the bitter cold on the docks, he decided that he had experienced enough of New York. He reasoned that being poor in the warmer South was not as horrible as being poor in the freezing North, so he came home.

Shortly after his return to Savannah, my father received word that his youngest brother, Uncle Tommy, had been killed in the line of duty while serving in the New York City Police Department. The news was devastating for the family. It was thought that Uncle Tommy had escaped to a better life in New York and that had given some hope to the rest of the family. Now, he was gone.

My father began to drink more heavily than ever and the tension at home mounted to unbearable levels. I had to clean up the vomit when my father imbibed to the point of throwing up and passing out. I tried to mediate when the quarrels between my parents became bitter. I tried to keep peace between my siblings. I tried to keep peace between my parents and the children. It seemed that everyone looked to me to be the family hero and peacemaker and to keep the family vessel afloat.

Not only was Dad drinking heavily, he began selling moonshine from the house since he could not find a job. My mother strongly disapproved and worried about the illegality and the immorality of the operation as well as possible exposure of us children to unsavory customers. Until one has walked a mile in their moccasins, it is difficult to judge the actions of desperate people who sometimes resort to desperate measures in order to eat, to feed their children and to keep a roof over their heads.

The booze was disguised in a large hot water bottle in which it was stored. One night, the authorities raided our house. My mother had just moments to dive into bed clutching the hot water bottle to her abdomen, feigning illness and groaning loudly. The policemen feared being exposed to some lethal disease and left rather quickly after a cursory look around with their flashlights. Fear chilled my bones and humiliation and shame overwhelmed me. My parents could have been arrested and jailed had the moonshine been discovered. We children might have been put into the juvenile justice system or into foster care.

After that incident, Mom issued an ultimatum to Dad. There would be no selling of moonshine or any illegal goings on in her home or else. Or else what was not clear, but that was the end of Dad's brief bootlegging career.

EYES ON THE PRIZE

We experienced some hungry days after that. The newly installed electricity was cut off, eviction was threatened and parental quarrels became loud and frequent. I felt enveloped in a blanket of shame and embarrassment. I buried myself in school work and housework. I had long ago learned to escape with books and the radio whenever possible. The world of imagination was a needed and welcome respite from the harsh realities of life.

Without my ability to imagine and find temporary escape, I think my sanity might have taken flight. My young soul struggled to keep from drowning in the torrent of silent tears. "Who am I?"

"What does this all mean?" "When will it end?" "How can I change it?" "What are my options?" I sought to use whatever tools I had to solve problems rather than give up or give in but with both limited resources and experience, this was not always easy or even possible.

I was always hungry but my mother said I was greedy, not hungry. I was always tired too, but my mother said I was just lazy. "Darn," I thought, "I could have sworn I was hungry and tired!" My stomach growled and sometimes, I was so exhausted that I could hardly stand it. But, my truth seemed invalid and I was trapped within the truth of those around me. Perhaps my mother was in denial about my condition or perhaps she simply found it too painful to acknowledge the truth when there was nothing she could do to make things better.

Being defined by others and having my reality challenged was confusing and frustrating, leaving me feeling disconnected and unanchored in a world that sometimes did not feel quite real around me. Many years would pass before I learned to trust my own truth about who I was, how I felt and what I was experiencing. Maturity and spiritual evolvement gradually brought me to the realization that indeed I was a worthy piece of the puzzle of humanity, deserving of the same dignity and respect afforded others.

There was no access to resources that might help me unravel the tangled family constellations or to make sense of the unresolved trauma, anger and grief resulting from the pathology of a society characterized by Jim Crow, apartheid, racism and internalized racism. Coming to terms with all of this was a slow, painful and tedious process without therapeutic support of any kind. The strength of the human spirit is remarkable and cannot be underestimated when one keeps one's eyes on the prize.

My sister Bunny's health was fragile and the other children were too young to be of much help with duties around the house. Some sibling rivalry developed between Bunny and me. There was also great love between my sister and me, just eighteen months apart in age. Understandably, Bunny did not like being told what to do by a sibling so close in age and expressed this in hurtful ways by pointing out and ridiculing my perceived flaws of darker skin marred by acne and features that were less delicate than hers. Bunny had the lightest skin of the siblings, close to my mother's complexion, and her beauty was often noticed and commented upon.

I desired peace at almost any price and internalized many of the negative feelings that surfaced during these times, hiding my hurt and wounded self-esteem. I began to feel overwhelmed and my mother sensed my distress. I became very thin and had begun having nightmares. Perhaps my mother was afraid that I would collapse as I had at ten years of age and have to be hospitalized again.

My mother had graduated from a Methodist boarding school for Negro and Indian girls and she began to talk with me about going away to that school after graduating from the ninth grade at St. Benedict's. That was just the motivation that I needed to give me hope in a seemingly hopeless situation. I was energized and inspired to reach my highest level of achievement. I kept my eyes on the prize. By the end of the school year, not only did I have a stellar academic record but I had a leading part in the school play and was valedictorian of the ninth grade class of 1947.

This made for an impressive application and transcript and the principal of Boylan-Haven Boarding School in Jacksonville, Florida was eager to welcome me to the student body of this rather elite Methodist institution for high achieving Negro and Indian girls. Pocahontas Little Dove was about to spread her wings. It was time to soar.

A MIGHTY FORTRESS

September 1947 in Jacksonville was quite warm and I was flushed with excitement as my mother and I got off the Silver Meteor, the train that we had taken from Savannah. The train ride itself was an exhilarating experience. I had never been that far from home before, except to visit my grandparents and a few other relatives in Georgia and the Carolinas. Most of that travel was by Greyhound or Trailways bus. Although we had taken trains a couple of times, I had never been on anything as sleek and streamlined and as smokeless as the Silver Meteor.

The older, smoke belching, blackened iron horses that passed through my early childhood neighborhood on the wrong side of the tracks were dirty and graceless. We used to run and watch the passing trains and wave to the passengers. Some of them waved back and others just stared through the windows or looked away. I enjoyed looking at the well dressed white women who wore hats and waved their daintily gloved hands. I wondered who they were and where they were going and I made up stories about them in my head. I was sure that I would dress that way someday when I was educated and no longer poor.

From the windows of the rear cars of the segregated trains appeared dark faces, the faces of Negro people. They always waved back and smiled.

My mother and I exited the train station in Jacksonville and hailed a taxi to take us to the Boylan-Haven School campus on Jessie Street. We had checked my foot locker and my mother carried my small suitcase. The taxi driver was a friendly Negro man who helped to locate my foot locker in the baggage area and loaded it into the trunk of the taxi along with my suitcase. We rode for what seemed like a long distance and I wondered how much it would cost since we had always had to frugally account for every penny.

The driver finally stopped at a heavy gate made of black wrought iron grating, the entrance to the campus of Boylan-Haven School, which was surrounded by a six foot stone wall. The grass-carpeted campus was scattered with majestic trees and colorful shrubs and flowers. Rising four stories into the air was an imposing gray stone building. It looked massive to me, like a mighty fortress that had stood for many years.

I was later to learn that this building's two upper floors contained the dormitories and would be my home for the next three years. The offices, most of the classrooms, the library, the dining room, the parlor and the auditorium were all located on the first floor of the building. The basement held more classrooms, a home economics center, a small science laboratory, the laundry, the beauty parlor and a small gymnasium.

Behind this massive main building was a much newer annex that housed a kindergarten room and several other classrooms. At the far end of the campus was a basketball court that doubled as a badminton and volley ball court.

It was mid-afternoon when we entered the gate and were directed to the office of the school superintendent, Mrs. Edith May Carter. Mrs. Carter was beautiful with kind, soft brown eyes and a melodious voice. She wore her long, dark, wavy hair in a bun softly pulled back from her lovely face framed with a touch of gray at the temples. Her features were similar to those of my mother although Mrs. Carter was Caucasian.

The taxi driver deposited my foot locker and suitcase in the luggage room so that I could unpack them later. First day classes were already in session so I was instructed to bid farewell to my mother as another student was summoned to escort me to my tenth grade Civics class.

My mother and I hugged and kissed each other good-bye and promised to write soon since my family did not have a telephone. My mother followed Mrs. Carter into her office without looking back and I smoothed and adjusted my navy blue jumper and white blouse as I followed the escorting student down the long corridor to the classroom. The Civics teacher, Miss Glenna Owens, welcomed me and introduced me to the small class of about sixteen students. Miss Owens was an attractive, willowy, Negro woman of light complexion. I had not had a Negro teacher since kindergarten.

After school, a couple of my roommates showed me my bunk and locker in an open bay dormitory and helped me unpack before supper. I would move to a smaller room with three other girls before the end of the first quarter.

Upperclassmen were housed on the third floor. Mrs. Childs, whom we called Mother Childs, was our dean, housemother and school nurse. She was a fair and impartial no-nonsense person who expected adherence to the rules. Her son, a practicing physician in Jacksonville, was our school doctor.

Mrs. Josie Ayers or Mama Josie, a very warm, affectionate and motherly woman, served as dean and housemother for the younger girls on the second floor and was also a nurse and the school dietician. We loved Mama Josie.

The talented, predominantly female teaching staff was racially and ethnically diverse. With dedication, they provided a secure, protective environment and caring parental guidance for developing girls. The atmosphere was nurturing and supportive with a sense of mutual respect, devoid of the humiliation and corporal punishment of the Catholic parochial schools of my earlier years. Expectations were high and discipline was strict but not implemented in the cruel, authoritarian way exercised by some of the nuns.

I had positive feelings as day one drew to a close. It was not until I crawled into my bunk that night that I fully felt the gravity of the separation from my mother and the rest of my family. At home, I had always had to share a bed with at least one younger sibling so it felt a bit odd to have a bed all to myself. A few silent tears fell on my pillow as I drifted off to sleep.

A NEW DAWN

Morning came early at 6 AM as the dorm came to life at the sound of the wake-up bell that reverberated throughout the building. As nearly as I can recall, we had about an hour to make our beds, wash up and dress for breakfast. I did not miss fetching bath water from an outdoor faucet and heating it on a wood or kerosene stove as I did daily at home. I adapted quickly to modern indoor plumbing with sinks and mirrors, toilet stalls, bathtubs and showers.

Around 7 AM, another bell summoned us to the large, bright, welcoming dining room where healthy, balanced and reasonably tasty meals were served. Breakfast began with a communal grace led by Mrs. Carter, the school superintendent.

After breakfast, work duty assignments were performed. Perhaps there was time to freshen up or to review homework before the first chapel bell sounded at 8:40 AM. At 8:45 we were in our assigned seats and tardiness was not an option. No one wanted demerits for infractions of the punctuality rule.

Often, outside speakers of various races and backgrounds were invited to address us on relevant topics during chapel services. These speakers included local clergy, civic leaders, visiting academics and others of note. Once, a panel of three white men from Alcoholics Anonymous spoke to us and engaged us in a question and answer session. This was information I desperately needed considering my father's addiction to alcohol. My deep sense of shame led me to guard that family secret throughout my high school years. During another chapel program, we were addressed by a rabbi and a young Holocaust survivor. The impact of that program has remained with me from that day forward.

At other times, various faculty members presented chapel programs, sometimes with student participation. At other times, juniors and seniors were afforded the opportunity to hone public speaking skills during chapel services, or the Drama Club gave some meaningful presentation. The varied programs were rarely boring and almost always of value in some way. The programs always involved prayer, scriptures and the singing of soul stirring, spirit lifting hymns.

The morning class cycle began immediately after chapel and lasted until noon when lunch was served in the dining room. Afternoon classes began shortly after lunch and concluded at 3:45 PM.

We were expected to manage our time wisely throughout the day, studying and taking opportunities to listen to the news on the radio or on television during breaks or to squeeze in a few minutes of piano practice or to get outside for a bit of warm Florida sunshine and fresh air. Dinner was served at 6 PM.

Since idleness was the devil's workshop, or so we were reminded, after-school hours were filled with activity. There were extra curricular activities, a welcome break from work and study. I joined the Drama Club and the school chorus. Drama Club gave me a creative outlet and the chance to write some scripts and direct or participate in dramatizations. I do not recall every detail of the daily schedule but I remember brief periods of downtime when I enjoyed shooting a few hoops and playing badminton or volley ball.

Since I was on a work-scholarship, working my way through school again, I did not have a great deal of leisure time. I studied between loads of linens and towels while working in the laundry after school and on Saturdays. We had a large industrial sized washing machine and dryer and a mangle on which we ironed the cotton sheets, pillow cases and dresser scarves. Towels were fluff dried and folded along with the linens for distribution to faculty and students. This was not easy work but we took pride in a job well done as we did the linens for faculty and about one hundred fifty dormitory students. We often had fun times just chatting and socializing while we worked.

I was never really robust physically and I did tire from the rigorous schedule of work duties and studies. I have often wondered if this constant stress and overwork with little time to really relax was a prelude to the fibromyalgia and chronic fatigue syndrome that I developed later in life.

At one point, Mrs. Carter recognized that I needed a change and she gave me a break from laundry duty and assigned me the task of cleaning her room and hand washing her laundry. I was nervous about doing a satisfactory job. She never complained or demanded better so I assume that she was pleased.

After dinner, Mrs. Carter and faculty members took turns leading evening devotions in the dining room and we sang beautiful hymns and spirituals. In warm weather, we gathered on the front steps of the main building and sang hymns, spirituals and folk songs to the delight of the neighbors. Mrs. Carter had a beautiful contralto voice and I wanted so much to sing as she did. My opportunity would finally come in college.

GIRLS OF BOYLAN-HAVEN

The Boylan-Haven student body consisted of girls of color, including Negroes of every hue, Indians of several tribes and degrees of blood quantum, and Latinas, primarily from Cuba and Mexico. Differences were accepted and appreciated and we learned diversity by living it.

We numbered about one hundred fifty residential students with another fifty or so day students. Everyone knew everyone else which made for an intimate, close knit community. Older students took younger ones under their wings and it was quite amazing the way we all got along. During the three year period that I spent at Boylan-Haven School, I recall only one physical fight between students. It broke out after church one Sunday afternoon in the dining room at dinner. One girl had to be taken to the hospital emergency room to get stitches in her forehead after being hit with a water glass that shattered upon impact.

The argument was a carryover from Easter vacation when both girls from the same hometown got caught up in an angry dispute. We were all shocked and visibly shaken. Tears rolled down Mrs. Carter's cheeks, unashamedly. Our Boylan-Haven family was wounded. Faculty, like good parents, united in an effort to help us heal and put the disturbing event behind us. What we learned about relationships and non-violent conflict resolution from that incident was taken very seriously.

Some of us, perhaps most of us, as young women of color had experienced trauma of one kind or another. That was a given by virtue of growing up under the racist conditions of that era. Many of the collective traumas created deeply wounded individuals who needed to grow and heal and learn what our mentors and teachers were helping us to discover under their strong yet gentle guidance and tutelage. Our young lives, some already displaced and shattered, were set on a path toward wholeness and healing that would forever affect and define whom we became.

Many of the girls came from privileged families. Some were the daughters of doctors, lawyers, clergy, teachers, business people etc. Others, like me, were from more humble beginnings. Some were fellow work scholarship students who had to maintain high academic standing in order to keep our scholarships and enjoy the privilege of remaining students at Boylan-Haven School.

One student and her sister came from a local family of Negro insurance millionaires. She went on to earn a doctorate and became a professor of anthropology at a prestigious university in New England. She ultimately became the president of Spelman College and Bennett College respectively. She served in many outstanding capacities during her long and illustrious career. Whenever she appears in the national media, I feel a deep sense of pride at the achievements of my Boylan-Haven sister. I refer of course to the accomplishments of Dr. Johnetta Betsch Cole. Her sister, Marvyne Betsch graduated from Oberlin College and became a world renowned opera singer.

In addition to a sound academic foundation, we got a liberal and inclusive spiritual grounding at Boylan-Haven. We learned to think critically and to ask questions, not simply to accept and regurgitate information given to us. Ecumenicity was embraced and racial and religious tolerance and appreciation were encouraged. We celebrated the Jewish feast of Passover with a Seder where attendance was voluntary. We attended a choice of two Methodist churches on Sundays. Prayer cells met once a week. This too was voluntary, unlike Sunday church attendance which was mandatory.

CULTURE, SOCIAL AND LIFE SKILLS

Our broad education included etiquette and learning the social skills that characterized refined young women. We were schooled in proper hostess conduct and dressed formally for Sunday afternoon teas several times a year. We organized and attended formal proms as well as square dances and informal social dances that helped us develop grace and graciousness. I loved chairing decorating committees and seeing my creative ideas come to fruition.

There was an art and a science to getting dates at an all girls' school. Our day student sisters were skilled at finding and setting up blind dates for those who lacked escorts for these events. The boys at Stanton High School, a local Negro high school, were honored and pleased to be invited to enjoy the company of the elite group of girls at Boylan-Haven. They came with their best manners and appropriately attired. Naturally, we were carefully chaperoned at all times and had lots of good, wholesome fun and healthy social interaction.

My junior prom date came down with chicken pox. One of the day student sisters had just introduced him to me a few weeks before during visiting hours one Sunday afternoon. Edward was a handsome, brown skinned young man with striking hazel eyes and a keen intelligence. The few acne scars did not detract one iota from his good looks. He was an outstanding student at Stanton High School and had a quiet but charming and outgoing personality. I was infatuated almost immediately.

When he called from his sick bed to apologize I was devastated but I kept my composure and sincerely wished him a speedy recovery. After I hung up the phone, I was hit with a ton of doubt that maybe he had simply changed his mind because I was not pretty enough. All those long ago self-esteem issues seemed to bubble to the surface no matter how hard I tried to ignore them. I cried in the arms of Miss Lewis, my English teacher who lived in our dorm.

Miss Lewis assured me that I was smart and pretty and that any young man would be pleased and lucky to be my date. But I still had only a week to find another date for the prom. It would be so embarrassing to have no prom date, no one with whom to dance, no corsage, no one to compliment me on my lovely gown, no nothing. Miss Lewis said she had an idea. She had a godson who was a year younger than I but he was very tall and could pass for being older. He was good looking and an excellent dancer she said and she thought he would consider it an honor to be my date. She got on the phone with Alex and I hardly recognized myself as the lovely young woman whom she described to him. His voice was deep but I could only imagine what he looked like. We did not have time to meet in person.

On prom night, when my name was called in turn and I gracefully descended the grand staircase, Alex was standing at the foot of the stairs like a bronze prince in a tuxedo, holding a beautiful corsage that matched my gown perfectly. I thought I must be dreaming. His dazzling smile was topped by a sparse silky mustache which did give him a more mature appearance. No one had a clue that he was a year younger than I. We had a marvelous time. I saw Alex a couple of times after that before school was out for the summer.

Edward called to apologize again after the prom and seemed happy that things had worked out for me. I was pleased when he asked to see me before I left the campus for the summer. He showed up with a box of candy and a scattering of healed chicken pox marks on his arms and face. We had a lovely visit, wished each other well and said our farewells as he would be off to attend Howard University before I returned from summer vacation.

INTRODUCTION TO CIVIL RIGHTS AND SOCIAL JUSTICE ACTIVISM

At Boylan-Haven, we were exposed to and took advantage of a wide variety of educational and cultural experiences. In my junior year, I entered an oratorical contest that was judged by Mary McLeod Bethune, A. Philip Randolph and several of Jacksonville's local Negro clergy and community leaders. I entered the contest for the practice of writing the speech and for the public speaking experience. I had received praise at school for my writing and public speaking abilities and I was confident that I would not make a fool of myself but I did not think that I had much of a chance of winning a city-wide contest judged by such notables as Mary McLeod Bethune and A. Philip Randolph. The title was "What America Means To Me". Even then, I was an independent thinker and could not envision myself in segregated America giving a saccharin speech pretending that I was not suffocating under the constraints of racism and drowning in the river of oppression. I spoke passionately about how America's promise was inconsistent and not congruent with its reality. I spoke of my dream that someday my country would live up to its ideals and of my faith in the possibilities of the nation that I loved to truly become the land of the free, where all would be entitled to justice and equality regardless of race, color or creed. I hardly expected the burst of applause and the presentation of the winner's prize by Mrs. Bethune and Mr. Randolph when I finished. Mrs. Bethune embraced me and I felt anointed and appointed to inherit and carry the torch that she and Mr. Randolph were passing to my generation. I felt it my duty and calling to help create the kind of America that I dreamed America could and should be.

A. Philip Randolph was a handsome, imposing and charismatic man. He made clear to us youngsters in his ringing, baritone voice that freedom is never freely given; it must be won. He was a prominent twentieth-century African-American civil rights leader, labor leader and the founder of the Brotherhood of Sleeping Car Porters. Through his efforts and leadership, he sought to win fairness and equality for all. A. Philip Randolph later helped to organize the 1963 March on Washington during which Dr. Martin Luther King, Jr. delivered his famous "I Have A Dream" speech.

Mary McLeod Bethune, the daughter of slaves, began her career as a civil rights leader and educator, founding the Bethune Educational and Industrial Training School for Negro Girls in Daytona Beach, Florida in 1904. The historic school later merged with Jacksonville's Cookman Institute for boys and eventually became the four-year institution, Bethune-Cookman College in 1941, evolving into Bethune-Cookman University in 2007.

Mrs. Bethune was an adviser to President Franklin D. Roosevelt during his administration and a valued and respected friend of both Eleanor Roosevelt and the President. She was not only a Black educator but an American educator, working with tireless concern for the education of all children, regardless of race, color or creed. She was a dark skinned woman with a commanding presence. She exuded a calm dignity and intelligence. There was a certain handsomeness about her that defied conformity to the fair skinned standards of beauty of the day. She radiated faith and extended a caring embrace to all humankind. I was impacted by her greatness and forever changed.

I spent part of each summer on campus at Boylan-Haven attending youth seminars and convocations and soaking up knowledge like a sponge. I felt I had so much catching up to do, bursting out of my small world and gradually developing a national and global consciousness. I missed my family but I somehow knew that I no longer fit the tight confines of my life in Savannah, Georgia. I wanted more. I needed more and I had to have more or die.

I chafed against the restrictions of discrimination and segregation and my spirit struggled to break free. My heart cried out with the unknown poet, "I'm tired of sailing my little boat, far inside the harbor bar. I want to go out where the big ships float, out on the deep where the great ones are. And should my frail craft prove too slight, for the waves that sweep those billows o'er, I'd rather go down in a stirring fight than drowse to death by the sheltered shore."

The "warrior woman" inside of me made me too brave and too stubborn to succumb to the assaults on my personhood, or to be crushed because the accepted standards of beauty told me that I was ugly. The wounds of racism cut deeply and the ugly scars would not be made whole without the healing balm of justice.

I remembered the wise example and counsel of Mrs. Bethune and Mr. Randolph about the power of forgiveness. The cruelty of racism and the pain of segregation and discrimination enraged me but I knew that in order to survive and to triumph over them, I had to develop the capacity to forgive and to rise above it. Otherwise, the anger would destroy me, stunt my potential for growth and development and prevent my positive contributions, whatever those might be. I determined that I must become a victor and not a victim. I firmly believe that love is stronger than hate and that those who choose love will ultimately win. This in no way means passivity but the practice of loving activism.

UNTIL JUSTICE ROLLS DOWN LIKE A MIGHTY STREAM

I will forever chafe for as long as racism exists and I will work against it and speak out against it "until justice rolls down like a mighty stream".

In our society, if one speaks out and tells the truth about racism and its ugly history, many will accuse him of reverse racism. In the year 2008, shortly before the election of Barack Obama as the first African American president of the United States, The Rev. Jeremiah Wright was demonized for such truth-telling about the history and legacy of institutional racism in America.

Voices of reason sought to explain the justifiable anger that many like Rev. Wright feel. Journalist Bill Moyers observed: "The pulpit was a safe place for black men to express anger for which they would have been punished anywhere else. A safe place for the fierce thunder of dignity denied, justice delayed. I think I would have been angry if my ancestors had been transported thousands of miles in the hellish hole of a slave ship, then sold at auction, humiliated, whipped and lynched. Or, if my great-great-great grandfather had been but three-fifths of a person in a Constitution that proclaimed 'We, the people'. Or, if my own parents had been subjected to the racial vitriol of Jim Crow, Strom Thurmond, Bull Conner and Jesse Helms."

Yes, we have many unresolved feelings and issues, both blacks and whites. Our white brothers and sisters generally have a hard time understanding or dealing with black anger. It scares the hell out of them. They find it hard to understand that anger at the system is not the same as anger at individual white people. They find it difficult to comprehend that because we are frustrated and angered by a centuries old system of racial inequities, that does not mean that we are angry with every white person as an individual or that we dislike white people.

Often, when we run out of patience in the struggle or express strong emotions, we are labeled "angry black people" and some whites will use that stereotype as an excuse to close off and stop listening. Many of us, therefore, repress our feelings and hold them inside until the stress of it kills us with strokes, heart attacks, emotional breakdowns or other stress related diseases. Every day becomes a challenge to live authentically with faith, strength and courage in a hostile land.

We recognize the abolitionists of the past and the modern day anti-racists who have fought beside us for justice, decade after decade, some giving the supreme sacrifice. We fully acknowledge their loyalty and commitment.

Most of us have white friends and neighbors whom we love and respect. Some of us have white husbands and wives and other relatives whom we deeply and dearly love. Our anger is not about bitterness or hatred. It is about the desire for equality and justice. It's about wanting racism to end. We're tired of suffering and want to know what equality, dignity and respect feel like before we die. We're angry because we have played by the rules, done more than what was asked of us, but have still been dehumanized and denied our place in time. Our anger is justified and whites should be as angry about these injustices as we are. We're frustrated that they are not. If they were, things would change.

Many whites fail to understand that *good* people can be prejudiced. They think that only *bad* people are prejudiced so they are horrified if they are called on their unconscious racism, finding it hard to confront or change. We know that racism, conscious or unconscious, is part of the fabric of American society. It's in the very air that we breathe as a people. No one escapes its effects entirely, victims or perpetrators.

I don't think that righteous anger is necessarily a negative when it shocks people into reality and makes them examine their flawed thinking and misdirected actions. There is a time for anger as long as we do not dwell there and we use it to bring us full circle into forgiveness, reconciliation and deeper understanding.

It is a bit idealistic, I think, not to allow ourselves to be fully human and to beat ourselves up emotionally whenever we veer from the impossibly perfect path of never experiencing anger. We cannot re-victimize ourselves as not being good enough just because we sometimes fall short of that ideal. Even Jesus had a meltdown with the money changers in the temple. Following his example, we pull ourselves back to the right path and are enriched by the growth the experience has offered and are wiser and better able to cope the next time we are confronted with free-floating hate and ego and to not take those impostors personally.

We strive to reach the ideal but we must remember that God loves us just as we are, warts and all. As long as our intentions are pure and as long as with all our hearts, we truly seek justice, then we shall surely find it. We shall overcome hate with love.

It is said that for every "Aha moment" that a white person experiences in regard to racism, a person of color has paid a tremendous emotional price. Yes, the lessons that we teach come at an extraordinarily high cost to us.

The sin is not that people are biased or prejudiced but that they are in denial about it. People too often pretend that they are not prejudiced and fail to address the inequities that prejudice creates in society. Until we admit them and confront our biases and prejudices honestly, we cannot overcome them.

Healing the wounds of racism is a long, hard and often painful process. Who will have the courage to stay the course; to grow through the pain and triumphantly come out on the other side? Many will become frightened and run and hide and miss the joy to be gained if only they would stay with the discomfort, the tears and the disagreements until transformation, forgiveness and healing occur. It is so rewarding and so worth it to finally evolve into that sacred space of acceptance and appreciation of the other. We must stay firm in our conviction, tender in our mercy and unyielding in our faith.

It does appear that it is not so much the crimes of racism and genocide that bother us as a nation but the remembrance of those crimes which we would rather forget. But, we must never forget.

Conservative talk show hosts and commentators whipped their audiences into a frenzy throughout 2009, openly voicing their vitriol and their wishes for President Obama to fail. Others were not so open about it and continue to hide behind code words like saying it is the president's "policy" that they oppose rather than his race. Former President Jimmy Carter said what many others were thinking and he was demeaned and ridiculed for speaking the truth. Carter acknowledged that much of the opposition to President Obama was race-based because of our country's history and unsolved racial conflicts. Those who dare to speak the truth on these issues risk being either ridiculed, ostracized, forced to recant or risk being accused of reverse racism.

It is difficult sometimes not to give up on my beloved country. I have to keep believing that "truth crushed to earth shall rise again". It's difficult not to become downright cynical, angry or depressed at times when the battle seems so hopeless. Having come this far by faith, quitting is not an option as long as I have breath. There has never been a time when I have not had to fight for my place in the sun so there is no choice but to soldier on.

Some of my own critics react with anger to my truth-telling and distance themselves from me. If this is the price I must pay for living with integrity, my choice is clear.

Some brave white people risk censure and condemnation for speaking out too boldly against racism or openly acknowledging white privilege. Our country, at all levels of society, seems still unready to address these topics with honesty and to deal with the issues and seek to solve the problems of racism once and for all. It is the conversation that America refuses, so far, to have. My personal list of heroes for racial justice is long and includes people of all hues.

I and most other people of color know that not every white person is a virulent racist and that throughout history, there have always been abolitionists and allies who fought for justice. I would not presume to question the purity of their motives. What I find troubling is the passivity of those who sit on the sidelines and do nothing, either because they do not care or because they live in denial and cannot see, choose not to see or pretend not to see both the visible and the covert racism all around them or to recognize the privilege that they enjoy by virtue of being white. Their empathy is impaired, their vision faulty, their consciousness dulled and their inaction thundering in its silence. We can unlearn racism if we have the will and the intention.

Though I continue to try and educate and to influence with kindness and understanding, I sometimes feel impatient with having to carefully chose and censor my every word in order to avoid being accused of reverse racism or labeled an "angry black woman". I rein myself in when I feel the urge to shout, "Wake up and do something! Don't just talk the talk. Dare to walk the walk!" We are all children of God, sisters and brothers who must learn to live together as such, or as Martin Luther King Jr. said, we'll die together as fools! It would do no good to shout or to show impatience as this would only cause alienation. Maybe there is still some hope in a softer, gentler approach. But racism is neither soft or gentle for those of us who feel its sting daily and I wish that the masses of white Americans would mature enough to face the ugly, bitter truth without flinching and expecting to be coddled and protected from reality.

The fact is that most people would rather be flattered and praised than confronted with truth and challenged to grow. My mother used to say that one can catch more flies with honey than with vinegar. So, the strategy of bargaining rather than challenging, even when it feels less than honest, may be the prudent thing to do in some circumstances. The Obama presidency seems to bear that out. Others may speak the truth about our country's racial disparities but our president strategically cannot. He cannot afford to be misunderstood. He must tread on thin ice, with measured words, and maintain a post-racial stance in an effort to unify the country and not lose majority support. As president of all the people, his hands are tied with the bonds of neutrality and the restraints of a still mythical "post-racial" America. There is also a generational divide regarding race and racism. People like me, born before the Civil Rights Movement, have a lot more forgetting and forgiving to do. Some of the younger people cannot relate to the racial trauma that we experienced. We paved the way for the progress and opportunities that they now experience. We crashed into walls and opened doors that they often pass easily through in the twenty-first century. They stand on our shoulders and reach new heights. For this, we are truly grateful.

The young who are also wise do not forget this. They study history and know that the battle for justice and freedom was often bloody and hard fought. They know that the struggle is not over though the tactics and strategies may differ in confronting the issues of the twenty-first century. They respect the long, hard climb that we made for their sakes more than for our own and they grab the torch as we pass it to their eager, waiting hands.

I am an old woman now and it pains me to know that I shall die never having known what it feels like to have my full humanity recognized by my country. To add insult to injury, I dare not express that sorrow openly lest I be censured and called un-American or unpatriotic. I love my country. It was mine first, through the blood of my Indian ancestors and largely built on the backs of my African ancestors and their descendants. Because I love America so passionately, I yearn to see her become the land that the Statue of Liberty and the U.S. Constitution declare her to be. I want her to overcome her flaws, heal her wounds and be the America of my hopes and dreams; the America for which I have worked and fought for a lifetime.

Our younger people may be the ones we have been waiting for; the ones who have the capacity to help heal the stubborn wounds of racism. They may be the ones who will show the world once and for all how to harness the power of justifiable anger and neutralize the bitterness that possibly contributes to the stalemate. They may be the ones to enlighten the privileged ones who tighten the yoke of systemic oppression, and to bargain with them to concede some of the power. The younger ones may be the ones who can lead us out of the wilderness and teach all sides how to make room at the table and write a new manifesto of peace and justice for all. May the God of our weary years and the God of our silent tears embolden them with wisdom and courage to build, to achieve and to pursue until victory is won.

COMMENCEMENT

My three years at Boylan-Haven School passed quickly. There were countless opportunities for growth and maturation, academically, socially, spiritually, mentally and even physically with my first chance to participate in physical education classes and to play some sports. I was not particularly athletic but I avoided being a klutz and managed a "B" average in physical education classes. Special emphasis was placed on personal growth and spiritual development and on living lives of usefulness and service, making a difference and helping to build a better world.

I blossomed in many ways in spite of my quiet manner as I developed strong leadership qualities. I was an honor student and I was elected to and enjoyed the privilege of serving as Student Council president during my senior year. I also became valedictorian of my graduating class, the Class of 1950.

Our school superintendent, Mrs. Carter, talked with me early that year about my future plans. I had none beyond returning home, finding a job and trying to figure out what I might study at Savannah State College part-time. I considered nursing, but the sight of blood made me dizzy.

Through Mrs. Carter's intercession, I was awarded an academic scholarship to National College, a Methodist liberal arts college in the midwest from which she and two of our teachers had graduated. I was thrilled and my parents were overjoyed. National College was originally founded by the Women's Division of Christian Service of the Methodist Church, now the United Methodist Church, in order to train missionaries and Christian lay workers for service worldwide. It had become a liberal arts college offering degrees in such areas as sociology, psychology, music, education and religious education.

Two of my classmates, Cecelia and Ora Lee, were admitted to National College also but as tuition paying students. They both dropped out after our freshman year. Initially, I thought I would be an Early Childhood Education major but decided on sociology and psychology instead.

That summer at home was to be my last visit of any length, though I did not know that at the time. I was physically tired but I wanted to contribute to the family income and accepted some housecleaning jobs in order to bring in a few dollars. I did not see much of my father who was a confirmed alcoholic by that time. I remembered the panel of white men from Alcoholics Anonymous who had come to Boylan-Haven to tell us about alcoholism. We still could not afford a telephone so I found the number for Alcoholics Anonymous in our neighbor's telephone book. I thought there might be some help available for my dad. When he asked for our location, the man on the other end of the line must have recognized it as a Negro neighborhood. In no uncertain terms he told me that niggers were not "alcoholics" but were "dirty drunks". I hung up the phone and sat there staring into space for a very long time. I could not wait to get out of Savannah.

My mother was working for a kindly dentist, Dr. Rubenstein, who advanced her money for my train fare to Kansas City when she confided that I was valedictorian of my class but that we were struggling to save enough money to get me to college where I had been awarded an academic scholarship. Dr. Rubenstein had trained my mother to assist him in his practice but she was not allowed to assist with white patients who were getting less quality care without even knowing it because the doctor could not have her assist. How ironic! He had segregated waiting rooms and the Negro patients had to wait until he was finished with all the white patients. He did not seem to have a choice regarding the matter if he wanted to keep white patients.

The optometrist, who had been my mother's previous employer, had only one waiting room. He took Negro patients only on a certain day of the week to avoid the problem and not lose white patients who were no doubt better able to pay.

THE FACE OF EVIL

As my mother toiled away at the dentist's office, I took care of my siblings and other responsibilities at home. I was home alone one late July afternoon when a cousin by marriage stopped by for a family visit. He had visited often enough with my beautiful cousin, his wife. I told him that my mother would be home from work shortly and that I would tell her that he had stopped by. Instead of leaving, he brushed past me and sat down in the living room. He was an older relative after all and I was trained to be courteous and respectful. It was a hot day in early July so I thought nothing of it when he politely asked for a glass of cold water.

I had graduated from high school in June so I proudly pointed to my class picture on the mantle as I left the living room and went into the kitchen. He could examine the picture while I used an ice pick to chip some pieces from the block of ice in the icebox. I filled a glass with water from the nearby water bucket using the long handled dipper that hung on the wall near the stove.

As I started to turn around I was startled by the heavy breathing and the husky voice of my cousin saying, "You're the prettiest girl in your class." I had not heard him enter the kitchen. He was so close behind me that I could feel his hot breath on my neck. I moved away quickly and sat the glass on the table telling him again that I expected my mother any minute. He ignored the glass of water, grabbed me and pulled me close to him. The harder I resisted, the tighter he held me. My ninety-five pounds were no match for his strength and bulk as he began tearing at my clothing and trying to kiss me. His intentions were clear. Tooth and nail, I fought and wrestled myself away from him and ran out of the house through the back door. He stayed inside as I ran around the outside of the house to the front where I knew my neighbors would see him if he pursued me.

My fearful heart was pounding as I wondered what to do. I saw some of the neighbor women talking on their front porches so I felt safe as long as I stayed within their view on our front steps. Somehow, I thought this man's outrageous behavior was my fault though I had done absolutely nothing to provoke it. I was afraid to tell the neighbors or even to tell my mother when she came home a few minutes after the frightful incident. I thought she might not believe me or that she might think that I had done something to entice him or to invite such behavior. I was glad that this too would be behind me in a few weeks when I went off to college.

Keeping the toxic secret fueled the self-blame and guilt that I felt. I later realized that my younger sisters and others might become victims of this predator and that they might not escape as I did. I did not know enough at that time to do the right thing, to tell someone. Sex was a taboo subject, mysterious and spoken of only in whispers. At seventeen, I was still very naive, never having so much as kissed a boy. My first kiss would not happen until my sophomore year in college. The closest I had been to any boy was at the school dances at Boylan-Haven School where the chaperones always reminded us to maintain a distance of at least six inches between dance partners. That too was the girl's responsibility and I took my responsibilities very seriously.

COLLEGE BOUND

I slept very little the night before and awoke early that September morning with the urge to pinch myself to make certain that I was not dreaming. At mid-day, my friend and Boylan-Haven classmate, Ora Lee, was due to arrive by Greyhound bus from her home in Woodbine, Georgia. She was welcomed by my family and enjoyed staying overnight with us. We were leaving together for Kansas City, Missouri the following evening to attend National College.

Our house and the bedroom I was to share with Ora Lee were sparkling clean but I remember feeling embarrassed by our poverty and living conditions. Ora Lee never indicated in any way that she expected more. I had no clue as to whether her home situation was better or worse than mine. I knew that she lived with her father and step-mother in Woodbine and that she had been a scholarship student at Boylan-Haven also. Ora Lee was already nineteen and possessed a quiet maturity so I was thrilled to have a big sister.

The following day, my mother helped me finish packing, and then prepared a shoe box lunch of fried chicken, bread, grapes and pound cake for Ora Lee and me to share on the train.

Calvin, the young Sunday School superintendent of my home church told me that he would drive Ora Lee and me to the train station and that he would bring my parents and my sister along to see us off. My dad was nowhere to be found when it was time to leave so the rest of us loaded the luggage and piled into Calvin's car. He was a very courteous, industrious young man, a few years older than I, who aspired to become a Methodist minister. He was working part-time managing a delivery district for the Savannah Evening News and attending Savannah State College. He was a nice looking fellow with smooth caramel brown skin. He would have been much more attractive without the gold teeth that I thought spoiled his smile.

With my mother's permission and under her supervision, he had visited me at home about three times. He had taken his sister, my sister and me on a group movie date once during the summer. He knew that my mother would not have permitted me to go alone with him though I was seventeen years old and had just graduated from high school.

There was a very awkward moment as we said our good-byes at the train station. I hugged and kissed my mother and sister good-bye as Calvin stood politely on the sidelines. I shook his hand and promised to write. As we boarded the train, Ora Lee said, "He really wanted to kiss you good-bye."

The train ride was interminably long. We talked and read, we slept and ate. We realized that our food would not last if we ate as often or as much as we wanted to. I had two dollars in cash and Ora Lee had little more than that. We needed to save what money we had not knowing what lay ahead. We did not have money for supplemental nourishment so we tried to ration the food but it was not nearly enough to last for the approximately thirty-six hours that it took the train to reach Kansas City. We shared the last piece of chicken around daybreak on the day of arrival. Our excitement and anxiety overrode our hunger as the train pulled into the Kansas City train station.

A NEW HORIZON

Both Ora Lee and I had been assigned big sisters who were upperclassmen at National College and they met us at the train station. Ora Lee's big sister, Virginia, was a beautiful young Negro woman. Her lighter skin matched Ora Lee's complexion. By conditioning, I became aware that again, I was the darker sister. Patricia, my big sister, was young and white, a gentle, soft-spoken blond woman from Nebraska whom I perceived as a plain and pleasant mid-westerner. Her kind, soft, blue eyes twinkled when she smiled. We had exchanged letters with our big sisters over the summer but race was not mentioned. They had seen our pictures in the admissions office when we were assigned to them so they had the advantage of knowing what we looked like and recognized us immediately.

We knew that National College was predominately white with just a handful of Negro students and quite a few international students. It was 1950 and the Civil Rights Movement would not come for more than another decade. Southern culture permeated Kansas City. Segregation was strictly adhered to though there were some blurred areas that made things even more confusing. For example, we were allowed to sit anywhere on the city bus from the campus to town but restaurants everywhere were segregated. We could attend classical performances at the Kansas City Music Hall but the movie theaters were segregated. We had to guess about whether or not we would be admitted to any given place or turned away. As we retrieved our baggage, pangs of hunger gnawed at my stomach and I wondered when the next meal would come.

We arrived on the lovely hill-top campus of National College just in time for lunch. A beautiful chapel stood at the pinnacle of the hill, its spire rising heavenward against a clear autumnal sky. As we entered the marble-floored lobby of the residence hall and took the elevator to our dormitory rooms, we overheard a young white woman student say to another, "Niggers are okay as long as they stay in their place." Their soft giggles were unsettling as Ora Lee and I exchanged knowing glances. Mrs. Carter had not prepared us for this and we knew we had to grow up quickly and learn to cope if we were to survive.

Ora Lee and I were each assigned Negro roommates and our rooms were on the same floor but at opposite ends of the hall. We placed our luggage in our rooms and went to the lovely, spacious dining room to have lunch with our big sisters and to meet other students and faculty members who dined with us. The dining room seemed luxurious and vast compared to the one at Boylan-Haven School. The entire campus was like nothing I had ever experienced.

We did not hear any other racial comments. If there were any, they were kept out of our hearing range. Students came from all across the nation and from various parts of the world. Most were friendly and welcoming enough on campus and as we became better acquainted, there were overtures of friendship and relationships began to develop. The separation came when we left the safety of the campus and had to deal with the culture of the town which we had not yet learned to negotiate. We could not join white students as they socialized at the local hamburger joint across the street from the campus. They never thought to ask if they could bring us take-out food, soft drinks or fountain drink offerings and we were too proud to suggest that they do so. Instead, we walked a couple of blocks to the grocery store and bought bottled soft drinks, fruit, cheese and crackers or deli for sandwiches.

There was a conspiracy of silence and no one spoke of these strict boundaries but we felt them and to nurture real friendships across these lines felt strained. Relationships with our white counterparts remained cordial but superficial for the most part and everyone played by the dishonest rules and pretended that the boundaries did not exist. We simply did not talk about them openly. The Negro students talked about the situation among ourselves and encouraged and supported each other.

We were a strong and determined core group of young Negro women who knew that we needed each other in order to survive but who were determined not to self-segregate. We endeavored to participate in campus life as fully as possible. We felt called to be examples and to lead the way in teaching and demonstrating that interracial friendships were possible, enriching and desirable. Had we not heard repeatedly that we must be a credit to our race? Sometimes, we shed secret tears but remarkably, most of the time, we joked and maintained a sense of humor about the ridiculousness and the stupidity of racism. Occasionally, the subject came up among white students during Negro History month or in some sociology or psychology class.

On the afternoon of our arrival at National College, the president of the college, Dr. Lewis B. Carpenter, summoned Ora Lee and me to his office. He was a personal friend of Mrs. Carter, our Boylan-Haven School superintendent. He told us that he had promised Mrs. Carter that he would do all that he could to see me through college as long as I maintained at least a "B" average, the prerequisite for keeping my academic tuition scholarship.

The arrangement was that I would work to earn my room and board. These jobs included working in the library, operating the telephone switchboard, doing some cleaning chores and waiting tables in the college dining room. I could earn spending money by doing laundry and housekeeping for faculty members or baby-sitting their children. I wondered when I would have time to study and maintain the required "B" average. I had met challenges before and had become somewhat skilled at time management at Boylan-Haven School so I felt pretty confident that if anyone could pull this off, I could. I was certainly no stranger to hard work and I firmly believed in the formula that prayer plus work equals success.

Dr. Carpenter explained that he would not be able to offer Ora Lee much in the way of scholarship aid since help was need based and she had family who would pay part of her expenses. He told her of a Jewish family who needed someone to serve as a companion for their sixteen-year-old daughter and to assist their Negro cook and maid with light housekeeping for a small salary plus room and board. The family owned a restaurant in downtown Kansas City and lived in the suburbs, a convenient bus ride to and from the campus.

Ora Lee took the job and moved off campus. We had most of our first semester classes together and spent part of our lunch time and study periods together. We missed an important campus social, a get-acquainted event, because we did not have appropriate attire and felt we would stand out and be too uncomfortable among our well dressed peers. I remember that we cried and comforted each other as we sat alone in my dormitory room while everyone else attended the event.

Ora Lee telephoned her adult brother collect the very next day. He immediately wired her what to us was a generous amount of money. She took me shopping with her the very next weekend and bought us each a good basic dress that could be dressed up or down with accessories and made suitable for almost any occasion. She bought each of us dress shoes and matching handbags. There are no words to describe how deeply touched I was that she would share so generously and unselfishly with me. Hers was the kind of compassion that true friendship is made of and the kind of loyalty that kept the Negro students able to withstand the exclusion and the experience of otherness.

UNREQUITED LOVE

My friend Calvin faithfully wrote me encouraging letters during those first months at college and sent me an Elgin wristwatch for Christmas. He expressed his disappointment that I would not be home for Christmas but I never told him that I could not afford the train fare. I wrote back, mostly about school and to thank him for the watch. I had never owned a watch before. My friends were impressed and I think some may have been slightly jealous that I had such a caring boyfriend with good taste in jewelry.

When Valentine's Day rolled around, Calvin sent me a beautiful, wood carved jewelry chest filled with delicious assorted chocolates and a lovely, romantic card. Again, I was surprised and my girlfriends were impressed. Calvin was probably the dream beau of many a girl but I was never attracted to him as I had been to some other boys. I admired his character and his ambition but my feelings were purely platonic. I had no idea how to handle the situation and I was too ashamed to talk to anyone about it. I certainly did not want to lead him on under false pretenses or to take advantage of his generosity.

Knowing that his interest was romantic upset me. I was angry that he had to go and spoil our friendship. I wrote to him stupidly and not very tactfully asking him not to write to me again and I offered to return his gifts. Calvin must have been hurt and disappointed to receive such a childish letter from me but he was gracious and said that he understood. He told me to keep and enjoy the gifts and to take all the time I needed to adjust to college life and the whole process of growing up in a strange environment. He said he hoped I would write to him again when I was ready.

I never became ready to write to Calvin again but I will always regret that I was not mature enough to be kind. He did not deserve my callousness and rudeness. Years later, my sisters told me how broken-hearted Calvin had been. They said he had fallen deeply in love with me. I wondered how! He had never spoken of love until that Valentine's Day gift and card. We had never kissed or even held hands. I was still afraid of boys and certainly was not ready to deal with young men. I liked them from a distance and became scared when they attempted to get close. I thought that every relationship inevitably led to marriage and I was not ready for that. I did not yet know that I could set limits and boundaries or tactfully end relationships that I felt were not right for me.

When I eventually heard years later that Calvin was happily married and had a family, I felt relieved and less guilty and exceedingly glad for him.

SEX AND SEXUALITY

My well meaning mother had instilled such an irrational fear of boys and men in me that here I was a college student with absolutely no idea of how to relate to the opposite sex in a healthy way. My fear looked to others like aloofness and coolness. I know now that my mother was afraid I might become pregnant and ruin any chance I had of finishing college and having a career and/or finding a husband who would spare me the pain that my father had brought her. She did not know how to verbalize this or how to prepare me so that I would not fall prey to these mistakes. Most parents did not speak openly about sex and sexuality in those days. I guess they hoped that somehow, we would figure it out on our own or be taught by someone else. It was a trial and error way of learning and the miracle is that we managed to survive at all and avoid catastrophic results.

As a child, before I even knew where babies came from, I was bombarded with constant negative messages about sex and reinforcement of the belief that pregnancy out of wedlock was the greatest sin and the ultimate disgrace that could befall not only a young girl but her family as well. Yet, no one taught us anything useful about how to avoid teen pregnancy or about what normal teen relationships with the opposite sex should be. We puzzled over our feelings and over the physical changes in our developing bodies with a sense of shame and uncertainty.

As a seventeen-year-old college freshman, I combed through volumes on biology, physiology, anatomy and human sexuality in the library. I then discovered books on psychology and relationships and I listened carefully as my peers discussed their relationships and those of others. Since our college did not turn co-ed until my senior year, there was no immediate pressure to relate to male counterparts on campus, so I had time to read, listen and learn and eventually to fit some of the pieces of the puzzle together.

After Ora Lee moved off campus, I felt very lonely and longed for the warmth and community we had felt at Boylan-Haven where there were some teachers and many students with shared experiences who looked like me. The social separation at National College was awkward and taxing. There was the constant pressure to behave always in such a way as to be a credit to my race. That was an unfair and unimaginable burden to place upon anyone. I could never act as an individual without the weight of my entire race on my back.

I was not comfortable with the idea of being asked to teach white people about Negro hair or about why the Negroes as a people had a wide variety of skin tones. I was asked questions like, "Do you put shoe polish on your hair to make it shine?" "May I touch your skin?" "Does your color rub off?" "Why are your hands white on the inside and brown on the outside?" or "May I touch your hair?" It felt demeaning and insulting, like being a laboratory specimen.

I was caught totally off guard and cornered in the elevator one day when a young white woman blurted out, "You Negro girls have such full, luscious, kissable lips!" She was rumored to be a lesbian. I was still trying to figure out heterosexuality and understand boys so this was an even bigger mystery to me. I quickly changed the subject and created a distraction until the elevator reached my floor.

I still do not feel as though I am knowledgeable enough to comprehensibly discuss homosexuality and gay rights. I can only state my opinion about the inalienable rights of every human being. I believe in the inherent worth and dignity of each individual regardless of sexual orientation. I do not believe that homosexuality is a choice or that it is voluntary. I believe that it is an inborn orientation along the whole broad spectrum of human sexuality. I respect each person as they were created and fashioned by the Maker of all life, deserving therefore of equal human rights.

I suspect and it was rumored that several women students on our campus and certain faculty members were homosexuals. To my knowledge, they were not openly gay and there was no discussion beyond the occasional allusion put forth by someone in private conversation.

Since that time, I have met and included openly gay people among my friends and associates and, as a justice-loving, truth-seeking, social activist heterosexual, I have come to realize that the oppression that people suffer because of sexual orientation is extremely painful and unfair. While not the same, it is comparable in many ways to religious oppression and also to the racial oppression which is all too familiar to me. All oppressions are a cruel insult to the human spirit. Our collective goal as a just society must be to recognize the dignity and worth of each individual and to afford the same human rights and privileges to all human beings. Morality and spirituality demand it, even as our laws lag in implementing justice and equality.

COMMON BONDS

As the college experience continued to unfold, Ora Lee and I were both making a wider circle of friends. I was adjusting to dormitory life and bonding with other students, both white and Negro. On

Saturday mornings, the few Negro students on campus would gather around the piano informally in the recreation room and sing hymns and Negro Spirituals for perhaps an hour or so. There was something about that time together, that common sharing, that sustained us throughout the week and we looked forward to it.

Sometimes, a few white students would stop at the door and listen but not intrude upon the harmonies and spiritual atmosphere that the melodies created. Oddly, they never asked to join and we never invited them. There seemed to be a mutual understanding that we needed this time alone. Our souls felt fortified after these sessions. It was like putting on spiritual armor in preparation to meet the challenges of the week ahead.

We would share experiences of the past week, offer encouragement and coping strategies and enjoy the safety of our own spontaneous support group. At other times, we tried hard not to self-segregate but to be full participants in extra-curricular activities and campus life. We could not avoid the task of educating our white peers about race. It came with the territory so with candor, humor or whatever it took, we maintained our dignity and set about doing that for which we had no model. There were no faculty members of color to advise us and we were removed from the Kansas City Negro community except for Sunday church attendance and student service to the segregated churches that we attended.

Eventually, we found a social outlet at the Negro YMCA. A warm, chubby, walnut brown skinned, middle aged woman at the "Y" adopted us and we all called her Mama Julia. The young men affectionately looked to Mama Julia for guidance and nurturing also and she chaperoned us, supervised us and planned many enjoyable events such as socials, picnics, dances, masquerade parties and the like. We had lots of good wholesome fun. These were mostly group dates though a few couples paired up in time. The courtship and eventual marriage of one of my best friends, Gloria, came as a result of our YMCA affiliation.

I was a very graceful dancer, thanks to the practice at Boylan-Haven School, and I was a big hit at a masquerade party at the "Y" when I dressed as Latina singer Carmen Miranda. Accompanied by the band, I sang songs in Spanish for the entertainment of all. I had discovered my singing voice by that time and enjoyed singing in the a capella choir at college. I had been awarded a voice scholarship in addition to my academic scholarship and felt honored to be a choir soloist. Performing brought out the best in me. It transformed me and I felt empowered by my ability to establish a rapport with an audience and feel a strong mutual connection.

In time, I accepted a movie date with one of the young men from the "Y" whom I had invited as my escort to a campus event prior to that. I knew that I would find an excuse not to see him again if things started to become too serious and uncomfortable for me as I still did not know how to handle normal male advances.

I was blossoming and becoming somewhat more comfortable and socially at ease around the opposite sex but not ready for romance except in my dreams. I did think about romance a lot. I sang about it, read about it, daydreamed about it and wrote poems about it. I experienced my share of secret crushes on male professors, all of whom were white. In one's daydreams, one could easily cross the boundaries of race through flights of fancy. I discovered that blond hair could be quite attractive on a man and that blue eyes could be quite alluring. I had to stay academically focused with two scholarships at stake so through determination and will, I relegated the romantic thoughts to their own mental compartments, at least most of the time.

I do remember the shock and disappointment that I felt when over the course of my college career, I learned that three of our professors were involved in affairs with female students. Two of them subsequently left their wives, resigned and married their mistresses. My faith and trust in people took a hit as I came to grips with yet another facet of life in the real world.

DIPLOMACY AND SOCIAL ACTIVISM

Throughout the year, I was invited to speak and sing at area churches in Missouri and Kansas as part of the public relations efforts of the college. February was Negro History month and it was especially difficult to keep up with the many requests for speaking and singing appearances and not neglect my studies. Sometimes Hatsumi, my Japanese friend, accompanied me on the piano. Other times, I had brief rehearsals with an accompanist provided by the church. It worked out well most of the time. If there was any doubt, I simply chose to sing some spirituals, a capella. The spirituals are so beautiful unaccompanied as they were originally sung by the slaves and by the congregations in the early Black churches. I sought out some of the beautiful arrangements performed by famed contralto Marian Anderson.

My speeches were described by many who heard them as inspiring and eloquent which made me feel very humble while giving me confidence and the desire to reach others in ways that would make a difference, impacting their lives by bridging the gaps between the races and creating deeper understanding, appreciation and acceptance.

Once on a Race Relations Sunday during Negro History month, I was asked to speak at a church in Abilene, Kansas, the home of President Dwight D. Eisenhower and of the J. C. Penney family. I took the Greyhound bus from Kansas City early that Sunday morning and some of the Penney family who were members of the church met me at the bus terminal. They seemed eager to make me feel at home, so immediately upon our arrival at the lovely, pristine church, they told me that there was someone I just had to meet. Wondering who it could be, I followed them to the basement of the church where they proudly introduced me to the Negro janitor. His was the only other Negro face that I saw during my visit. I'm sure it was their misguided way of trying to establish a rapport of some sort.

My speech was well received despite the brief interruption when a small boy spontaneously yelled out from the congregation, "Hey Mom, look at the nigger!" The child was quickly silenced by his embarrassed parents and I did not miss a beat as I continued with my prepared speech.

After the service, the Penneys invited me to their home for dinner where they told me stories of their ancestors and gave me a photograph of old J.C. himself. When dinner was over, they drove me back to the bus station for my return trip to Kansas City. There is no way of really knowing the effectiveness of visits such as these but I always did my best to bring a meaningful and unifying message in speech and in song. Dr. Carpenter continued to receive requests to have me appear so I guess I must have been doing something right.

Once, my friend Sigrid, an international student from Germany, was asked to speak at a rural church event in Kansas and I was asked to sing. A staff member who was driving us to the event suddenly became ill and blacked out at the wheel. The car hurtled off the highway, down an embankment and stopped a couple of feet short of wrapping itself around a tree. I, who had been riding in the back seat, was thrown forward and came to rest on the dashboard. What stopped me from going through the windshield, I shall never know but my faith in miracles and guardian angels increased exponentially. That was before the advent of seat belts.

The three of us were doused with the coffee we were drinking and had to borrow clothes from nearby congregation members in order to appear at the event. Some men saw us go off the road and came to our rescue expecting the worse. They could not believe that none of us suffered any physical injuries. They managed to tow the car back onto the road. Neither Sigrid nor I knew how to drive. We were just minutes from the church but cell phones had not been invented yet either. We had no way of notifying the church. Our driver felt confident that she could drive the distance and we made the undoubtedly unwise choice to continue on.

We arrived at the church without further incident. How we got through our presentations with frayed nerves and borrowed clothing is a mystery. We took the Greyhound bus back to Kansas City, Missouri with grateful hearts that we had all escaped tragedy.

My singing always brought great joy to me and often moved others to tears, especially when I interpreted the poignant spirituals with emotion and pathos. The great African American contralto, Marian Anderson, was my idol and I actually met her backstage after one of her concerts at the Kansas City Music Hall. She was lauded worldwide for her moving renditions of the Negro Spirituals. She broke many barriers including becoming the first Negro to sing a major role with the Metropolitan Opera Company in 1955 as a regular company member. Anderson performed the role of Ulrica, the Gypsy fortune-teller, in Verdi's opera "The Masked Ball."

In 1939 when she attempted to give a concert in Constitution Hall in Washington, D.C., she was refused because of her color. First Lady Eleanor Roosevelt resigned from the DAR (Daughters of the American Revolution) because of this incident and arranged that Miss Anderson would perform instead at the Lincoln Memorial, where she sang before an audience of 75,000 cheering people. Her marvelous voice was described by Arturo Toscanini as one that comes along perhaps once in a century.

I drew courage from Marian Anderson's story and sought to emulate her poise and dignity in the face of racism and injustice.

I enjoyed singing classical music, especially in Italian. I favored sacred music, especially the oratorios and I liked the spiritual feel of the Latin on my tongue when I sang the masses and hymns. The Latin reminded me of my Catholic school days and felt warmly familiar and comforting. The flirtatious Spanish songs allowed me, in character, to be coquettish and coy. I experimented with various genres of music and quickly discovered that Country music was what I did least well and that it should be forever eliminated from my repertoire.

My friend Hatsumi was an excellent accompanist, a concert pianist who often played for our choir when we rehearsed and performed. We became friends and enjoyed joining three other Japanese students to cook tempura and other Japanese foods while we did house sitting for some of the faculty members. We shared a mutual respect and perhaps the fact that we were all outsiders from the dominant culture made for a deeper level of trust, comfort and rapport. This was true with some of the Latina students and other international students also.

On the other hand, some of the international students had apparently learned how the system of racism worked in America and were even more distant than some of the native born whites. Some of the darker skinned internationals did not want to be associated with Negroes, perhaps for fear of being mistaken as Negro and being denied privileges accordingly. Though I understood their fear, it hurt nevertheless to be maligned by other people of color. Even more disconcerting was the fact that they as foreigners were granted privileges and rights in my country that were denied me as a Negro American citizen.

Occasionally, we were able to address some of these issues in our sociology classes. Once in a Race Relations class we hatched a scheme to borrow a sari from a student from India, dress me in it and have me pass at a local restaurant when we presented ourselves as a multi-cultural group of patrons. To our amazement and amusement, it worked! We were admitted and served.

Emboldened by the experiment, the group next passed me off as an African princess, dressed in African regalia, at a different restaurant. When challenged, one of my white companions countered in a whisper to the manager, "Do you know who she is? She is Princess Omolola. We're honored to have her visiting at our college. It would be very bad publicity for your restaurant if you created an ugly international incident by not admitting her. Her father is probably meeting with the President in Washington D.C. as we speak." I guess we must have been either convincing or not worth the bother because we were graciously served.

When the group visited a third restaurant, we went as ourselves dressed in our regular neat co-ed apparel. We were immediately asked to leave. We peacefully sat there while patrons poured ketchup, mustard and sugar on our heads as they mocked us with insults and laughter. This was 1952. We had no model yet for how to conduct a non-violent sit-in or any other kind of protest so we were not sure what to do next as we sat there dripping of red and yellow condiments with sugar granules sparkling through. We were actually relieved when a lone policeman walked in and said, "Why don't you girls go on back to school. You don't want to get in trouble and mess up your careers and upset your parents." We had been taught to respect the law and we were so frightened by then that we were glad for a face-saving way out of the situation.

In our inexperience and relative innocence, we had not thought through the possible scenarios or recognized that violence might be perpetrated against us. We had not sufficiently organized, sought allies or advice as our sociology professor pointed out to us when we revealed our misadventure in class. It is said that God protects fools and babies. Someone was watching over us.

INEVITABLE CHANGE AND GROWTH

I could feel myself changing and growing. I stretched and tested boundaries, shedding many limiting beliefs but it would take time and work to overcome some of the psychological wounds of earlier times and the challenges imposed by a flourishing Jim Crow system.

After my freshman year, I spent the summer in a social work capacity at Orchard Center camp for migrant farm worker families under the auspices of the National Council of Churches. This was an opportunity to earn some money and to earn some valuable experience before returning to Kansas City for my sophomore year at National College.

The camp was located near the town of Bridgeton, in southern New Jersey. The migrant families traveled there in buses, trucks and ramshackle vehicles from Florida and other points south following the harvests. There were also people from as far away as Jamaica, and Hispanics from several places. They harvested crops for Seabrook Farms, producers of Birdseye Frozen Foods.

As far as I could tell, the factory was manned primarily by Japanese and Estonian immigrants; Negroes, Caribbeans and Hispanics seemed destined for the arduous work in the sun-baked fields.

I traveled by train from Kansas City to Lancaster, Pennsylvania where the training for our service to migrants was to take place. I remember looking and feeling very professional in my navy blue gabardine suit. Thanks to Ora Lee and a few generous friends, my wardrobe had improved since our first train trip to Kansas City.

I hailed a cab at the train station in Lancaster. The driver was a friendly, middle aged, slightly balding white man. I had heard that the North was more liberal and that segregation was not a matter of law. I gave him the name and address of the training site, The Evangelical and Reform Theological Seminary. He was full of questions about who I was and why I was looking for the seminary and I saw no harm in explaining that I was a missionary in training and what our summer mission would be. He explained that he was also a believer, Baptist by faith.

It seemed we had driven all over Lancaster by this time and I asked how much farther it was to the seminary. He said he was not quite sure and that he would stop and ask Maybelle because she knew where all the Negro church institutions were. So much for the liberality of the North. He had automatically assumed that I must be looking for a Negro institution. He stopped in what was clearly a Negro neighborhood and got out of the taxi. He walked over to a shabby storefront and talked with a fat, very dark-skinned middle-aged woman who pointed as she gave him directions. I could not hear the conversation from where I sat in the taxi.

The driver was strangely quiet as he returned to the taxi and we headed off in the direction which Maybelle had indicated. It didn't take long for me to realize that the taxi driver had made assumptions about me and about where I was going even though I spoke articulately and was impeccably and professionally dressed. Soon, we came upon an expansive, beautiful campus with velvety grass, blooming flowers and stately trees. I gave the driver the map showing directions to the building where I had been instructed to report. We passed several white people who smiled and waved as we approached the building and white people greeted us at the door. The driver apologized for getting lost and seemed to fairly deduct that part of the fare after he placed my luggage in the lobby.

The training was comprehensive and professionally done and the trainers were experienced and skilled. The agenda was well planned, with ample time for recreation, socializing and getting to know the participants who were of various races and were from all over the country. They were mainly college students or recent graduates. There were a few older humanitarian "Peace Corps types", who wanted to mentor and serve with the young people.

After a few days, armed with new skills and knowledge, we were off to the mission field. Our Orchard Center staff was comprised of two young ordained ministers and their wives, a teacher, a social worker, two nurses, the Center manager and his wife and several part-timers. I was the youngest staffer and the only college student in our group.

The married couples on staff were housed in two-room, rough hewn wooden cabins. To me, the cabins looked like pictures I had seen of slave quarters. The migrant farm workers were housed in similar cabins with a single naked light bulb hanging from the ceiling. There was no indoor plumbing and communal outhouses were strategically placed on the camp grounds.

We staff members enjoyed the privilege of having our own communal outhouse and sinks with running hot and cold water had been installed in each of the staff cabins. That was a welcome convenience and the larger staff cabins even had showers. The single people could share cabins but since I was the only single girl, I had a small, one room cabin of my very own with a sink and running water but had use of the shower at the cabin occupied by the nurses. I bought inexpensive curtains and a cheap bedspread and made my cabin into an adorable and comfortable sanctuary.

My colleagues were impressed when I invited them to my open house. They all spoiled me since I was the baby of the group but I was determined to pull my weight and prove that I was not a spoiled co-ed and that I was serious about this important work. That was soon evident and I was commended for my hard and productive work. I was a motivated self-starter who learned quickly and applied myself with willingness and enthusiasm.

It was demanding but rewarding work with a cohesive and dedicated team of social activists and missionary types. We all doubled as childcare workers, church schoolteachers, literacy educators, arts and crafts teachers, recreational leaders, coaches, counselors and more.

The female staffers took turns picking wildflowers to decorate the chapel for religious services and the ministers delivered sermons to encourage and lift the spirits of the migrant people whose lives were brutally hard. Religious services were well attended. I led congregational singing and often served as soloist during services. After a couple of weeks, I formed a little choir to help with the music and one of the staffers played a small portable organ. One of the ministers sang and played guitar.

Our childcare center was well organized and we took care of infants and children ranging from three months through five years of age. Our staggered shifts began at 5:30 AM and officially ended at 5:30 PM, though it was usually 6:00 PM before the last field-weary mother rushed in to pick up her child or children.

The nurses held a well-baby clinic and all of the children were examined and screened for immunizations, health, dental and eye problems. We held pre-school and kindergarten classes. We cooked and fed the children healthful snacks and two nutritious meals per day. Prior to our coming, mothers had to take these children to the fields with them. If they were lucky, they might find a shade tree where they could leave the babies with older children to look after them. That was a dangerous arrangement but without someone to advocate for them, the migrant workers were not in a position to demand safer working conditions, fair pay or any other basic human rights. Children were endangered and a few had actually been killed or lost limbs as a result of accidents involving farm machinery.

Our team spoke in local churches, wrote letters to or had meetings with national, state and local officials and advocated in whatever ways we could to create awareness, to raise funds and to obtain help for these forgotten and abused children of God.

To show their gratitude, the migrant women sometimes brought us fresh produce from the fields. We often wondered if they would be punished if caught or if they were allowed to pick leftovers. We used the produce to supplement the meals we prepared for the children and we sat down and had family-styled meals with them twice daily. The children were so lovable and we could see their progress in the three months that they were under our care. The parents trusted us and looked to us for guidance and encouragement.

For the first time in my life, I saw first-hand that as difficult as my life had been as a child, there were those who had even less and who suffered even more. I didn't know how yet, but I knew that I wanted to make a difference in the lives of the less fortunate and disadvantaged in our world. One had to admire the fortitude and respect the determination of these hard working people, and I did.

The courage and resilience of the human spirit showed in the eyes of many of these men and women who walked with dignity and took advantage of our literacy classes and other activities to relax the toil-worn body and to feed the mind and spirit. Like other human beings, they wanted a better life for themselves and for their children. Also, like other human beings, a few fell through the cracks, dragged down by hopelessness, despair and alcoholism. One could feel only empathy, not judgment, for those who succumbed, for who is to say that they themselves would not falter under such deprivation and duress. "There but for the grace of God go I."

GAINS AND LOSSES

Ora Lee had been preparing to leave National College to spend her summer vacation at her brother's home in Florida as I set out to learn about the plight of the migrant farm workers in New Jersey. We did not write over the summer as I had not yet received my post office box and I had somehow lost her brother's address. She was the first person I tried to call when I returned to campus in September. We would have so much to talk about!

I wept when I discovered that Ora Lee would not be returning to college. The family who had employed her in Kansas City said that she went to Florida to study nursing and that she had left no forwarding address. Of course, I blamed myself thinking that if only I had not lost her brother's address, if only I had written, I might have persuaded her to return. Her former employer assured me that this had not been a hasty decision, that Ora Lee realized that National College was not the path to a career in nursing and she had become convinced that she wanted an R.N. degree. National College had no nursing program.

The woman also mentioned that Ora Lee had been lonely with the limited social life available to her and was disillusioned with a set of associates who encouraged her to take up smoking and a lifestyle which was not in her best interest. She assured me that she felt Ora Lee had made a wise decision to go to Florida and study nursing. Blaming myself would do no good. Sometimes, things are meant to happen as they do. I had gained a summer of experience and enlightenment that would last a lifetime but I had sadly lost a friend.

Ora Lee's employers seemed like good people, trapped in the culture of the times. Ora Lee often ate with the kitchen help in their restaurant on the way home from school. They gave her tickets for the two of us to see some of the outstanding performances at the Kansas City Music Hall. We saw the memorable "Lost In The Stars", the musical adaptation of South African novelist Alan Paton's poignant and revealing "Cry The Beloved Country", starring the unforgettable Todd Duncan.

We ate dinner with the kitchen help at the restaurant before heading to the performance. I felt uncomfortable in the kitchen but the food was excellent, what I could taste of it under the circumstances. The kitchen workers were all Negroes. The waiters and waitresses were all white as were the patrons.

Those memories all came flooding back and I knew that I would miss my friend and our many shared experiences, both the good and the bad.

I did not hear from Ora Lee again until the late 1960's when I received her address in Lynn, Massachusetts from a mutual acquaintance. We were both married with children by that time and enjoyed a visit when Ora Lee came to Philadelphia with her family to visit in-laws. She had indeed become a nurse.

We lost touch again a few years after that and I did not find her until around the year 2000 after I learned to use the Internet. Through a people search engine, I located three people by that name and wrote to them all. My Ora Lee responded with a telephone call. She was a widow living in South Carolina, suffering from diabetes and losing her vision. She declined my offer of a round trip plane ticket to visit me in Arizona, as she was no longer able to travel. She sounded depressed during our last telephone call and her letters ceased after that, even though I wrote and called repeatedly leaving messages on her answering service.

I have no idea how she is or why she stopped communicating. Perhaps life and illness took their toll. I shall always love and miss her and it hurt deeply to lose her yet again.

"IN HIM I LIVE AND MOVE AND HAVE MY BEING"

My years in college seemed to pass so quickly. I maintained a good grade point average, more than sufficient to keep my scholarships, and I truly enjoyed most of my studies. I became a sociology/psychology major. I had a keen interest in learning about people, what made them tick, how we function in society and how I fit in. I searched for understanding and insights about myself. There were not too many good self-help books around in those days.

In spite of my excelling academically, performing notably in choir and as a soloist, gaining recognition as a public speaker and achieving in many ways, success was not sweet. I could not relax enough to enjoy it. Each minor triumph that I attained left me more haunted than ever by my inability to rescue the less fortunate whom I was forced by circumstances to leave behind. I worried about my family at home and was conflicted about my ambivalent feelings. I was relieved in a sense to be away from some of the problems, especially my father's alcoholism.

I looked forward to the infrequent letters from my mother but at the same time they depressed me. I tried to encourage my mother and give her hope as best I knew how. I never mentioned my troubles or trials and shared only good news as I felt she had plenty of trouble and trials of her own.

When I didn't hear from her or my siblings, I sometimes felt abandoned and unloved. I wrote regularly and expressed my love and appreciation for them all and I wanted and needed some indication that the feelings were mutual. I encouraged and praised my siblings for their achievements and I felt empty and sad that there seemed to be no reciprocity and no one in my corner to cheer me. No one in my immediate family had come to my high school graduation. A great aunt who lived in Jacksonville came and heard me deliver my valedictory address. No family members came to my college graduation. No one could; I knew that. There was no money.

Still, I shed secret tears after both occasions, then, I beat myself up for selfishly wanting and needing affirmation and recognition. I couldn't figure out how to be a savior and rescue my entire family. I also could not figure out how to fill the hole in my heart and the ache in my soul.

Even in my shining moments, I was plagued by the pangs of survivor's guilt. Would I ever be able to forgive myself for having escaped some of the hardships and for managing to achieve a small measure of success while leaving them behind? I wondered if I would ever feel deserving of the fruits of my labor or of the blessings and serendipitous breaks that came my way. Was I destined always to feel like an imposter, afraid of being found out? Would I forever fear losing it all; having my happiness snatched away in an instant? Would I ever feel good enough? Would I ever feel at peace?

Yes! But not as the world gives peace. Through personal growth and prayer, I would journey toward a peace that transcends understanding and casts out fear.

My spiritual journey continues to take me in search of a deeper faith and a closer walk with the Source of Strength who has sustained and guided me through the years. I have come this far by faith and I hold tightly to the belief that with God, all things are possible. I have to believe that I am strong enough and smart enough, that with His help, I will continue to be able to handle life's inevitable challenges, recognizing that no life is immune to suffering.

My faith in the Creator continues to grow, as does my faith in myself and my ability to face the uncertainties of life with a measure of equanimity. God's amazing grace has been there through the tumultuous storms, a Rock of Ages, solid, safe and sure. Divine love sustained me when I could not love myself and the Everlasting Arms held me up when I was not strong.

This I know for sure. God is in control. We human beings are all inextricably connected and bound to one another. What affects one affects all. Whatever happens to one human being could possibly happen to any other, including me. We all have a purpose, however large or small, a reason for being. In all actions of my life, I endeavor to remain mindful and aware that "In him we live and move and have our being". (Acts 17:28)

I know that the world does not owe me anything. Rather, I owe the world and should strive to make it better than it was before my arrival on the planet. I have learned that life is not a rehearsal, nor is it a spectator sport. You get one chance to live boldly and unafraid. So, if I cannot leave a significant mark upon the world, grant that I may at least leave a small scratch that will make a difference.

STRANGERS ON A TRAIN

My college career was quickly progressing. So much to learn; so little time! I spent another summer working in service to the migrant farm workers at Orchard Center in New Jersey and one summer as an urban social worker at Mother's Memorial Center in Cincinnati, Ohio.

My classmate Mona was returning home to South Carolina so I was happy to have company at least part of the way on the long train trip from Kansas City, Missouri to Cincinnati. We had a two-hour layover in St. Louis, Missouri. We were the picture of what Emily Post probably described as properly attired young women in tailored navy blue suits worn with scarves, hats, gloves and understated jewelry. We each carried matching purses and carry-on make-up kits.

As we walked through the train station in search of food and beverages, we were approached by two handsome, young American soldiers. They were striking in uniform with polished brass, spit-shined shoes and military bearing. They courteously addressed each of us as Ma'am and introduced themselves as Hank and Jimmy. Hank was the shorter of the two, caramel-skinned with wavy hair. Jimmy was ebony-skinned with long eyelashes and soft brown eyes. He reminded me of Joseph, my grade school crush.

It seems as though they had been observing us and had already decided who should pursue whom. Hank paid for Mona's snack and soda and Jimmy paid for mine. We got acquainted and learned that the young men grew up together in Chicago and were meeting others of their unit in Indiana and shipping off to the war in Korea.

The four of us talked until it was time to board the train together. We talked easily, conversation punctuated by the train's sounds of metal against metal and the occasional blast of the whistle. No one spoke of time being of the essence but we all must have known, even in those moments, that this story's ending was uncertain. At any rate, we exchanged mailing addresses and promised to write. After that, Hank held Mona's hand and Jimmy held mine as we sat closer, our bodies rocking side by side with the motion of the train. That was probably the closest I had ever voluntarily been to a man.

Hank and Jimmy gathered their belongings as the train neared Evansville, Indiana. As the train pulled into the station, Jimmy embraced me tenderly and kissed me on the lips. I was only vaguely aware that Hank was kissing Mona also. Jimmy's lips were so soft and warm and the sensation was more pleasant than anything I had ever felt before. It was my very first kiss, a kiss from a stranger on a train. Just that quickly, they were gone. Mona and I pressed our faces against the window panes of the train trying to get a last glimpse of them but they were already out of sight.

We were quiet for a while after that and I wondered if Mona was praying as I was that Hank and Jimmy would remain safe and not die in Korea.

Surely enough, the letters from Hank and Jimmy arrived regularly over the next months and Mona and I compared notes as we answered them. The soldiers' letters were upbeat but there was loneliness between the lines. Mona transferred to another college at the end of the year and we lost contact with each other. I continued to be a cheerleader, writing encouraging letters to Jimmy. Eventually, his letters stopped and I have always wondered what ever happened to him and if he and Hank made it home from Korea. If my prayers had anything to do with it, I am sure they both did. Who knows, perhaps they each met Korean brides and lived happily ever after.

OPERA AT THE ZOO

Another summer of service as a student brought me to Cincinnati, Ohio. The conservatory of music in Cincinnati was a wonderful find and the opera season on the beautiful grounds of the Cincinnati Zoo was unforgettable. Notable artists of the day including Richard Tucker, Jan Pierce, Renata Tebaldi, Rise Stevens, Eleanor Steber, William Warfield and David Poleri performed and I was privileged to attend at least half a dozen operas that season.

I was introduced to Victor, a handsome young tenor who was studying at the conservatory of music in Cincinnati. We became good friends and spent many evenings practicing music and singing together in the parlor of Mother's Memorial Center where I lived. Victor was a decent pianist. We loved each other's voices and enjoyed singing duets and listening to each other sing.

One evening as we were bringing our session to a close, Victor said to me, "Let me sing something special for you." He burst into an art song by Rabindranath Tagore:

> *Do not go, my love, without asking my leave.*
> *I have watched all night,*
> *And now my eyes are heavy with sleep;*
> *I fear lest I lose you when I am sleeping.*
> *Do not go, my love, without asking my leave.*
> *I start up and stretch my hands to touch you.*
> *I ask myself, "Is it a dream?"*
> *Could I but entangle your feet with my heart,*
> *And hold them fast to my breast!*
> *Do not go, my love, without asking my leave.*

I could hardly contain myself. His voice was ethereal and the words left me breathless. I tried not to read too much into the performance because Victor had never showed a romantic interest in me. We were pals all summer and I eventually concluded that he was gay. I never found out for sure, but I tossed that night, sleeplessly dreaming that we were lovers. Of course, when summer ended and I left to return to Kansas City, Victor and I were still just pals. We never wrote to each other and I soon got over the crush.

OVER THE TEACUPS

My life on the campus of National College continued to expand. Singing and drama club infused my life with great joy and immeasurable fun. I wrote scripts for some of our class productions and performed in others. My voice scholarship was awarded during my freshman year when I sang on a dare during a Christmas program.

When our drama club presented "Over The Teacups", a play in two acts, I played the role of a formerly wealthy widow, cousin to another formerly wealthy widow. We were keeping up appearances of wealth as we entertained our friends over tea. Since this was a campus performance, no one seemed to notice or care that the student cast as my cousin was white. The issue came up when we decided, after great reviews, to enter a local drama competition. Our faculty adviser pointed out that we would probably not be permitted to perform a play in which a Negro and a white woman were cast as cousins. Never mind that I grew up with knowledge of white relatives in real life! But this was Kansas City in the 1950's.

Our adviser investigated as to whether or not this would present a problem with the people sponsoring the competition and was told that it would. They gave us the option of recasting the play so that the white cast members were related and the Negro cast members were related to each other. That would mean learning each others parts as well as not being as well suited for the new roles. The unanimous decision was not to enter the contest.

This was a teachable moment but no one took advantage of it. Perhaps no one knew how.

THE CIRCLE OF LIFE

My friends described me as sedate but well rounded with a droll sense of humor. I kept them in stitches during some of our late night dorm room sessions.

A number of those college friendships have endured until the present day. Sadly, death intervened, placing others in a spiritual realm. Love is eternal and the memories are very much alive. I treasure the memory of my dearest friend and former roommate, Gloria; ebony-skinned and willowy with a winning smile and the most beautiful, warm, brown eyes that reflected the kindness of her spirit. She died of breast cancer when we were both young mothers in out thirties. The loss was devastating and never quite reconciled until closure finally came in the spring of 2005. It was then that three of Gloria's daughters and her granddaughter came to visit my husband Gene and me in Arizona. We held a memorial service for Gloria at the beautiful Shrine of St. Joseph in Yarnell, Arizona, an hour's drive from our home in Prescott.

We all participated in a private ceremony sharing memories, readings, songs and whatever we felt moved to express. Gloria's second daughter, Debra, a professor of dance and theater arts at St. Cloud University performed and led us in a dance celebrating Gloria's life. Evelyn, the eldest daughter, an ordained minister, gave an invocation and reading. Carolyn, the third daughter, read a piece she had written for the occasion expressing her love and memories of her mother. Desiree, the granddaughter who was not yet born when Gloria died, moved us to tears with her poignant reading about her dream of what might have been had her grandmother lived and the amazing legacy that she inherited.

We all regretted that Linda and Pamela, Gloria's youngest daughters, could not be there. I sang what I had known to be Gloria's favorite hymn, "His Eye Is On The Sparrow". Gene shared his regret for never having had the opportunity to know the friend who meant so much to me and who was such an integral part of my life throughout my college years and beyond.

A stunning gold and black butterfly circled among us as I began reading a poem, "Perhaps you are the morning bird singing joyfully at sunrise, or the butterfly that dances so carelessly on the breeze". Coincidence? I doubt it. We were momentarily frozen in awe and wonder.

Gloria's girls check in periodically via e-mail and it is always a special joy to hear from them, to counsel them and to take pride in their achievements and accomplishments. They are my adopted nieces, for their mother and I shared a bond much closer than that of many biological sisters. The Circle of Life brought Gloria's daughters and me back into the circle of love and light.

Evelyn, Gloria's oldest daughter wrote the following e-mail to me in the year 2009.

Hi Poco and the gang!!!

I have attached the original letter I got from you Poco. I remember reading it a few years ago, and I remember the tears streaming down my face as I thought about Mama.

Thanks again for being one of her best friends, and thanks to you and Mary for searching to find Mama's children, my sisters and me.

In reading your letter again, I now realize where Debbie got her "African Dance" stimulation. I also realize where Pam got her "Comedian" skills. I see also the passion and compassion for the human race in all of us. I see the drive in Debbie and me to make a difference.

Wow what an amazing letter! Thanks for your love.

–Evelyn

November 12, 2004

My dearest Evelyn Marie,

I can't tell you how thrilled I was when Mary Chaney Williams called from Philadelphia and told me that she had been able to contact you and your Dad! Over the years, we mentioned to each other many times how much we wished we had not lost touch with your family. She remembered that Rev. Gray was still in Kansas City, MO and asked him if he would try and track Smitty down. We were hopeful but were afraid to get our hopes up too high.

After my heart stopped racing for joy, my husband Gene and I got busy on the computer copying the photos of your Mom and Dad so that I could send this packet to you. I hardly know where to begin;

there is so much to say and so many loving memories going through my mind.

Your mother Gloria was at that time the person closest to me in all this world. Unfortunately, there was a lot of chaos in my birth family so Mary and Gloria were my surrogate family. The three of us bonded in sisterhood in sort of a "three of us against the world" fashion. I was the youngest of the trio, so Gloria, because of her nurturing nature and our compatible personalities, took me under her wing and became my closest big sister.

The world was a very different place in those days before the Civil Rights Movement. We were a few students of color on a predominately white campus and we turned to each other for strength and support. There was no Black Student Union or any other support system in place and it is a miracle that we survived and flourished in that sink-or-swim environment.

Fortunately, with National College being a Christian school, we didn't have to face physical threats and we did not know enough to know that we needed emotional support. We confided in each other and figured out coping mechanisms on our own. We shared our fears and misgivings, hopes and dreams and encouraged each other, prayed together, cried together, shared soap and tooth paste when our funds were low and created as "normal" a college life for ourselves as we could.

Everything was segregated. We could not go to the hamburger joint across the street from campus. There was a grocery store a few blocks way; we used to go there and buy cheese, lunch meat, sodas and snacks from time to time. There was a Black theater but if we wanted to go to the white theater with schoolmates, we had to sit in the balcony, that we called the crows nest. We dealt with those indignities with grace and humor. Gloria had such a great sense of humor! We were roommates for a while, she, Mary and I. Then we decided that we should integrate the dorms. It was a daring thing that had never been done before. We were invited after a while to join liberal white roommates, and things worked out fine.

Often we gathered with the few other Black students and sang hymns and spirituals and just enjoyed the understanding and camaraderie of each other. It sustained us and enabled us to thrive and achieve. Sometimes in the dorm room, Gloria would entertain us with some "African" dancing and singing and we'd make up steps and words and join in dancing until we all tumbled on the bed exhausted and laughing. What a tension reliever! Gloria had that way of looking on the bright side of things and enjoying life. I tended to be kind of shy and serious in my youth and she taught me to lighten up and play more.

Everybody loved Gloria, whatever his or her race. Her humor, kindness, compassion and understanding endeared her to all who knew her. That melodious contralto speaking voice of hers was so recognizable and matched her inner and outer beauty. Her spirit shone through those soft brown eyes that seemed to look deep into people's souls and know when they needed a word of cheer or comfort. She was truly giving and unselfish. I still miss her so much and when I pray, I talk to her.

In those early days, we all thought we would grow old together, Gloria, Mary and I. Life goes by so quickly; I'll be 72 in January!

The last time I saw Gloria was around 1956 when I was in the U.S. Air Force and passed through K.C. on a trip from Wyoming to Ft. Worth, Texas. Your sister Debbie was a baby and you were just a toddler. I enjoyed a visit of a few days with my big sis, Gloria, and my big brother Smitty and got the biggest kick out of playing with my precious namesake Evie Marie and with little Debbie. You clung to me like white on rice and I loved it! After that, we communicated by letter and the occasional phone call. After I got married, we were both busy raising our families but kept in touch on a regular basis and just knew we'd see each other again when the kids were a little older and the money more readily available.

I was so worried when the cancer was first discovered but being so young, I was sure Gloria would beat it if anyone could. Then the reality finally hit me. She told me that it was terminal and my world shattered.

I was, at the time, in a very dysfunctional marriage trying to hold it together, with three young children of my own. I couldn't go to her to help and comfort her and just be with her. Your aunt, "Little Ollie", was there but I wanted to be there. It tore me up to know that I could not, after trying everything I knew, make the trip to properly say goodbye to my big sister. I worried about you kids but finally had to trust God to care for all of you as He apparently did, and I am so grateful.

Even in our last conversation, just days before she died, Gloria was comforting me and those around her. She told me not to worry and she was calm and ready to transition and meet her heavenly Father. I know we'll meet again. I know she'll be there to greet me when I cross over.

Well, Evie, I've gone on and on. My heart is so full and I am so joyful to have found you. How are Smitty and your sisters? How is "Little Ollie"?

I want to know about all of you, where and how you are. I hope that your lives have been blessed and happy. I will call you and your Dad soon and hope you will feel free to call or write me when you can.

After I divorced my children's father in 1978, God gave me a second chance at happiness. I eventually met my wonderful husband, Gene. We have had fifteen glorious years together. We moved to Arizona when we retired six years ago and are leading a full, happy life of volunteer work, travel etc. Our sixth grandchild, Allison Elizabeth Gertler, was born last night so we'll be going to California to visit her and the proud parents toward the end of the month. My three children and Gene's four give us a combined seven, scattered all over the country. We visit them and they visit us.

I could write for hours more but my precious husband has returned from doing some errands and I think he needs a good hot meal.

I'll look forward to talking with you or hearing from you soon. Give my love to my Big Brother Smitty and to the rest of the family.

Oh, Pocahontas is the name my parents gave me at birth to honor my mother's Indian heritage. The nuns changed my name to Evelyn when I started Catholic grade school and I kept it until I reclaimed my birth name when I got divorced in 1978. Most people call me by my nickname, Poco.

With dearest love and prayers,

Poco

A TRUE SISTER/FRIEND REACHES FOR YOUR HAND AND TOUCHES YOUR HEART

I treasure all my sister/friends from National College. Two of us integrated the dorms in our junior year. There had never been interracial roommates on campus before Margaret and I decided to share a room. Margaret asked me and I said yes. We were classmates and friendly but not especially close at the time and quite different in personality and temperament. Margaret was very extroverted and outgoing while I was quiet and more of a studious introvert. She was fair, blond and robust while I was nut brown, demure and petite. We would not be able to borrow each others clothes and make-up.

Everyone said it would never work, pointing to our personality differences rather than our racial differences, but we bonded, and never had any serious disagreements. Margaret did tell me about the racist attitudes of a fellow student whom she had known from her hometown in Drumright, Oklahoma. That student was no longer on our campus when Margaret disclosed this.

My Negro friends thought I should be the one to integrate since I had proved myself to be very adaptable and prone to pioneering. They encouraged me to take the risk. In the years that followed, interracial roommates became common on the campus of National College. Thanks to Margaret and me, the unwritten rule was dismantled and no longer taken for granted.

Margaret's married sister lived in town and came to our room to meet me when she visited the campus. She seemed friendly and Margaret never mentioned any problem. Later in the year, when her mother and father visited, Margaret said they asked her why she had not chosen a lighter-skinned Negro if she wanted to room with a Negro. They said I looked as though I had Indian in me and they were not too thrilled about that either. Coming from Oklahoma where there are many tribal communities, Indians were not among their favorite people.

I wish I had dared to ask Margaret how she responded to her parents' questions and comments about me but I suppose, as comfortable as we thought we felt with each other, there were prudent boundaries. I had even fixed Margaret's hair in a French twist at her request though I had not invited her to touch my hair and she had not asked. She often admired my French twist and remarked about the versatility with which I styled my hair. She wondered why her straight, Caucasian hair seemed not to conform as easily as mine did to certain styles. I avoided becoming deeply involved in the hair conversation except to say that in general, Negro hair and Caucasian hair were different in texture.

A teachable moment? Perhaps, but at the time, I didn't see the point or have the inclination to bridge that particular cultural divide on something so personal and so controversial as Negro Hair. This exploration would have to wait many decades until comedian Chris Rock's 2009 movie, "Good Hair".

THE CHOSEN TWENTY-SIX

As our college careers came to a close, Margaret and I both decided to become home missionaries in service in the United States for two years. For Margaret it was probably a free and clear choice to serve in the US-2 program, similar to the more recent Peace Corps but administered by the Board of Missions of the Methodist Church. Margaret had spent a couple of summers doing urban social work in Philadelphia and Memphis during college and saw this as an opportunity to commit to two more years of service through the church.

For me, the decision was somewhat more complicated. Graduation from college would propel me into adulthood without a safety net. I was immediately expected to be an independent, self-supporting twenty-one-year-old. I had been so focused on just getting through college that I had not sought or even known where to seek career guidance or how to go about finding a first job. I did not have the worldliness or sophistication of some of today's twenty-one-year-olds. My life had been rigidly structured to that point, and staring freedom and personal decision-making in the face for the first time scared me.

I had made a commitment to serve the church for at least two years in compensation for the college scholarship funds that I had received. So, when I heard of the US-2 program, which met that criterion, I applied, passed the Mission Board exams and was accepted. The six weeks training course for US-2 service was held on the National College campus beginning about a week after graduation. This was hardly the fast track to a career in religious service. It offered only subsistence pay but provided a safety net of sorts. I would be housed and fed for my two years on the job while I decided what to do with the rest of my life.

A total of twenty-six of us recent graduates from campuses around the country gathered for six weeks of intensive training to go out as rural and urban social workers, teachers and religious education workers, across the nation from cities and hamlets to Indian Reservations and urban ghettos. We dubbed ourselves "The Chosen Twenty-Six" and made up a group song to the tune of "The Battle Hymn Of The Republic". "Glory, glory, we're the Chosen Twenty-Six, We've passed the Mission Board!"

The US-2 program has survived for decades and continues today. Service in other countries drew graduates from all over the nation also. K-3's served in Korea for three years. A-3's went to Africa, J-3's to Japan and so on. I was not ready to make a three-year commitment or to go to a distant country but thought that might be a future possibility.

I requested Hawaii as my US-2 assignment. I had read about the multi-cultural and multi-racial makeup of Hawaii. However, assignments were need-based and I was told that they needed me at Bethlehem Community Center in Charlotte, North Carolina. I did not reveal my disappointment and trepidation about going back to the Southeast to face segregation and Southern racism again. Assignments were made in military fashion and with Christian zeal so, in submission, I answered, "Here am I, Lord. Send me." I thought of being more assertive and requesting a Northern assignment but doubted that the Board composed of dedicated and consecrated white people would understand and would doubt my commitment to serve. Besides, they might send me to the frigid remoteness of Alaska instead.

GOING SOUTH, AGAIN

My co-workers, two middle aged white women, met me at the train station in Charlotte, North Carolina. The center supervisor, Margaret, was a stern looking woman from West Virginia who wore sensible shoes and had her graying hair pulled back rather severely into a bun. She seemed humorless and I could feel little warmth emanating from her. The other woman, Lola, wore a shy smile but exuded a warmth and friendliness. There was a gentle, childlike quality about her. Lola hailed from Buffalo, New York.

Margaret drove us to Bethlehem Center, gave me the introductory interview and talk and the grand tour of the big old two story structure that housed the agency situated in the poor Negro section of town across the street from the YMCA. The first floor of the building held an office, group meeting rooms, recreation room and classrooms and there was a playground out back for the children. The upper floor provided living quarters for the staff and had three bedrooms, two bathrooms, a kitchen, a small library and an office for Margaret's use.

A dignified, older Negro woman from the area was employed as cook and housekeeper. She came five days a week and served Margaret, Lola and me a hearty and delicious mid-day meal and always made enough for them to have leftovers for supper. I was responsible for providing my own breakfast and supper out of my subsistence pay so I tried to eat well at the mid-day meal. The center took care of my rent and bus transportation.

Margaret showed me a bedroom and bathroom that I could use during the day at the center but quickly explained to me that it was illegal for white and Negro people to live in the same household in Charlotte, NC at that time. Therefore, I would live in a nice Negro part of town with Mrs. Tucker, a very fair-skinned Negro widow who rented rooms with shared kitchen and bath facilities to young, professional, single Negro women in the area.

To her credit, Margaret helped Lola and me get acquainted with the town, accompanying us to the bank where we could open accounts, showing us where to shop, how to use the public transportation system and other essential services. She then drove us to Mrs. Tucker's home where I would live.

Mrs. Tucker had a lovely, spacious, well furnished home on a broad, tree-lined street, next door to a professor and his family and very near Johnson C. Smith University where the professor taught. The bus stop was about two blocks away and I would travel by bus to and from work daily.

I was actually relieved to be living away from the center, as I could not imagine working all day with these older women and then being stuck with them twenty-four/seven. Lola seemed so happy to have me join the Bethlehem Center team and we began to bond almost immediately in spite of the difference in our ages.

Margaret seemed to try at times to get beyond her aloofness but I suppose that was just the nature of her personality and who she was. She felt the need to remind me regularly that the younger workers lacked the dedication of the older missionaries and were distracted by social life and secular involvements. Some even left their assignments, she said, to get married!

My housemates were all very attractive, light skinned, sophisticated, well-educated young women from privileged backgrounds. They seemed to have supportive families whom they visited regularly in their hometowns around the state. Alice was a high school social studies teacher. Christine was a kindergarten teacher and Penny and Marion were both school librarians. We got along very well. I was the youngest and they all became nurturing and protective toward me, much like big sisters. They endearingly called me Li'l Indian.

Alice and I shared a passion for classical music, an interest that drew us together almost immediately. We were also closer in age and not in committed relationships. Penny and Marion were in long-term relationships and Christine was engaged to be married.

Mrs. Tucker was refined and maternal. She respected our privacy but required that we behave respectfully, follow house rules and maintain our own rooms on the second floor. She arranged for our rooms to be deep cleaned periodically, upon notice. We had our own house keys and of course, no male guests were permitted beyond the parlor on the first floor.

LITTLE BLACK SAMBO AND UNCLE REMUS

Being my own adaptable self, I quickly adjusted to the routine at the center. Our regular hours were 9 AM to 5 PM. Not being a morning person, I generally arrived between 8:30 and 8:45 AM but almost always stayed late just to prove that I was dedicated and not eager to rush off as I thought Margaret expected.

Lola held kindergarten classes in the morning. I often assisted her and played the piano when she had the children exercise to music and sing. I loved storytelling and reading to the children and always tried to choose stories that would teach as well as entertain. Our small, limited library at the center fell far short of providing books with positive images for and about people of color. All the heroes and heroines in the stories were white. If Negroes were mentioned at all, it was in a derogatory way. I came upon copies of "Little Black Sambo" and "Uncle Remus". The characters had coal black faces and huge red lips. I felt a torrent of rage rise up within me as my mind flashed back to the doll fitting that description that my father gave me when I was a small child.

As far as I was concerned, exposing the children to those books was tantamount to child abuse. My rage melted into a dull and familiar ache, an ache caused by racism and the strain of getting past it as constructively as possible. I had already placed the books in my tote bag with the intention of discreetly destroying them. I felt certain that Margaret, my supervisor, would not understand if I tried to explain to her that these books damaged the psyches of Negro children and nurtured racism and negative stereotypes in the minds of others. She had probably purchased the books herself since she had run the center for many years.

Though I felt powerless, I could not accept powerlessness. I resisted in a way that would not bring retribution. I destroyed the books. I felt safe expressing my outrage to Lola. It had not occurred to her that the books were offensive but she became concerned and seemed to understand why I objected to them. She readily agreed that she should not perpetuate the spread of racism or inflict psychological damage upon the children. She cared enough to respect and honor my feelings about the matter.

Sometimes, a small win is all that a situation permits but continual resistance is important. The oppressed learn ways to resist that may look like passive resistance but which may in actuality amount to powerful psychological subterfuge. There are many recorded examples of how the slaves resisted, ranging from subtle tricks and deceptions to open rebellion.

I recall drinking from the water fountains designated "White" when I thought no one was looking. I got away with it except for the one time when I was five. Those acts of defiance and civil disobedience made me feel empowered as a child even when no one knew about them except me. It reaffirmed my personhood to drink cold water from a clean fountain rather than warm water from a rusty, dirty fountain that was placed there to humiliate people who looked like me.

That was long ago but the psychological warfare continues in the twenty-first century. Racism has morphed into forms that are sometimes less recognizable and are therefore even more dangerous and damaging to the psyche. The tactics are more subtle and covert but I and virtually every other person of color wage the daily battle to maintain the integrity of soul, heart and mind in a society where racism is still pervasive and insidious. Although we continue to resist, and often more openly today, the dull and familiar ache remains long after the rage subsides.

ADJUSTMENT AND ADAPTATION

Lola often assisted me with my Girl Scout troop and other after-school groups. When I had planning to do or reports to file, Margaret assisted Lola. We all shared the responsibilities for adult programs and my training and work with migrant families proved to be very useful.

Some mornings I made scheduled home visitations. We were supposed to get to know the families in the community and try to establish a rapport so that members of various ages would participate and find value in center programs and activities. We were a source of referral to other social service agencies for specific needs and coordinated with the schools in some instances.

I did not feel safe entering some of the dark hallways and stairwells during home visitations. Clients were not always reachable by phone so that they could meet me at the entrances. I talked with Margaret about this and later discussed it with Mrs. Tucker who was on the board of the center. She and Mrs. Dooley, the board president, agreed that considering the neighborhood, it did seem foolhardy for a young woman alone to be exposed to possible danger. We would do home visitations in pairs in the future. Margaret always sent Lola and me. Lola had not learned to stand up for herself and she felt pushed around by Margaret. I did not want to get caught up in their disputes but the tension between them was palpable at times.

Soon after my arrival, Margaret insisted that I meet the minister of the local Negro Methodist Church, sign the membership roll, participate fully, make a financial pledge and attend services regularly. She said that as a Methodist Missionary, that was what was expected of me. She and Lola had done the same at the white Methodist Church. Lola was being micro-managed also and seemed to become more unhappy with the arrangement each day.

Margaret invited me to be a guest soloist at their church one Sunday and she took great pleasure in flaunting me as her protégé. I enjoyed singing but felt the need to do it on my terms.

Margaret's controlling personality began to make me feel that my life was not my own and I did not like the feeling. I assumed that she had freely chosen to be a spinster missionary. I had not, and being a US-2 had not obligated me to do so. I never knew what circumstances brought Margaret to her place in life; therefore, I could not stand in judgment of her. I knew only that I was no longer a happy camper and after the first year and a half I knew that I could not continue to participate in perpetuating my own unhappiness. I had to take charge of my life.

I communicated with other US-2 friends around the country who were having fun, dating and living their lives normally and fully while doing their service for the church. The local Negro Methodist Church bored me and I did not fit. Besides, I could not afford a financial pledge to it on the subsistence salary I was receiving. I was trying to send my mother a small check each time I got paid and was barely making it from one payday to the next with enough money left to buy food, toiletries or to replenish needed items in my wardrobe.

I liked going with my friend Alice to the Sunday chapel services at Johnson C. Smith University. Alice was competing with who knows how many other women for the attentions of a handsome young professor at Johnson C. Smith. I enjoyed looking at and interacting with the young men on campus but most of them were younger student types and dating fellow students. There was a scarcity of eligible Negro men in Charlotte and the competition was stiff. I felt no inclination to jump into the fray even though I had looked forward to opportunities for male companionship since I graduated from college.

Alice and I went to the movies at the neighborhood Negro theater almost every Sunday evening. That was our main social outlet along with attending educational and cultural events on the campus of Johnson C. Smith University. We did enjoy our sisterly relationship though I never revealed to her or to my other housemates the secrets of my poverty stricken family or the circumstances under which I had lived.

I often thought of my childhood years during which I frequently daydreamed that I was an adopted child looking forward to being rescued by my biological parents who would turn out to be sober, kind, loving and rich. There would be no more hunger, cold, quarrels or poverty. They would have a car and I would have lovely clothes, many books, a bicycle, a piano and my very own room in their beautiful house. I would be kind and share with poor children, especially the dark ones whom no one seemed to love. I dreamed a dream of no more dim, eye-straining kerosene lamps by which to read and no more chopping wood for inefficient stoves on which to cook. I dreamed of no more smoky fireplaces lacking enough fuel for warmth. I dreamed of not having to heat irons on the stove in order to iron my school clothes and of hauling water no longer to do laundry by hand in galvanized tubs.

I sometimes wondered what I would do if someone from Savannah emerged and revealed the secrets of my wretched past. I feared having to cope with the shame of having been born into abject poverty and of having a poor and dysfunctional family, still stuck in the throes of my father's alcoholism.

When Dr. Butler and his family relocated from Savannah to Charlotte, my fear of being found out loomed before me. Should I beg them not to tell or should I break the silence myself? My siblings and I had attended St. Mary's Parochial School with Dr. Butler's younger brother and I knew that the Butlers were an intact family, leading a comfortable middle class lifestyle.

I tossed and turned all night the day before Dr. Butler, his wife and young son moved into Mrs. Tucker's vacant room to await the arrival of their moving van. Their home would be ready the following week but I doubted that I could avoid them until then.

Besides, Mrs. Tucker had already told them that one of her young ladies, as she called us, was a social worker from Savannah. They were eagerly waiting to meet me when I came home from work the following day.

Dr. Butler was very brown like me though his brother who had been my schoolmate had much lighter skin. He and his wife were very friendly and we conversed easily. It was not long, however, before the dreaded questions arose. Where had I gone to grade school, high school and college? I could relate those facts without shame and they were impressed that I had been awarded an academic scholarship to college. I tried not to change my expression when Dr. Butler asked if my family still resided in Savannah and inquired as to where they lived.

I had already decided that I would not lie. Savannah was not that big, especially the Negro communities, and not that far away. The Butlers still had ties there also. I would rather tell the truth than be caught in a lie later. I knew that the truth would set me free. It might embarrass and piss me off first but ultimately, it would free me to be accepted on my own merit. The Butlers showed no reaction when I told the name of the street on which my family lived and we continued to converse for a while longer.

As I left for work the following morning, Dr. Butler was relaxing on the chaise lounge on the front porch. We exchanged greetings and he began to tell me that his brother had sent greetings to me when they talked the night before. His brother remembered me well from St. Mary's and St. Benedict's Schools and had told Dr. Butler that I was valedictorian of my class and about the leadership qualities and academic excellence I had shown from an early age. Dr. Butler seemed genuinely impressed.

As I thanked him and asked him to return my greetings to his brother, he said, "I think you know how remarkable you are and that you don't have to play second fiddle to anyone." I was stunned for a moment as he continued, "It's not so much where people come from but rather where they are going that matters." I thanked him again for the vote of confidence and started on my way as he nodded in approval and said, "I like your outfit. It's very becoming!"

I think I floated all the way to the bus stop instead of walking. Needless to say, I was beaming all day.

As far as I know, the Butlers never revealed information about my humble background but they became friends and mentors for the remainder of my stay in Charlotte.

My relationship with the Butlers gave my confidence a boost and increased my sense of self-worth and self-esteem. I realized that it was no longer fear and shame that kept me from revealing my past but rather a matter of principle. I did not need to tell everybody everything. I could set boundaries and reveal, if I wished, on a need-to-know basis. My housemates did not need to know. Our relationships did not have that level or depth of intimacy.

I was living my truth with authenticity and integrity, practicing my values, making decisions and choices based on what I thought was good for me and on what I believed rather than on pleasing people. I felt a tremendous sense of freedom and inner pride about my growth and accomplishments, my sense of self-worth and value, my self-determination and my growing confidence and maturity. I could be humble and nurture myself without showing arrogance and let my true spirit shine through.

My housemates and others with whom we associated seemed to assume that my background was very similar to their middle class upbringing. Alice and I talked a lot about men and strategies for meeting the "right" kind of men and getting dates. Dates were as scarce as hen's teeth with the absence of eligible men. We were invited to an occasional house party but the men who showed up always had wives or girlfriends in tow. We were definitely not into the bar and club scene where the same ratios existed and the "right" kind of men were unlikely to be hanging out in those places anyway.

DEEP IN THE HEART OF DIXIE

Living with the restrictions imposed deep in the heart of Dixie felt like living in a universe parallel to the rest of humanity. I wanted to join the rest of the human race and enjoy the rights and privileges automatically given to everyone else. Why should I be denied them by virtue of the color of my skin?

The middle class Negro community in Charlotte was close knit and embraced me. At times, I enjoyed the camaraderie. I admit that sometimes it felt a bit too bourgeois for comfort but more than that, I was bothered by the fact that the racial separation and limitations were imposed and legally sanctioned. There were no choices or options. I wanted to spread my wings, to compete on an equal footing, on a level playing field, to not feel the otherness of being Negro, to not endure the consciousness of exclusion and of being treated as less than and inferior to white people.

The world in Charlotte seemed all black and white, very small and suffocating. I did not encounter people of other cultures or other ethnic groups. There was minimal interaction with white store clerks, bus drivers and bank tellers as I went about daily life and little beyond that. I was referred only to Negro doctors and dentists when the need arose. There was something about this system of apartheid that seemed so unnatural and unsettling.

This and work drained me so much that I felt I had nothing left to offer through volunteering beyond the occasional involvement at church. I began taking voice lessons again and I joined a community chorus giving me opportunities for exposure as a soloist. Music was also good therapy as it relaxed me and alleviated some of the loneliness that I felt. I found great joy in music, and Mozart could always bring sunshine into my cloudiest day.

Some parts of my job reminded me of working with the migrant farm workers. Many of the client needs were similar and demanded the same kind of emotional investment from the professionals who worked with them. We were all at risk for emotional burnout without proper support systems in place or lifestyles tailored to balance the demands of work. I had none of those.

I visited my family at Easter and Christmas when my housemates went back to their hometowns and families but that increased rather than reduced my stress. The last Easter that I visited my family, my father was so intoxicated that he fell on my foot and broke it. When I returned to Charlotte with a broken foot, I lied and said that my father was ill and had fallen as he tried to get up to greet me. I did not mention that the illness was alcoholism. That stretching of the truth got me some sympathy and saved me the embarrassment of revealing the family secrets that I had harbored for so long.

With treatment, my foot healed and I needed to get on with figuring out what to do with my life. My US-2 term would not be up for several months more but I began to look at my options. I suddenly remembered that I had been quite impressed when a Boylan-Haven School friend came to visit Ora Lee and me at college. She described the career and travel opportunities offered her by the United States Air Force and she seemed so fulfilled and happy. She looked stunning in her Air Force uniform. For a while after that, I pictured myself in Air Force blue and thought it a possibility worth considering. The G.I. Bill was appealing and offered the opportunity for me to go back to school for a master's degree. I also found it very appealing that the military was racially integrated.

THIS IS MY COUNTRY

I come from a long line of patriotic Americans on both the Indian and the Negro sides of my family, many of whom served faithfully in the military of the United States at home and abroad, in times of peace and in times of war. Perhaps that explained my latent desire to serve my country.

My first patriotic memory is the singing of "Three Cheers For The Red White and Blue" in kindergarten. My mother explained to me in age-appropriate terms the meaning of the American flag. American Indians have had a long history of strong patriotism despite the fact that America has not treated them fairly. We love this land and it was ours first. We have come to its defense to protect our piece of Mother Earth even when our government has denied us our rights and often our very humanity. The Code Talkers, Ira Hayes and many other American Indians have served our country with dedication, devotion, dignity and valor.

My love of country always gave me hope and faith that in time, my country would ultimately treat all of its citizens equally, with liberty and justice for all. So much of our country was built on the backs of my Negro ancestors, who never received compensation for their slave labor. Their blood and the blood of their descendants has been shed around the world in heroic defense of our country. The Buffalo Soldiers, the Tuskegee Airmen and Dorrie Miller were real African American heroes. This is my country!

Patriotism, not nationalism, fueled my passion to serve. My patriotism includes my love of country and my love for all humanity. It is an inclusive love and respect that envisions and embraces peace on earth and promotes brotherhood and healing of shattered lives around the globe.

At college, I first heard "A Song of Peace", sung to the tune of Finlandia, by composer Jean Sibelius. The words of the song resonated so deeply in my heart that even now, in our war torn world, those words resound and echo from the depths of my very soul.

> *This is my song, O God of all the nations,*
> *a song of peace for lands afar and mine;*
> *this is my home, the country where my heart is;*
> *here are my hopes, my dreams, my holy shrine:*
> *but other hearts in other lands are beating*
> *with hopes and dreams as true and high as mine.*
>
> *My country's skies are bluer than the ocean,*
> *and sunlight beams on cloverleaf and pine;*
> *but other lands have sunlight too, and clover,*
> *and skies are everywhere as blue as mine:*
> *O hear my song, thou God of all the nations,*
> *a song of peace for their land and for mine.*
>
> *May truth and freedom come to every nation;*
> *may peace abound where strife has raged so long;*
> *that each may seek to love and build together,*
> *a world united, righting every wrong;*
> *a world united in its love for freedom,*
> *proclaiming peace together in one song.*

Since the days of my youth, I have evolved into a pacifist. War is not the answer! In the modern world and perhaps in all times, war has solved nothing. Mainly poor people have fought and killed other poor people all over the world. Brave Americans, thinking that they were fighting for duty, honor and country, later discovered that much of the brutal sacrifice, genocide and occupation are for the benefit of corporations like Northrop, Exxon Mobil and Halliburton. Would to God that we could find a saner and less primitive way to solve humanity's conflicts and problems!

LOOKING AHEAD

There seemed no reason, on that warm November day in Charlotte, not to gather information about the Air Force. I looked up the local Air Force recruiting office in the telephone book and made an appointment to talk at length with a female recruiting officer that very evening after work. She encouraged me to apply for Officer Candidate School since I was a college graduate. She explained that not many women were being admitted as officer candidates but that I had nothing to lose by trying and that I could always join as an enlisted person if I failed the test or was not accepted for whatever reason. I said I would think it over.

When I walked out of the recruiter's office that evening, I was almost certain that I would call her back soon and arrange to take the Officer Candidate School test. I was also almost certain that I would enlist in the United States Air Force if the OCS option fell through. I told my boss that I needed to go home for a couple of days to see my ailing father and off I went to Fort Sumter, South Carolina, near Charleston, to take the OCS test.

I arrived on base in the early evening the night before the test. I spent the night with my door double-bolted in the bachelor officer's quarters so that I would be ready to report for testing early the next morning. Right on schedule, I received a wake up call. The caller seemed surprised to hear my female voice on the other end of the line but wished me luck with the testing.

I felt confident and stunning in my attire reminiscent of outfits worn by Audrey Hepburn. I wore a flattering, form fitting, charcoal gray tweed dress, medium high-heeled black leather pumps with matching handbag and a white cloche hat and gloves. In the 1950's, this manner of dress was considered professional and ladylike. It was also an indication of class and reflected good taste and breeding.

I had been instructed to report to the mess hall for breakfast and then to the testing room where I was the only applicant. The uniformed man administering the test was friendly but very professional and did everything with military precision.

After the academic portion of the test, I was allowed to take a break while my test was scored. I was pleased when I was informed that I had passed and done exceptionally well on the academic portion of the test. Now, it was time for the personality portion of the test. I had no idea what a military officer's personality should look like. I suspected it would be assertive but not overly aggressive.

At any rate, I decided that I should answer the questions honestly and I could see that the same information was being asked in many different ways so that trying to outsmart the test was virtually out of the question. Also, I reasoned that if I were not suitable for Officer Candidate Training, I would not want to be stuck in a situation in which I would be incompatible and unhappy.

The test consisted of a series of multiple-choice questions. One went something like this. In your leisure time, would you prefer to (a) read a book (b) crochet a lace doily (c) cook a meal or (d) clean a carburetor. Let us not even mention the fact that I did not know what a carburetor was. I only knew that it was on a car somewhere.

The gentleman administering and scoring the test tried to break the news to me gently. He actually blushed as he told me that the test deemed I was too feminine. "Darn!" I thought. "I should have checked (d) clean a carburetor."

"You are very smart, Ma'am," he said. "You would make an excellent school teacher. If you really want a military career, you can enlist and work your way up through the ranks. You could choose to retake the test within a specified period of time if you desire." He pointed out that there were military jobs as an enlisted person suited to my personality, temperament and abilities. Actually, I was not too disappointed. I was not accustomed to failure but somehow this didn't bother me too much. I blamed it on sexism and I did not regret being feminine. I enjoyed being a girl! I learned much later that race may have played a part and that the military, in spite of all its progress, was not free of racism.

When I returned to Charlotte later that day, I made an appointment with the recruiter to take the enlistment test the following day. I aced it with ease. The few questions that posed difficulty had to do with mathematics, always the area in which my aptitude was weakest. I passed the physical examination although the doctor suggested that I gain about five pounds. He added that on the military diet, I likely would anyway.

I set a tentative enlistment date for January, right after the holidays, so that I could spend Christmas with my family. I was informed that I could be sworn in early in January. For the next three years, I would belong to Uncle Sam. Nothing was cast in concrete until I was sworn in but barring anything unforeseen, I was ready to proceed.

It felt good to have a plan and I looked forward to a new and exciting adventure. I savored it as I mapped out my exit strategy. I needed to write letters of resignation to my supervisor Margaret, to the board of Bethlehem Center and to the Methodist Mission Board. I needed to break the news to my friends and family and I wanted especially to talk with Dr. and Mrs. Butler. The Butlers gave me their blessings. Dr. Butler had served in the military and thought that the Air Force would offer me a wonderful opportunity to expand my horizons and help me realize my potential. He agreed with me that Charlotte, at that time, offered me little in the way of incentive, motivation and possibilities, that it had been a stopping off place that had served its purpose and that the world beckoned me to move on.

I felt good about my choice. My family approved though there were raised eyebrows among some of my friends and acquaintances. Some seemed of the opinion that nice girls did not join the military. They had the idea that women who joined the military were sexually promiscuous and immoral. I knew myself well enough to know that my set of values would serve me well wherever I was, in or out of the military. There were all kinds of women in both places. It was a matter of choice and character. I trusted the character building that had shaped me to that point in my life and I did not doubt my capacity to make principled, moral choices.

I think a little jealousy was at work in the cases of some of my critics. I chose not to stay stuck in an unhappy situation that was taking me nowhere while some of my contemporaries let fear hold them back from taking any kind of risk, even when they knew they needed to make changes. Being a pioneer did not intimidate me. Perhaps I was too young and inexperienced to know enough to be afraid.

In my letter of resignation, I asked the Methodist Mission Board to send me a bill for the prorated cost of my early departure. It had been detailed to us in US-2 training that if we left before the full two years of service were up, we would have to pay back proportionately the cost of training for the time not served. My bill came to $89.00 exactly, a cheap price for my freedom. I arranged to make two payments of $44.50 each from my first two military paychecks. Free at last!

With that financial obligation behind me, I was able to send a little money to my mother on a more regular basis. My mother and father had divorced by this time and I wanted so much for her to have a happier and better life.

INTO THE WILD BLUE YONDER

Some might say that committing to the military for three years was not freedom, but I had freely chosen it as a pathway to greater freedom. Women did not serve in combat in that era, so I would likely not be in any greater danger or incur any greater risks than I would in civilian life.

My housemates had not yet returned from Christmas vacation so there were no tearful goodbyes as I readied myself for the flight to

Basic Training at Lackland Air Force Base in San Antonio, Texas. I said my farewells to everyone before we went our separate ways to celebrate the holidays.

Mrs. Tucker thoughtfully prepared an intimate little going away dinner just for the two of us. My friend Bob, an insurance agent with whom I had gone on two dates, offered to drive me to the airport. I laid a nice "Audrey Hepburn" ensemble out on my bed before dinner and double-checked my room to make sure I had not forgotten anything. After dinner, I bathed, dressed and spent some time in prayer and quiet reflection. I had been sworn in earlier that day so there was no turning back now.

I assembled my suitcase and cosmetic kit near the front door and chatted with Mrs. Tucker as we waited for Bob to arrive. He was punctual as usual but seemed rather subdued as we drove to the airport. He saw me to the check-in counter at the airport, then escorted me to a comfortable seat in the waiting room where I sat with my cosmetic case in the seat to my right. I thought Bob would sit in the vacant seat to my left and perhaps wait the twenty minutes with me until my flight was called. To my surprise, he remained standing and said a hasty goodbye without so much as a handshake. It was a deja vu moment, a flashback to Calvin, except there were no promises to write. I recognized that it was the end of another chapter in my life, so in an instant, I was fully present in the moment, staring into the open door of my future.

In a few minutes, we were airborne, and I was reaching for the stars as we soared across the January night sky under the Wolf Moon.

ARRIVING AT LACKLAND AIR FORCE BASE

My trip to Fort Sumter, South Carolina for the Officer Candidate School test had given me a glimpse of what a military base looked like, but there I had been housed in the bachelor officer's quarters and had eaten from plates in their dining room. I was hardly prepared when my name was called upon deplaning to line up with a bunch of twenty or thirty raw, rag tag, new male recruits. I was the only female in sight, in high heels a la Audrey Hepburn, carrying a purse, a make-up kit and a suitcase.

I cannot begin to imagine what must have been going through the minds of the Training Instructors who met us, but after a brief huddle, they called me Ma'am and asked me very politely to step out of line while they barked orders and herded the male recruits onto a bus for transport to the base. I sat in the front seat behind the driver and across from the two training instructors. Our first stop was a chow hall. I assumed the troops must usually arrive hungry. I was too excited to feel hunger. It all felt surreal and I remember feeling on high alert and somewhat numb with so much adrenaline pumping through my body. Pure shock is what it was!

I followed the lead of the guys in front of me in the chow line. I did not hesitate. I grabbed a stainless steel tray with divided compartments and moved down the line as servers plopped scoops of food into various compartments on my tray. Some of the food was recognizable and some was not. The G.I. servers worked fast and did not look up until my thin wrists and feminine hands appeared on either side of my tray. I met their curious gazes as I tried to maintain a pleasant but neutral face. A smile played around the lips of some of the G.I. servers while surprise bugged the eyes on the faces of others.

The food was not gourmet quality but was quite basic and quite edible. I could survive on it I was sure. During my lifetime, I had survived on far worse. After the hasty meal, we got back on the bus. The male troops were taken to wherever they take male troops.

I was taken to the orderly room of the 3743rd WAF Training Squadron. After completing the sign-in process, I was escorted by a WAF (Woman in the Air Force) to a barracks where Flight 173 was preparing to go to the chow hall. My first thought was, "I have to eat again! I can't! Suppose they force me, or shoot me if I refuse!"

I was given permission to take my bags to the room that I would share with two other WAFS and I quickly exchanged my high-heeled shoes for flats. I had not realized how uncomfortable the high-heeled torture chambers had become until I took them off.

My fellow flight members told me later during Basic Training that I had arrived looking smashing, like a celebrity, and they all wondered who I was. The recruiting sergeant back in Charlotte had not given me a clue about what to wear so I was dressed for a job interview.

I never regretted putting forth that initial image of class and professionalism. Making a good impression served me well throughout my enlistment. I was respected but flexible and adaptable enough to be down to earth, accepted and well liked. I was one of two college graduates and one of five Negro WAFS in our flight of seventy-five Basic Airmen. We were still called Negroes as it would be nearly a decade before we would become "Blacks" and longer still before we became "African Americans".

BASIC TRAINING

On that first day, we had not yet learned to march so we were instructed to line up by two's in size order and to walk in silence to the chow hall. My stomach was more relaxed now and I discovered that I was actually hungry since I had eaten very little in the male chow hall upon arrival.

My home training, the Catholic schools of my childhood, Boylan-Haven School, and National College had all served to prepare me for this day. I was accustomed to discipline, orderliness and following directions, which translated into obeying orders in the Air Force. The recruiter in Charlotte had explained the rigors of Basic Training to me. I knew that I would get through it and through technical school and that the rest of my service would be not exactly but much like going to work each day in the civilian world.

Basic Training turned out to be challenging but actually enjoyable for the most part. I had a mind set that told me that attitude is crucial, so during the weeks of marching, spit-shining shoes, marching, policing the area, marching, cleaning and laundry, marching, white glove inspections, marching, attending classes, marching and prison-like restrictions, my mind and soul were free. My feet were tired from all the marching but my heart recalled Richard Lovelace's final verse of "To Althea From Prison":

> *Stone walls do not a prison make,*
> *Nor iron bars a cage;*
> *Minds innocent and quiet take*
> *That for an hermitage;*
> *If I have freedom in my love*
> *And in my soul am free,*
> *Angels alone, that soar above,*
> *Enjoy such liberty.*

My mind felt liberated, with no worries about food, clothing and shelter, and I was delighted that I would be able to send a few more dollars home periodically.

My social group work experience made me a good organizer and my singing experience made me a natural for teaching my flight members marching songs and leading group singing during times of relaxation and recreation.

Who could not enjoy marching and counting cadence to silly rhymes such as these, especially when we looked sharp and marched in excellent formation past our male counterparts.

> *(1) "I got a guy in San Antone; we make love by telephone.*
> *Hip-o, hop-o, wring out the mop-o*
> *Left-o right-o left."*

> *(2) "I got a guy in New York City, he's cross-eyed and thinks I'm pretty.*
> *Hip-o, hop- o, wring out the mop-o*
> *Left-o right-o left."*

I entertained with a mini-concert at our flight's farewell party before we shipped out to technical school after Basic Training ended. It was truly an honor to be asked to sing "You'll Never Walk Alone" and "The Lord's Prayer" during our impressive flight graduation exercises the following day.

The career guidance people who helped us sort out fields suitable for our aptitudes, talents, abilities and skills determined that I would be a perfect candidate for Chaplain Services Specialist School. The Negro interviewer who assigned me explained that there were very few Negroes chosen to serve as Chaplain's Assistants. I was being asked to be a pioneer again.

President Truman had desegregated the military in 1948 but it would take decades for full integration to be realized. I began to notice that there seemed to be disproportionate numbers of Negroes in food service and in the supply area. Commissions and promotions seemed slower and harder to achieve by Negro airmen and sexism was very common. Still, the military seemed ahead of the 1950's civilian society from which I had come.

There would be many occasions for hellos and good-byes during my Air Force career. One had to get used to them. The bonds and comradeship that formed in just a few weeks of Basic Training were amazing. As my flight dispersed, some would go on with me to technical schools in Wyoming, some would go together to other locations while others would never meet again but hold a special place in each other's hearts forever.

SNOWBOUND IN WYOMING

The calendar said it was spring but the snowdrifts and packed ice in Cheyenne, Wyoming disputed that fact. My friend and fellow WAF Shirley, and I, had traveled by train from Basic Training in sunny San Antonio, Texas through Omaha, Nebraska and on to the frigid land that is Cheyenne. When we arrived in the middle of the night, two intoxicated cowboys were slugging it out in the middle of the train station. We thought we had time-traveled backwards into the Wild West. Still experiencing culture shock, we called the base motor pool at Francis E. Warren Air Force Base as instructed and two male airmen picked us up promptly. They took us to the WAF orderly room where we signed in and were escorted to a frigid open bay barracks. We later discovered that water would freeze overnight if left sitting in a container near our beds on the floor of the barracks.

The uniform of the day was announced before breakfast each morning so that airmen would be appropriately dressed for the bitter cold weather. We were forbidden to wear civilian clothing off duty during the coldest months to prevent hypothermia and other diseases or illnesses caused by exposure.

Fire guards were assigned to guard the fire all night in the ancient coal furnace so that the flame would not die out. I pulled fireguard duty only once. Guards had an emergency number to call if the fire seemed in danger of going out. That meant staying awake and alert all night. Needless to say, that was not my favorite Air Force duty assignment.

Our military overcoats were long and warm and heavy. We looked like Russian soldiers marching through Siberia in hoods, winter pants and overshoes. They did the job and we did not feel the weather through them as we marched daily to our technical school classes.

I had never learned to touch-type so the typing class was my most challenging course. I managed to hold my own in math, excelled in English, Military History and studies related to the duties of a Chaplain's Assistant. Again, my background in social work and psychology proved to be invaluable.

We had well qualified instructors, all white, but most were more like kindly professors than military superiors. My typing teacher, Sergeant Bob Hutter, was a most kind and patient man, a real gentleman, who admired my scholarship and did all that he could to help me, a novice typist, improve my skills. I was accurate but slow. I passed the typing test but not by much and he assured me that I would pick up speed on the job with practice.

I became friends with Sgt. Hutter's wife and daughter and we kept in touch until his untimely death from lung cancer in the 1960's. So many of the male and female airmen were heavy smokers. Fortunately, stuffing burning leaves into my mouth never appealed to me so I never took up the habit. Bob's wife eventually remarried and we gradually lost touch as she moved frequently to accompany her new military husband.

THE EQUALITY STATE

Wyoming is nicknamed the Equality State because of its early advocacy of issues related to women's rights. That equality did not yet extend to rights for minorities.

Some establishments in Cheyenne had signs forbidding equal access to services. Several posted signs that read "No Negroes, Indians or dogs allowed." Two out of three; not good odds. My Lakota Sioux friend Red Feather and I decided to dress in full uniform and push the envelope. "Here we go again!" I thought. We pretended not to notice the sign and seated ourselves in a restaurant booth. It took a few minutes but eventually, a waitress came and took our orders. They may have spit in our food in the kitchen but we decided not to worry about that which we did not actually see. Could it be any worse than what may or may not have happened in the chow hall kitchens?

The next time we were in Cheyenne, Red Feather and I happened to be wearing civilian clothing. Again we entered the very same restaurant and were denied service. We were not surprised though we were not sure whether the Negro, the Indian or both were being denied. We seemed to encounter less discrimination when we were in uniform although I cannot say for certain that this was universally the case.

What I can say for sure is that prejudice and discrimination always inflicted wounds; it always hurt. We used humor to deflect some of the barbs of racism, and humor served as a healing balm, much as it had throughout my life. Sometimes the humor came after the release of rage in private and sometimes it came before, depending on the nature and severity of the humiliation suffered. Red Feather was a quiet young woman with a brave and beautiful soul. She never lost her dignity and bearing. I learned from her perseverance. We prayed for strength and we prayed for the perpetrators as I had always been taught by my parents to do. Red Feather's strong traditions seemed to provide a spiritual shield that kept her strong. We both believed that someday, the Creator would set things right.

In an integrated Armed Forces, there were more choices than in the civilian world of the 1950's. One could more readily choose one's friends according to common interests and compatibility regardless of race. There was even a fair bit of interracial dating. Many people brought their prejudices with them but overt racism was frowned upon and had consequences. There were more opportunities for people to learn and to get to know each other as individuals and see each other as just people. We depended upon each other and needed each other to get through many tasks and challenges. Cooperation was a must and teamwork was crucial. In military situations, our very lives could depend upon one another and we were made keenly aware of this.

It was not a perfect world but it certainly was an improved one where interracial friendships could be nurtured. As with campus activities in Kansas City during my college years, on-base activities presented no problem but venturing off base could present uneasy situations when interacting with some of the intolerant townspeople.

Spring was late in coming to Wyoming. I remember celebrating Memorial Day in the mountains with a group of WAF and airmen friends. We roasted hot dogs and marshmallows on an open fire as we shivered in our shoes. We wanted to celebrate even though the ground was covered with snow and more flakes fell from the sky. This was our tailgate celebration party to honor my service as Barracks Sergeant and the awards we received for outstanding barracks inspections under my leadership. We cooked our food and warmed our hands over the fire and then raced back to the vehicles to thaw out, warm up, laugh and eat.

In a matter of weeks, it would be time for the next series of good-byes. Technical school was nearly over and we would soon receive orders to report to our permanent duty stations. I was assigned to the Strategic Air Command (SAC) at Carswell Air Force Base, Fort Worth, Texas. What was it about the South that would not let me go? I seemed to keep circling back to it. Perhaps there were lessons that I needed yet to learn. Perhaps my fate and future were somehow tied up with that part of the country from which I longed to escape.

GOING SOUTH, AGAIN!

The bus ride from Cheyenne to Denver, Colorado was beautiful. In Denver, I connected with the train and I would later be passing through Kansas City, Missouri, my college stomping ground. I had written to my National College sister/friend, Gloria, that I would like to spend a few days with her and her family there. She was seven months pregnant and also had a toddler who was named Evelyn after me. Gloria's husband Smitty was like a big brother to me. I looked forward to seeing them and they were thrilled that I was stopping for a visit. Gloria and I had such fun. That was the very last time that I saw my beloved sister/friend before her untimely death. I am so glad we had that time together.

I was initially assigned to Chapel #1, the Protestant Chapel at Carswell AFB. There were several Protestant Chaplains and a Jewish Chaplain at Chapel #1. They all seemed like good caring men but it was the sense of humor and the intellect of Chaplain Jacobovitz, the Jewish Chaplain, that impressed me. We had some conversations and he seemed impressed by the thoughts I shared on various issues. This created a deeper level of trust and rapport. I knew little about Judaism but felt drawn to know more. I still carried the medal given to me by my little Jewish friend, Aaron, on that night long ago when his father helped my family escape from the Klan. I had read "The Diary of Anne Frank" during my late teen years and I had so many questions about the Holocaust and various aspects of the Jewish experience.

There were four other Protestant assistants so the workload was very light and I was often bored. Our supervisor seemed to be constantly trying to find busy work for us to do. I jumped at the opportunity to substitute for the Catholic Chaplain's Assistant who was dispatched to the flight line on TDY (temporary duty). With my ecumenical leanings and familiarity with Catholicism, I welcomed the opportunity to volunteer since the other assistants, all Protestant, seemed hesitant to do so.

It did not take long for word to spread that there was a cute new Catholic Chaplain's Assistant on duty. It became almost comical when calls started to flood the office with airmen wanting to make appointments to see the Catholic Chaplain. Several were attracted to my telephone voice and came to the chapel out of curiosity, unaware of my race. When they met me in person, race mattered to some but seemed not to matter to others. Many of the airmen called me Sister (as in nun) and became my very protective big and little brothers.

I felt very comfortable at the Catholic Chapel, Chapel #2, and asked if I might remain even after the senior Chaplain's Assistant returned. Permission was granted. After a few months, I decided to convert! It felt right and I did not have to take the classes for converts since nine years of Catholic Parochial school had taught me all I needed to know in order to become a Catholic. The priest sent for my transcript from St. Mary's School in Savannah and was impressed with it. I reviewed the Mass, prayers and other rituals, studied the familiar Baltimore Catechism on my own and was ready for Baptism shortly thereafter. Two friends served as my sponsors or godparents.

It was like coming home; saying the Rosary, attending the Miraculous Medal Novenas, setting up and dismantling the altar, laying out the priest's vestments and attending daily Mass and Holy Communion. I was not too fond of Confession. I felt embarrassed confessing even venial sins because I knew that the priest would recognize my voice. I resigned myself to trying to overcome pride and vanity but I sometimes went into Fort Worth with friends to a church where I could confess anonymously.

The young airman, Francis "Frank" Toman, who served as one of my Baptism sponsors seemed very devout and served Mass almost every day. On Saturday mornings, he taught the altar boys the liturgical Latin and trained them to serve Mass. He could be counted upon to do other chores and volunteer tasks around the chapel also. He even substituted for the hired organist from time to time. We became good friends so when he asked me out to a movie at the base theater, I accepted. The senior Chaplain's Assistant, a sergeant who lived off base, invited us to her house for Thanksgiving dinner.

DEVELOPING RELATIONSHIP

My friendship with Frank seemed to easily and naturally evolve into a dating relationship. It felt comfortable because he did not pressure me for sex. I trusted him because he seemed sincere in his religious practice and values. He was a cute enough guy with golden blond hair and blue eyes, very talented artistically and played the accordion well enough to win several Air Force competitions. He often performed at the Airmen's Service Club, the NCO Club and at the Officers Club. He was good at math and assisted me with the chapel's monthly financial reports. The priest seemed very fond of him and the parents of the altar boys respected him and were very appreciative of the training he gave their children.

As our friendship developed, Frank and I began to exchange some confidences regarding our families and life experiences. I was appalled to learn that he had been severely mentally, emotionally and physically abused by his domineering and harsh father while his mother was too frightened and passive to intervene. He was a deeply wounded soul and I did not know until much later just how deep those wounds really were.

He said he wanted to have a large family some day and he swore he would never be like his father. I watched and admired his easy interaction with the altar boys and imagined that he would make a loving father. My observations soon told me that Frank could use a few pointers on discipline and setting boundaries when the boys became too rowdy and rambunctious in the chapel. He received my suggestions graciously and implemented most of them.

Our attachment continued to grow. I do not know how much of my feeling for Frank was motivated by empathy, compassion, pity and protectiveness. I tried to back off. It bothered me that I was three years older than Frank. I convinced myself that he was mature and he assured me that age did not matter to him, that he loved me. In my own way, I was carrying deep scars and wounds from the past also, and wanting so much to be valued, loved and appreciated clouded my judgment. Frank gave me little gifts, cards, and love notes on a regular basis. No one had ever made me feel loved and appreciated that way before. I felt really special for probably the first time in my entire life.

I had missed most of the developmental adolescent experience of dating and had never gone steady. I did not know how to relate to boys and suddenly, I was thrust into adulthood and trying to relate to young men. I had no role models of what healthy relationships should look like. Books, magazines and movies are poor substitutes for real life experience and trusted mentors. Who does a twenty-two-year-old woman go to and say, "Teach me how to date?" I felt embarrassed and retarded as I pretended and tried not to show my naiveté.

Word of our relationship spread and there was harassment from some sectors because of concerns over racial issues. Some more sincere people advised me to break off the relationship, saying that Frank was not good enough for me, not as well educated, not financially secure and probably not mature enough to handle an interracial relationship should we become seriously involved or take it to the level of marriage. The more the outside pressures assailed us, the more we clung to each other; us against the world. We were not wise enough to know that two broken people who had not healed from past trauma had little chance of building a secure relationship, even absent the racial complications.

Our squadron commander called us each in separately for a meeting. His concerns were purely race-based. He was born and bred in Dixie. Shortly after that, he issued orders for Frank to ship out to McDill Air Force Base in Florida. We were both heartbroken with only a few days left before his departure. Had our relationship ended there, the course of our lives would have been different but who is to say whether they would have turned out better or worse in the long run. We felt we were in love and that we would show the world that love conquers all.

Frank presented me with a beautiful garnet engagement ring, my birthstone set with tiny diamonds on either side. We pledged our love and spent our last night together huddled in the chapel office until his departure at daybreak.

For many days after he left, I felt an empty ache inside but life had to go on. We wrote to each other every single day and telephoned regularly. Long distance romances can sometimes be out of touch with reality but we did not realize that and created things in our minds as we wished them to be. I ignored the signs of immaturity and instability that began showing up in Frank's letters. He was having difficulties with authority figures, always insisting the problems were not his fault and that he was being persecuted. He never took responsibility for his actions and always found someone else to blame.

Blinded by loyalty, denial and what I deemed was love, I always came to his defense. We went on, recklessly disregarding the danger signals and planning our future. We set a wedding date for July 1957, when we would each take authorized leave and meet in Philadelphia where I had friends. Interracial marriage was still illegal in the South and forbidden under penalty of imprisonment. Someone informed Frank's parents and they were enraged that we were considering marriage. His father issued threats, spewed hate and raged like a wounded bull elephant.

Father Bede, the interim priest at the Catholic Chapel, was an older, very saintly man who empathized with our story and knew nothing of the red flags and warning signs that had surfaced regarding Frank's behavior. He helped us obtain a dispensation from Rome because we were spiritually related since Frank was my sponsor or godfather at Baptism. Without a dispensation, the Church would not permit us to marry each other. Father Bede also contacted the Catholic Church in Philadelphia where we were to be married and made arrangements with the priest who was to perform our wedding ceremony at a predominantly Negro Catholic Church. The priest at the predominantly white Catholic Church that he contacted initially refused to marry us because we were an interracial couple.

GETTING MARRIED

On the day that we were to leave our respective bases to travel to Philadelphia, Frank called to tell me that he had gone AWOL (Absent Without Leave). His legitimate leave orders had been revoked because of disciplinary action following an insubordination charge. He was on his way to Philadelphia and would meet me there despite the fact that this action would add serious charges leading to court martial when he returned.

My friend and fellow Chaplain's Assistant, Rose Marie, had gone shopping in Fort Worth with me and we found the perfect wedding gown, veil and accessories. I finished packing my lovely, waltz length wedding dress appropriate for our small, intimate wedding. Mary, my National College chum, her family and a few friends would attend. The dress looked stunning on my slender ninety-eight pound frame. Friends told me that I looked as though I were modeling for a bridal magazine.

My heart no longer felt light and happy as I took the train to Philadelphia. I could not be sure that Frank would be there or if he would be apprehended before he reached Philadelphia or before the wedding took place. I knew that he would face court martial in any case and perhaps serve time in the brig. I only hoped it would be after the wedding. My faulty reasoning told me that he must have loved me so much to take such a risk.

We both reached Philadelphia without incident. Mary's sister and parents, whom I called Mom and Pop, were so happy for us and were excitedly planning a nice little reception for us after the wedding. They were totally unaware of Frank's AWOL status. I pushed it out of my mind and forged ahead, denying the reality with which we would have to deal on another day. Mom and Pop had arranged for us to honeymoon at the home of family friends who would be away during our stay. They did not want us, as an interracial couple, to risk the humiliation of being turned away from a hotel on our honeymoon.

We applied for the marriage license, met with the priest and completed the necessary paperwork, met with our Catholic witnesses, ordered flowers, hired an organist and soloist and were ready to walk down the aisle.

Frank threw a temper tantrum when Mary and her mother told him he could not see the bride until after we reached the church. Maybe the stress of being AWOL had gotten to him but his behavior was way out of proportion to not liking that particular tradition. He angrily shouted to me up the stairs as I finished dressing, asking if I planned to let my friends run my life and tell me what to do after we were married. I was taken aback and began having second thoughts about going through with the wedding. Mom said it was just groom's nerves and that he would be all right once we got to the church. I too had thought initially that we would ride to the church together but after all, Mary's family was being supportive and doing so much for us that I could see no harm in letting them enjoy the occasion with a little tradition if it pleased them.

The wedding and reception were lovely and Mary had arranged for a friend who was a professional photographer to take pictures for us. We arrived at our honeymoon haven to find that the couple who had given us the use of their home had stocked the refrigerator and done all kinds of little hospitable things to ensure that we enjoyed our honeymoon.

We had three lovely weeks together. Had we stayed longer than that, instead of AWOL charges Frank would have faced upon his return a more serious charge of desertion. We slept in late most mornings, went to movies, did some sightseeing and shopping and kept a low profile. One morning, Frank went out early before I awoke and brought me a beautiful bouquet of roses. I felt like a queen!

Soon, it was time to say good-bye. We left a gift for our gracious host and hostess and secured their house. Frank would return to McDill AFB, Florida to face the music and I would return to Carswell AFB, Texas to try and support and encourage him from a distance.

Not long after that, Frank called me to tell me that his court martial was over and that he had received an early general discharge from the Air Force for psychological reasons. "Guess you married a mental case," he quipped. "Look what you're stuck with. I guess you want an annulment." He went on to say that he was found by the mental health professionals to have difficulty relating to authority figures, probably having to do with his troubled relationship with his father. Psychotherapy was their recommendation. I believed that we would support each other, get whatever help he needed, and that our love would see us through.

We had decided to make a home in Philadelphia when we were discharged. I still had six months to go on my enlistment. Frank went to Philadelphia in search of a job and an apartment with savings enough to live frugally at the YMCA until he was settled. There was no money for therapy but he assured me that he would begin as soon as it was feasible and I assured him that I would support his recovery from afar until I could join him in Philadelphia.

HONORABLY DISCHARGED

The following January, I received an honorable discharge from the United States Air Force. My friends at Carswell AFB gave me a farewell party and saw me off at the train station in Forth Worth, Texas. I arranged my train trip to Philadelphia by way of Savannah, Georgia where I stopped off to visit with my family for a week. I suspected that I would not see them again for a very long time and I didn't.

I was ready to begin a new phase of life, married life. I was still naive enough to believe that if I loved Frank enough, prayed fervently enough and tried hard enough, I could save him, rescue him, help heal any dysfunctions and build a healthy, happy marriage. What was I thinking?

I had been trained and conditioned to believe that love meant pain, sacrifice and suffering. My prior life experiences had underscored that. I had interpreted the teachings of the Church as meaning that martyrdom was noble and that duty and obligation were not to be shunned. I was determined to be a loving, devoted and supportive wife. I was sure that if I focused on being the perfect wife and soulmate that our twin flames would unite and set the world aglow.

As we began our life together in Philadelphia, Frank practiced pious habits of frequent and regular prayer. He attended Mass and Holy Communion daily, expecting that I do the same. This did not seem congruent with some of his secretive and inconsistent behaviors. At times, he seemed like two different people, sweet and gentle on the one hand and angry and explosive on the other.

I was unable to see that the jealousy, the clever manipulation, control and sociopathic behaviors were pathological. Instead, I believed that his possessiveness and wanting me all to himself were indications of Frank's love and devotion. I knew no terms for anti-social personality disorders and the condition was not described in the popular media for laypersons. Having no models for what a healthy relationship looked like and no recognition of just how unhealthy and co-dependent our relationship was, I could not see the danger in which I had placed myself. I blamed myself and constantly questioned myself about what I must be doing wrong.

OUR FIRST APARTMENT

Our cramped second floor apartment in a Negro neighborhood in Germantown was drab and bug-infested. We exterminated regularly but the bugs reproduced at an alarming rate. The place lacked even minimal amenities but the rent was affordable. There were no laundry facilities so I did our laundry in the bathtub. I did not complain because it seemed that Frank had earnestly tried to make it livable with a new coat of paint, some pictures, and some basic furniture that he had begun refinishing. Despite his innate talent for home remodeling and artistic design endeavors, I was to later learn that he started projects but rarely finished them. As a result, we often lived with chaos and sometimes with accommodations in dangerous disrepair.

Some would wonder how a presumably intelligent, educated young woman like myself could wind up in a situation like this. Some would call it stupidity. I did not wake up one morning and decide to become an abused wife any more than an alcoholic wakes up and decides to become an alcoholic or a diabetic wakes up and decides to become a diabetic. The causes are so much more complex than that and some of those extenuating circumstances still leave the experts puzzled. I had fought so hard against the odds all my life to succeed, to escape poverty, to get an education, to gain freedom and to eventually find a reciprocal and fulfilling love with a compatible husband.

I would ask only that those who might judge in haste pause for a moment. Until they have walked for at least a mile in my moccasins, I do not think that they can possibly know how I arrived at this place in time. I do not think that they are equipped to cast judgment upon those of us who were so wounded and traumatized as children that we carried the dysfunction with us going forward. We had to learn what normalcy was and what it looked like. We had to go through a recovery and healing process, find our true selves and create the balanced lives we deserved. We had to learn that we have intrinsic worth and value in the struggle to build a healthy self-esteem. My process took years but by the grace of God, I would not stop until I discovered my true strength and found wholeness.

I was very mature in some ways but so naive, innocent and unworldly in others, trusting too easily in the goodness of others and unwittingly giving away my power. I was a true believer and Catholicism, as I saw it, demanded submission to my husband and to the Church.

I harbored a deep sense of shame that I had not seen things clearly and that I had exercised a poor sense of judgment. I was still hopeful that I could turn things around. Finding a job, despite the fact that Frank did not want me to work, was a priority. I did not yet know that I was in the first weeks of a pregnancy that would prove to be difficult and disabling, making employment unthinkable and impossible. I was very ill and confined to bed most of the time throughout the duration of the pregnancy.

BETRAYAL OF TRUST

My illness, the lack of a support system and the isolation left me feeling helpless and alone as Frank began to use subtle ways of tearing me down mentally and making me feel worthless, flawed, stupid and crazy. I can give personal testimony to the fact that Stockholm syndrome is a real phenomenon.

Frank cycled through several jobs as a draftsman within a few months. He cited trouble with his bosses and was either fired or walked off the job. According to him, everyone else was stupid or unreasonable and he bore no responsibility. I was worried and scared to death, being ill and having a baby on the way.

Frank's mysterious, unexplained disappearances were unsettling and triggered outbursts of anger if I questioned him. I felt trapped with no phone, no friends, no family, no money, no resources of any kind, and no support system. The skillful manipulation that

Frank used almost turned me against my family. He knew how to work on my family issues and my issues of low self-esteem to my detriment. My family was in no position to help me anyway and I would never have asked them to.

He worked at isolating me from everyone, including Mary and her family, whom I considered my best friends locally. They were like family to me; besides, I felt I would always owe them for the support they had given us when we got married. Frank told me that they were not really my friends. Although he stopped short of saying that he had actually slept with Mary and her sister while I was completing my enlistment in the Air Force, he made insinuations and filled in enough details to leave me with that impression and I was devastated.

I felt abandoned by my friend Mary and her family, who were busy with their own lives and perhaps felt they should give us newlyweds space. Or was their pulling away caused by a sense of guilt on their parts? The cloud of suspicion hung heavily over the relationship and I had no real way of knowing the truth or the extent of the betrayal of trust. I was too ashamed to reveal to anyone that I was in such distress. I faked happiness on the rare occasions that we saw Mary and her family. Trust was destroyed and I was tortured by suspicions that would linger for years until I made the decision, with God's help, to liberate myself by letting go and forgiving unconditionally. Forgiveness was a gift I had to give myself for peace of mind and soul.

Any number of people had told us that interracial marriages do not work so I was certain that they would attribute any problems we experienced to race rather than to other causes. This magnified my sense of shame and strengthened my resolve to appear happy. It was Frank and me against the world and the burden of keeping us afloat was on my shoulders. I had to be strong enough for both of us. I could not allow the bigots and naysayers to be right.

Another horrendous blow soon followed at mid-afternoon on a beautiful autumn day. Our doorbell rang and I waddled downstairs heavy with child thinking that the mailman might be bringing some good news or that the Jehovah's Witness folks were making a call. I really did not care. I would have welcomed almost any human voice to verify that I was still visible and alive. It turned out to be a hefty neighbor woman who apologized for disturbing me. She hesitated, finally saying that she had no idea I was pregnant and that she hated to give me bad news in my condition.

She gave me the bad news nevertheless. She said that she and a couple of the other women on the block were alarmed because my husband had been flirting with their young pre-teen daughters, making inappropriate remarks and touching them. I told her there must be some mistake. She described Frank accurately and went on to say that she had caught him looking into her daughter's bedroom window, which was at sidewalk level. She said she had warned her daughter but had not told her husband who would probably kill to protect his little girl. She said she felt she should talk to me first and that if it happened again, she would have no choice but to tell her husband and to report Frank to the authorities. Negro people were hesitant to call the police if they felt they could resolve problems themselves. They generally had little faith in the justice system, given the gross failures of the past.

I told her I would talk to Frank and get to the bottom of it, maintaining that I thought there must be some mistake. How could I believe such a thing! I waited until after dinner to confront Frank. He neither confirmed nor denied the allegations but was much too evasive and arrogant to convince me of his innocence. I laid out the scenario to him of being arrested on child molestation charges and rotting behind bars while I gave birth to his baby, provided the fathers of those pre-teen girls didn't get to him first. He was very subdued for several days. I could hardly suppress my anger and my fear. I heard no more from the hefty neighbor woman but for weeks, I remember trembling with apprehension whenever the doorbell rang.

FIRST HOME AND FIRST BORN

Things began looking up at last. Frank had not been fired for a while and we had a few dollars in the bank. We needed to find a larger apartment, sans bugs, before the arrival of the baby. We discovered that the rent on a larger apartment would be about the same as mortgage payments would be if we could buy a row house on the G.I. Bill.

We would need very little money for settlement on a G.I. loan. We found a nice two-story row house in good condition on Clearview Street. It had three bedrooms, a fairly modern kitchen and bathroom, nice hardwood floors, a large front porch, a basement and garage. We hoped to have a car someday. The neighborhood was in transition with a few white families remaining. It was a quiet neighborhood and the economically stable middle class Negro families took pride in the upkeep of their properties. This felt like divine deliverance and I looked forward to living on Clearview Street for many years.

We moved in the middle of December and the baby was due in about three weeks. The new neighbors threw a very nice baby shower for me at one of their homes. My heart was filled with gratitude and a joy that I had not felt for a very long time. They gave us so many gifts that the baby would need. We had very little furniture but the important thing was that we finally had a home. We would furnish it gradually as we became able to afford a few items from time to time. I was overjoyed to celebrate Christmas in our very own home.

Christmas Day was clear, crisp and cold. Philadelphia had a trace of snow on Christmas Eve but the sky was now azure blue and the sun shone brightly upon neighbors and visitors going and coming and exchanging Christmas gifts and greetings. Our tiny tabletop radio played Christmas carols that echoed through our almost empty rooms. At eight months pregnant, I wore my black maternity jumper with a soft knit, antique gold blouse so that I could look as lovely as possible for my husband on Christmas Day.

We could not afford a tree but Frank brought home a few ornaments and used his artistic talent to create a festive centerpiece for the table. We were preparing Christmas dinner when I noticed that he seemed preoccupied and distracted. I checked the small turkey in the oven and basted it but in my condition, I could not lift it out of the oven. I asked Frank if he would please give me a hand with it.

He stormed into the kitchen, red faced and screaming, "Can't you do anything right! You're worthless! You can't even do a normal thing like having a baby without making a big deal out of it! You don't see other women complaining and getting sick just because they are pregnant. Some women have kids and they're back in the fields harvesting crops a few hours later. You're a disgusting namby-pamby!"

I just stood there in shock. I remember shaking all over and feeling in an altered state. Silent tears eased down my cheeks. "Stop that crying!" he yelled and slapped me so hard that I went deaf and blind for several seconds. I heard hysterical screaming, seemingly in the distance; then I realized that the voice was mine. I was screaming and gasping for breath. Frank knew that I had never been a whiner and did not cry easily so my screaming seemed to stun him.

Somewhere in my head, I thought of the baby and struggled to gain control. I did not want to go into premature labor or to harm our child. I begged God for mercy and a calm soon came over me. I sat perfectly still feeling so calm that it scared me. It scared Frank too and he was on his knees pleading, "Why did you make me do it?" "Why did you make me hit you?" He said it was my fault for getting so emotional.

He seemed repentant and gentle for the weeks that followed but never actually apologized or promised that such a thing would never happen again. He bought me a couple of small gifts. I believed he was sorry because I wanted to. I felt I had to believe he was sorry in order to maintain my sanity.

We sent my mother a round-trip train ticket and she arrived a few days before I went into a long, hard, protracted labor and had a difficult delivery on January 19, 1959. I had many stitches and was very weak from loss of blood. I had difficulty walking for weeks after the delivery. The obstetrician told us afterward that he had not realized that the baby was so big, eight pounds five ounces, and that I really should have delivered by Caesarean section considering my petite size. The information was not too helpful after the fact. I was in the hospital for five days and confined to one floor when I returned home unable to negotiate stairs.

Our baby's light skin confused the nurses in the hospital and at feeding time, they often looked in my room and said "Oops! Sorry, wrong room!" They returned with my baby and a look of embarrassment on their faces moments later. It was disconcerting not to be believed when I pointed out my baby in the nursery and was told by one of the nurses that I must be mistaken because they did not have any Negro babies at that time. They seriously thought that I was mentally deranged or believed that I was trying to steal a white baby from the nursery. By the time I had my third child, I knew the script and tried patiently to take things in stride.

LOST CONNECTIONS AND LOST BOUNDARIES

My recovery was slow and my mother stayed with us for a couple of weeks to help out after the baby was born. She loved her beautiful, healthy grandson, Francis Dominic, whom we called Dino. He was the most beautiful baby I had ever seen. My heart overflowed with joy, pride and love. In the hospital, the nurses called him "Gorgeous George" after a professional wrestler who wore his hair in ringlets. Dino's ringlets were dark, unlike the wrestler's blond ringlets.

My mother seemed restless and eager to return home because she sensed Frank's resentment of her presence. I loved my mother deeply but there was a disconnect between us that I did not know how to bridge. The separation began during my years away at Boylan-Haven School. I believe she was trying to protect me from the continued struggles at home while I was away and I tried to protect her by not burdening her with any problems that I encountered in my life after I left home. I felt great disappointment that we were not able to connect on a more loving and meaningful level.

I did not tell her that Frank had lost his job while I was in the hospital. He broke the news to me in my hospital bed the day after Dino was born. He told me that I needed to get out of the hospital as soon as possible because he had lost his job and we could not afford a big hospital bill.

Weak and in pain, I felt so alone. My husband seemed unconcerned about my health after I had gone through such a difficult time giving birth to our first child, our gorgeous son. Even so, I tried to reassure Frank that he would find another job soon. Then, I went somewhere else in my mind and focused on the baby and on trying to heal. I prayed that our meager savings would hold us until he found work again. I wondered if we should even bother unpacking the rest of our belongings in our new home or if we would default on the mortgage and become homeless. Would it ever end, this worry and insecurity over money and Frank's apparent inability to hold a job.

I tried hard not to give my mother any indication that my marriage was troubled or any hint of the struggles with which I was coping. Her divorce from my father had become final while I was in the Air Force. I needed to protect her from further pain. She had suffered enough in her lifetime.

My sisters Bunny and Gloria got married during my tour of duty in the Air Force and my mother lived with Bunny and her active duty Air Force husband. My brother Samuel joined the Navy and my brother Richard eloped to Florida and got married when he was a junior in high school. Richard later got his high school diploma and went on to earn a bachelor's and a master's degree in engineering. We were all concerned with not burdening our mother any further and with doing what we could to make her life easier.

My mother returned home to Savannah and I prayed that she had not been able to sense the depths of my painful secrets. My other prayers were answered and Frank found a job almost immediately as a technical illustrator. He had to work the night shift but the money was decent and we got caught up on the mortgage payments and avoided foreclosure on our home.

A telephone was one of our first expenditures as it had been most unsettling for me, still recovering and being at home alone all night with a newborn and no phone in case of emergency. We got a party line phone at a cheaper rate and Frank could call and check on us from work. Soon after that, we bought a car, a red Rambler with cream-colored trim. Buying a car made for a tight budget but we needed transportation. Philadelphia winters were brutal and frigid for traveling on buses with an infant. We were also concerned about Frank's safety, traveling home from work in the wee hours of the morning.

The job seemed stable and Frank liked his work. He appeared to be getting along with his boss and soon received a promotion. We still did not have much furniture but that was okay. Prior to the purchase of an affordable entertainment center with television, record player and radio, we had only a small, tabletop radio for entertainment. I read whenever I was not doing housework or caring for the baby. I napped when the baby slept. Frank and I never went out except to church and to shop for necessities so life became more bearable with the distraction of television and the enrichment of music.

HELL HATH NO FURY

My recovery from the birth of our son was slow. The doctor had me on vitamins and minerals to build me up and improve my health and stamina. He was a Catholic physician and a member of our parish church. After my postpartum check-up, he explained the rhythm method to us at my request; the Church's only acceptable form of birth control and family planning besides abstinence. Frank was not about to abstain. My periods were irregular and the rhythm method proved to be most unpredictable and unreliable.

During Confession, the priest told me that I had no choice but to comply with my husband's desires and that I had no right to refuse him under penalty of mortal sin. Even after explaining our circumstances, he said I would be a whore condemned to hell if I refused my husband sex or used artificial birth control. The priest told me that I had to have faith in these matters and trust God's will. He said that only God would decide how many children I should have. Catholicism had so brainwashed me that even with my health and life at risk, I did not dare disobey what I then believed to be the commands of God and His Church.

Fear of hell terrified me but so did another life-threatening pregnancy. In desperation, I contemplated suicide for about fifteen minutes when I discovered that I was pregnant again.

Surely suicide would send me straight to hell and besides, I could not leave my beautiful, sweet, precious son who had no one else to protect and nurture him. Suicide was quickly ruled out as an option. Frank exhibited abhorrent behavior more frequently and slapped our baby in the face once for crying.

That was the one and only time I have ever felt capable of murder and the cold, calculated look of murderous capability must have shown in my eyes. I told Frank that if he ever hit my baby again, I would have him thrown in jail if I didn't kill him first myself. He must have believed me because he never hit our baby son again. He said that I was crazy and probably crazy enough to kill him. Crazy like a fox, I was not about to correct him and have him call my bluff. I maintained vigilance and examined Dino daily for any signs of abuse. There seemed to be none.

KEEP YOUR SHOULDER TO THE WHEEL

One Saturday evening after I had put Dino to bed, I put on my lovely blue gown and robe set that had been a wedding present. I went downstairs to join Frank for what I thought would be a calm conversation about our future. Mainly, I wanted to address our marital issues and the possibility of couple's counseling. I was concerned about his anger issues and the emotional abuse heaped upon me. We would soon have two children to parent. We needed marital counseling desperately and to seek out the therapy that had been recommended to him by the Air Force psychiatrist. I needed support to help me find direction. Many things were going through my mind as I descended the stairs silently in my plush, soft slippers.

I did everything as well as I could, even when it was not easy for me, with a second baby on the way and with my body in less than optimal physical condition. I always kept myself well groomed and attractive along with making certain that we had a clean, sweet smelling, well cared for baby. I was a nearly perfect Suzy Homemaker, keeping an immaculate and tidy house, and so eager to please that I was probably becoming a Stepford wife.

I walked into the kitchen to find my husband peering through the venetian blind slats at our almost nude next-door neighbor, an attractive, older, forty-something-year-old woman, strutting around her kitchen in her skimpy underwear. "She's a slut!" He said, still staring. "She always walks around her house like that." "And do you always watch her?" I asked. "What do you expect?" He replied. "You are always walking around like a tub of lard and pregnant like a fat cow." Finally, leaving the window, he went on to tell me that this woman had asked him to make love to her when she had offered to baby-sit Dino while Frank and I went for my pre-natal check-up. I remembered that he had stayed there for a long time when he went to pick Dino up from her house. I had come straight home to lie down, never suspecting that this older married woman with two children of her own was seducing my husband.

How does a young wife and mother process and absorb such intense emotional pain and remain sane? How does one reconcile the fact that there had been so few respites from trials throughout one's existence? How much more could I bear when there seemed no hope? What options were there for finding a way out of a wilderness in which one was so deeply mired? I implored Heaven to tell me, "Where does my help come from?" There were no social services that I knew of and no shelters for abused women and children. I had become a victim of domestic violence which surely existed, often in secrecy, but did not yet have a recognizable name. I had no place to go for help and no one to whom I could turn.

I cried and prayed through the long days and lonely nights until my soul answered, "I will lift up mine eyes unto the hills, from whence cometh my help. My help cometh from the LORD, which made heaven and earth." (Psalm 121: 1-2). Only by His grace could I endure and ever hope to prevail. I did not give up. Giving up was not an option. I could not afford to give up. Faith kept me searching for answers and I would not stop until I had traversed the long, treacherous road to deliverance. I always remembered what I had overcome and that others have endured and overcome more. Someone was always worse off than I. I knew that ultimately I would find a way.

I had always smiled through my pain and others never knew the extent of it. I pretended and convinced others that I was invincible, happy and reasonably carefree. Even members of my birth family described me as skinny but strong as a horse. They and others who knew me quipped that I was a little piece of leather but well put together. I guess they wanted and needed to believe that so that they could demand even more of me and rely on me to carry even more of the family's burden. I dared not break down.

"Your younger sister is not strong," my mother always told me. "Bunny is the sickly one and you must help her with her chores and look out for her since you are the strong one." My mother was chronically ill herself so I tried to be strong for both of them. I felt I had to be strong for everyone.

Sometimes, I grew tired of having to keep up the facade, of having to pretend to be impervious to the onslaughts, the challenges, the demands and responsibilities that would bring any but the strongest to their knees. Yet I feared that if I let go and acknowledged weakness or exhaustion, my vulnerability would destroy me and I would shatter into a thousand bits and pieces, fragmented and irreparably broken open.

MEETING THE IN-LAWS

Frank's parents decided to come for a visit from their home in Ohio. I had never met them and was not sure that I wanted to after their bitter reaction to our marriage. They were second-generation Eastern European descendants. Frank's mother Helen was the daughter of first generation Polish Catholic parents and his father, Frank Sr., was the son of Czechoslovakian Catholic immigrants.

I prepared to receive them warmly. My intention was to take the high road, no matter what happened. Both of Frank's parents were enamored with Dino, our smart, alert, beautiful baby boy. He was their first grandchild and he looked almost as white as they did. I guess he caused their cold hearts to thaw a little and they began to remark about how much he looked like various members of their Toman family. They seemed to forget, at least temporarily, that he was a child of color.

Helen had nothing but praise for my housekeeping, mothering, my intelligence and me. She commented that I didn't talk like a Negro, whatever that meant, and asked if that was because of my Indian blood. I was quite stunned when I overheard her comment to Frank in all seriousness, "She is so well educated and attractive; what does she see in you? I guess she can't be that smart then, can she?" "Heh, heh, heh," he chuckled sardonically.

During their brief overnight stay, Frank Sr. refused to sleep in our house. He slept in the chaise lounge on the front porch, which was well elevated from the street, but still an odd place to sleep. Frank and I slept on mats on the floor of the baby's room and gave up our bed to his mother, Helen, even though I was very pregnant and uncomfortable.

Letters, cards and gifts for the baby arrived after their return home and Helen and I began to correspond on a regular basis. I never let on that our marriage was anything less than perfect. I concentrated on trying to build a relationship with Helen. I wondered what life had done to her and Frank Sr. to make them so hard and cold and mean. The brief display of affection they had shown Dino indicated that there was at least a small crack in their armor. It made me wonder if I too could help love them into softness and warmth and kindness. It seemed worth a try.

My maternal grandmother, Viola, had always advocated turning one's enemies into friends and allies. I believe that there is always hope for redemption, and Lord knows, I needed friends and allies.

The neighbor women with whom I connected were a little older than I but we exchanged occasional visits and phone calls. They passed on baby clothing and other items that their children had outgrown or maternity clothing that I could use. In most cases, their family planning was complete and these items were deeply appreciated and filled holes in our tight budget.

There were always showers of blessings and moments of grace to keep me going. Life was never hopeless, appearances aside. Sometimes, it was darkest before the dawn but dawn always broke eventually. I could not afford to allow excuses and blame to steal my dreams or to destroy my faith. "With God, all things are possible." I truly believe that and I had to walk my talk in order to keep going.

Life is filled with mysteries that I cannot begin to understand. I can only say that then and now, at any given moment, I try to the best of my ability to give to the world the best that I have. I trust the universe and the Creator to support me if I do my part for I believe that God helps those who help themselves. I never lost sight of that fact and I worked continuously toward becoming stronger and more self-sufficient. Inspirational and self-help books were my constant companions and nurtured my growth.

A DAUGHTER IS BORN

On December 8, 1959, our beautiful daughter, Lucinda Maria entered the world just eleven months after her brother, Dino. I went into labor while attending early morning Mass to celebrate the Feast of the Immaculate Conception, hence the name Maria. She weighed in at six pounds seven ounces and we nicknamed her Cindy.

Cindy looked like a lovely Polynesian doll with straight black hair. She was so beautiful that looking at her made me weep for joy. Her smaller size made for a much easier delivery with fewer stitches but recovery was slow and painful nevertheless.

My heart was filled with so much love for my son and daughter. I was consumed with thoughts about how to make life better for them. When I went for my postpartum check-up. I questioned the doctor about postpartum depression explaining that I was feeling overwhelmed, weak and exhausted from having two babies in January and December of the same year. He asked if I would like to see a psychiatrist whom he could recommend. I saw this as an opportunity to talk with a mental health professional and try to sort out some of our many complex problems.

I saw the psychiatrist twice and had absolutely no rapport with him. Actually, I did not like him at all. He sat with his eyes closed during our sessions and I could not tell whether he was asleep or bored or merely concentrating. I asked him and he said, "What do you think... and how does that make you feel?" For this, I was paying money that we could not afford! After the second session, I told him that we had financial problems and that I would not be seeing him again. He asked if I would like a referral to a clinic where fees were set on a sliding scale.

I was assigned a wonderful therapist at the clinic with whom there was almost immediate rapport. I felt a level of trust that allowed me to open up and talk about the painful secrets that were burdening me. Frank still would not agree to therapy of any kind. My therapist said he would work with me and that helping me cope better and gain some new insights might be enough to change the dynamics in my marriage. I felt I had nothing to lose and possibly much to gain. I felt more hopeful than I had for a very long time.

Unfortunately, the more healthy I became emotionally, the sicker and more abusive Frank became. The dynamics of the marriage were changing alright but not for the better. I felt stronger inwardly and sensed myself moving in a more positive direction though it would still take years for that growth to fully manifest itself. Those sessions had set me on a path to taking my power back and to keeping my eyes on the prize. I was evolving slowly but progressing in a positive direction nevertheless.

A SECOND BREACH OF TRUST

Cindy was six months old when Frank lost his job again. Our car was repossessed and our home went into foreclosure. We were harassed day and night by bill collectors and forced to move into a rented apartment. Mary's husband, the acting landlord, agreed to sublet the apartment to us and made a nice profit at our expense. We discovered this when a neighbor in the adjoining apartment and I were comparing rental fees. She was appalled when I told her what we were paying. I found it hard to believe that people who were supposed to be our friends were willing to exploit us and gain financially from our misfortune. We confronted the landlord and dealt with the realtor directly for a fairer rent.

This was a second breach of trust and Mary did not deny that she was fully aware of her husband's profiteering at our expense. It saddened me to know that our friendship would never be the same. Once betrayed; shame on you. Twice betrayed; shame on me. When people first show you who they are, it is best to believe them.

Eventually, Frank went to work for the Boeing-Vertol Company as a technical illustrator. A friend, who had moved from the apartment above ours, informed us of a house for rent near her new residence. It was a nice, three-bedroom row house with a basement, garage and a nice fenced back yard ideal for the children. We settled in and had a car again before long. This too was a red Rambler with cream colored trim. Frank had a penchant for red cars.

The children and I made friends easily in the predominantly Negro neighborhood, some of the friendships lasting a lifetime. My neighbors Claire, Barbara, Aloyse, Gloria and I became close. We baby-sat for each other, exchanged baby clothes and even borrowed an occasional cup of sugar from each other. Gloria and I took some adult evening classes together for enrichment. Aloyse, Barbara and their families were Catholic and we all belonged to the same parish. Barbara's husband was Italian and Gloria's husband was Puerto Rican so our interracial marriages created a common bond. Barbara and Gloria both died circa 2006 and both their losses were terribly painful for me.

Frank's anti-social personality disorder kept him from making friends in the neighborhood but people tolerated him because of the children and me. He was critical of my friends but I would no longer allow myself to be isolated and controlled. As a result, he said that I needed to be punished so he openly flirted and flaunted his attraction for my female friends in an effort to alienate and isolate me from them. He hinted at his relationships with women at work and anywhere else that he encountered members of the female gender.

It was sickening to endure as Frank spouted his false piety and shamed his family with his outrageous behavior, infidelity and cruelty. The rhythm method seemed to be working for a while and my health was slowly improving. I underwent several surgeries and was not yet healthy enough to hold a job. Cindy was three years old and I had not become pregnant again. I still kept my deepest secrets to myself. I am sure some of my closer friends suspected that I was concealing some troubles but most of them had problems of their own, though probably not as severe. We respected each others' privacy but tried to be there for each other when there was a need.

The Church still had me convinced that divorce was not an option and that I had to have faith that God would repair my marriage if I did my part. The unfairness of how the Church seemed to let the men off the hook seemed crazy to me. How did they expect a marriage of two people to be the responsibility of one person? How could the wives alone be held responsible without making husbands accountable? Something was terribly wrong with this sexist picture.

The therapy had helped me in its own way and I felt stronger and more able to understand and cope in my dysfunctional marriage. The therapist had respected the fact that I was Catholic. He was Jewish but he never criticized or encouraged me to go against my religion. He only asked questions that caused me to think and arrive at my own conclusions when I was ready. I missed his support when the sessions ended but I continued to use the lessons I had learned.

MARIO IS BORN

My third pregnancy proved to be the most difficult of all. I had toxemia and was so ill throughout the pregnancy that I could barely take care of the two children I already had. Frank's affairs were flourishing but I had to push them out of my mind and concentrate on my survival and on taking care of Dino and Cindy.

Mario was born three weeks early with an ABO blood incompatibility and had to have a complete blood exchange transfusion two days after he was born. He had become jaundiced and his yellow appearance was alarming. A local priest who served as one of the hospital chaplains was summoned to administer emergency baptism to my baby and we had him christened Joseph Mario. In the Catholic faith it was customary to name an at risk child after Joseph or Mary. We called our son Mario because I was a diehard Mario Lanza fan and loved the name and his music. I was sent home in a few days while Mario remained under treatment in the hospital.

Mario was a beautiful baby like his brother and sister before him. Cindy and Dino were such good little helpers when Mario came home from the hospital. He appeared healthy and seemed on his way to normal development. I pointed out to the doctor at his check-ups that his head appeared a bit lopsided to me and that one eyelid seemed to droop ever so slightly. The doctor said that Mario was healthy and that the lopsidedness was positional, that the baby probably slept on one side too much of the time and should be flipped over from time to time. I tried to be satisfied with that explanation but it worried me and I brought it up at every check-up.

The doctors at the hospital clinic almost convinced me that I was being an overly concerned mother but I could not ignore what my gut was telling me. Something was not quite right.

By the time Mario was around seven months old I was convinced that his development was slower than it should be. Again, I was told that each child is unique and that I should not compare his progress to that of Dino and Cindy. They said that the problems at birth may have slowed him down a little and that he would catch up.

Meanwhile, Mario's head seemed to grow more lopsided and I knew that it was not positional because I was flipping him like a pancake, day and night. At his next appointment, I refused to leave the hospital clinic until someone explained to me why his head was not rounding out and why his legs seemed weak and he was not able to stand or even to sit up alone. With Dino and Cindy in tow, we staged a sit-in. I refused to leave until they summoned a neurologist.

TWO SURGERIES

After a thorough examination and lots of questions, the neurologist told me that Mario had a premature closure of the fontanel, that the soft spot on the top of his skull had closed prematurely, forcing the brain as it grew to push against the skull causing it to become misshapen. Neurosurgery would be required to correct the condition. He said the prognosis was good that he would catch up and progress normally once the surgery was done.

I felt so upset and angry that Mario's condition had remained undetected by the doctors when I had repeatedly brought my concerns and observations to their attention. I wondered and worried that the outcome might have been better with prompt diagnosis and intervention. I blamed myself for trusting the doctors and for not having been more forceful with them.

Mario's surgery was scheduled for the same day that I was to undergo major abdominal surgery. I was advised to delay neither. My mother arrived to take care of Dino and Cindy as Mario and I were admitted to the hospital on the same day.

A woman in the hospital room across the hall from me died the night before my scheduled surgery. That was disconcerting to say the least. I survived my surgery and was given a pint of blood. I was released from the hospital about a week later to continue my recovery at home. My childbearing days ended with that surgery. I was afraid to feel liberated for fear that I would be punished by God. I had always wanted to be a wife and mother more than anything. I just wanted a loving husband to father my children and help nurture them and to be able to space our children far enough apart that bearing them would not ruin my health or kill me.

My mother returned home much too soon after my release from the hospital. She and Frank were like two hostile satellites revolving around each other and the stress was unbearable for us all. Although I was still very weak, I realized that the house was too charged with negativity for me to heal and that it was better for my mother to leave.

Mario remained in the hospital. He suffered some complications involving swelling of the brain and we were fearful as to what the outcome would be. Frank told me that he stopped at the hospital to see him after work each day. I only hoped he was telling the truth since I was not well enough to go to the hospital myself. I would question Frank about Mario's condition each night. One night, he told me that he had not stopped at the hospital. I became so upset that I started to call a taxi to take me to see my baby. I would summon the strength or die trying. To calm me down, Frank said he would go to the hospital and check on him instead. Mario was doing much better and was released from the hospital a few days later. He looked so vulnerable with his little shaved head but seemed happy and energetic. I worried and wondered if he remembered me but he responded to my voice and touch as he always had.

When Mario was finally allowed to come home, a friend lent me an extra crib so that I could have one upstairs and one downstairs. My doctor had told me to use the stairs only once a day for another week or so and to do no heavy lifting. Each morning after Frank left for work, I bathed and dressed myself and all three children and packed a suitcase with everything that we would need during the day. I gave my friend Aloyse a key and she stopped by our house after her duty as a school crossing guard and brought Mario to the downstairs crib along with the suitcase.

I knew that I could call her, Barbara, Claire or Gloria in case of emergency, but we generally managed until Frank came home from work. These women had their own family responsibilities and I would not impose upon their kindness needlessly.

Mario and I both continued to heal. He began making rapid progress, sitting up and finally standing. One day, he pulled up at a chair, turned around and ran across the room. He was a bit clumsy and seemed accident prone, falling frequently so I had to watch him carefully and keep things cleared away. No matter how cautious I was, Mario was active, bombastic and had such a zest for catching up on all the things he had missed that he had more than his share of spills, which could be very frightening.

It was difficult to curb my tendency to be overly protective. I worried that I would not have sufficient energy to make all three children feel nurtured and secure. I loved them so dearly and worried that I might not be able to compensate for their father's failings. I tried to show them love enough to make up for what he could not or would not demonstrate.

HUSBAND AND FATHER - MORE THAN BREADWINNER

Frank seemed to feel that being a good husband and father meant no more than providing food, clothing and shelter, not necessarily of good quality or of adequate quantity. Were it not for the hand-me-down clothing that the neighbors gave us, we would have been in dire straits.

I was a good manager and knew how to stretch a dollar, something I had done all my life. I learned about nutrition and made balanced meals a priority. I read articles and books on parenting, child psychology, relationships and other topics that I thought would teach me to be a better wife and mother. My children deserved that and I hoped that being the best that I could be would inspire my husband to mend his ways. I still felt capable of forgiving and moving on with our lives if he showed any inclination or desire to turn things around.

Days became weeks, then months and then years. My life and my marriage were to be endured for lack of viable options. I was in fragile health with no support system and nowhere to go with three children, the youngest of whom was developmentally delayed and no clear prognosis for him seemed likely for years.

I was undeniably trapped. Yet, I wondered what terrible fate awaited us if Frank decided to desert us altogether. The fear was paralyzing at times but I could not risk making a hasty or irrational move with the lives of my three beautiful children at stake. I needed a way and I needed a plan. I needed support and I needed resources. I loved my children too much to take a chance on getting into a situation worse than the one we were already enduring. At least we had a roof over our heads and food and clothing enough not to freeze or starve to death. My best option seemed to be to bide my time.

I was making each decision as wisely as I possibly could, praying unceasingly for guidance, strength and wisdom. Somehow, I knew for certain that God would help me make a way out of no way. I never lost faith that all this trouble would last but a season. It appeared to be an interminably long season but it had to come to an end eventually. The faith that had sustained me through all of life's trials had taught me that prayer plus work equals success and I continued to work as though everything depended on me to find a way out and to pray as though everything depended upon God to deliver us.

Dino and Cindy were soon eligible to attend the newly implemented Head Start summer program at the area public school. They were well behaved, bright and eager to learn. Mario and I walked them the few blocks to school each day and walked them home after their half-day session.

By the end of the summer, the military family from whom we rented the house returned from overseas and we had to move again. With luck, we found a comparable rental house that was quite nice underneath the filth and bugs left behind by the former occupants. It took a tremendous amount of work but I succeeded in turning it into a clean, comfortable, attractive home for our family before the start of the school year.

I enrolled Dino and Cindy in first grade at Holy Child Parochial School and we joined the parish church. We lived on the edge of the parish, too far for the children to walk and unsafe for them to cross streets that had a heavy flow of traffic so I escorted them to the school bus stop each morning and met them at the bus stop each afternoon. Through the grace of God, Mario remained safe when I left him asleep in the house on the coldest winter mornings as I raced to the bus stop. My heart pounded in my chest as I raced back home praying that he had not awakened during the few minutes that I was away. One morning, he awoke and put the safety latch on the front door, locking me out with a foot of snow on the ground. We could see each other through the glass in the door and he laughed as I shivered in the cold imploring him to open the door. He thought we were playing a game and he was delighted.

Finally, I waved good-bye and pretended to walk away. He opened the door calling "Come back, Mommy". The incident and the dangerous possibilities frightened me so much that no matter how brutally cold it was after that, I bundled him up and we all trekked to the bus stop together over ice and snow.

DOCTOR JEKYLL AND MISTER HYDE

The children and I were left to our own devices and Frank was more like a visitor than a member of the family. He disappeared for hours at a time and came and went as he chose. We had long since ceased to attend Mass together as a family. Mario was too hyperactive to sit through the Mass. He was a very loving and affectionate child but probably had undiagnosed Attention Deficit Disorder. This later manifested itself in problems all through school, never clearly defined in spite of rigorous testing by the Philadelphia School District and through the Albert Einstein Medical Center.

Frank told us that he was attending an early Mass alone on Sundays. I went to a later Mass with Dino and Cindy while Frank baby-sat Mario.

We had no social life or friends in common and I missed my friends in the old neighborhood. Our only family outings were an occasional ride to watch takeoffs and landings of small aircraft at an airfield just outside of town. The children seemed to enjoy that but the trips generally ended in an argument if I suggested stopping at a fast food restaurant to treat the children. I soon stopped suggesting.

In all of our years of marriage, Frank took me out to dinner once. I was pregnant with our first child and one of Frank's male co-workers and his wife invited us to come along and celebrate his wife's birthday. Frank said he provided food for us from the supermarket so we could make hamburgers or pizza at home and that there was no need to go to restaurants. I was sure he took himself out to eat whenever he chose and I did not want to know who accompanied him.

Frank was consumed with his own life and interests, which centered around other women and building model airplanes. I could not comprehend how any husband and father could be so cruel, insensitive and lacking in empathy, compassion and conscience. Sometimes I felt as though I was staring into the face of pure evil as I searched his eyes to try and find some spark of caring, regret or contrition. He would fake such emotions to get his wants and needs met as sociopaths do. His Jekyll and Hyde transitions sometimes made me question my own sanity as well as his.

I was struggling to keep our three children clothed and fed when Frank told me that he wanted us to take in a young single woman he had met who had a young child. In all seriousness, he suggested that since I had a college degree and she had none, I could get a job and she could take care of our collective children while I worked. He said she was having a hard time and that he had bought her child Buster Brown shoes. I could not believe what I was hearing or what he was suggesting. He actually wanted to move his woman into our house! Her child was wearing Buster Brown shoes that Frank had bought while my children were wearing cheap tennis shoes from the five and dime store.

He went on to tell me that he picked her up at her mother's house and drove her to work each morning and that this had been going on for months since they met at the real estate office a few blocks from us. He had gone there to inquire about a house we considered buying since he had been employed steadily at Boeing-Vertol for a while.

Needless to say, a mighty quarrel ensued and I broke the telephone receiver over his head as he tried to dial the woman. "Hit me and you're a dead man," I said coldly. He never mentioned the woman again and refused to respond to my questions about her. There were many other women up until the time I left him in 1978 during one of his office affairs.

DIFFERENT HOME, SAME PURGATORY

I could only assume that Frank was choosing to stay with us since he had not gone anywhere. He was home more often and began to talk about buying a house though he never would discuss our relationship or how to address our problems. He repeatedly rejected individual or marriage counseling but I gathered from other things he said that he was looking ahead to a future with me and our children. He seemed to enjoy keeping me guessing and off balance and seemed to calculate and time things in order to inflict maximum pain and hurt.

We had the opportunity to buy a nice two-story twin house in a middle class neighborhood that was in transition. Even so, we had to have a Jewish intermediary purchase the house then sell it to us for a dollar as the owner refused to sell to anyone who was not white. The Jewish people were making an Exodus as Black people began to move into the neighborhood. There was one other mixed race family on our lovely tree-lined street. The wife was Japanese and the husband was Black.

The neighbors took pride in their homes and lawns. Knowing that the white neighbors expected their non-white neighbors to be less diligent about property upkeep, I was immediately embarrassed that Frank took no pride in our property. The kids and I kept things up as best we could. A couple of the men on the block spoke to Frank about our overgrown lawn and the next-door neighbor whose property adjoined ours once cut our grass. Frank did not take the hint.

The church and parochial school that our children attended were just a block away and we were convenient to public transportation. I made friends and I felt strong enough to volunteer one hour per week at school. Eventually, I joined the church choir. It was wonderful to sing again and in time, I began doing duets and solos. Performing always gave me confidence and it began slowly to rebuild as my voice came back stronger, richer and fuller than ever. I knew that I must never lose my voice again and I sensed that I was literally singing for my life. My health was improving and there would be no more pregnancies. At last, I felt as though it was possible to emerge from the depths. It would be a long hard climb but there was finally a light at the end of the tunnel that was not an oncoming train.

Mario's learning disabilities made school very difficult for him. I think the special tutoring I was able to get for him helped a little. By this time, I was working three hours a day as a Reading Aide at the neighborhood public school. I paid the tutor out of my meager earnings and shopped at the thrift store for clothes to wear to work and for the kids to wear to school. I loved working at the school and was recognized repeatedly for my performance. I got on well with the teachers and other staff, the students loved me and my own children were very proud of me. The principal observed me at work with the children and encouraged me to return to school and become a certified teacher. Meanwhile, I became an officer of the Home and School Association and had many opportunities to speak and sing at school events.

I made the decision to transfer our children to the public school in which I worked. This was not an easy decision but I could not save any money while paying Catholic school tuition. This particular public school was still integrated, had high standards and offered quality education. Dino and Cindy did well there. Mario struggled academically but made progress and was outstanding in music, art and as an officer on the Safety Patrol.

Frank had no patience with Mario and made fun of him, unable to accept a child who was less than perfect, although Mario was playful, kind and charismatic. He made friends easily and people liked him. His head was still a little misshapen and did not finish rounding out until sometime in adolescence. Some children teased him at first until he won them over. He was very talented artistically and musically so I was able to arrange for free organ lessons for him and his siblings through the school. Mario was interested in and pursued music with a passion. He played percussion instruments in the band when he reached junior high and high school. Music and art were areas in which he could shine.

His hyper-activity probably contributed to the fact that Mario was accident-prone. He seemed unfazed by falls, scrapes, scars and bruises, but they made me very nervous and watchful. Even childhood diseases seemed more severe when Mario got them. His measles rash was much more severe and he had more chicken pox lesions than Dino and Cindy had combined.

Once, while playing with friends, Mario fell into a wrought iron gate shattering his eyeglasses. I thought I would faint as I held his hand in the emergency room as the eye surgeon picked shards of glass out of my son's eye. Mario was so brave and whimpered only a little, even after they had to bandage both eyes in the hospital and he could not see. After a couple of days in the hospital, they took the bandages off. Follow-up tests showed that miraculously, his vision had not been damaged. God bless Dr. T. Ramsey Thorpe, the esteemed ophthalmologist who so skillfully picked the bits of glass from Mario's eye and saved his sight. As Providence would have it, Dr. Thorpe was just about to go off duty in the emergency room that afternoon when we arrived. He remained on duty for as long as it took, reassuring me that all would be well.

Frank fled to a waiting area but abandonment in a crisis was what we had learned to expect of him.

A RAY OF HOPE

As I continued to work diligently at school, the principal once asked me, "Mrs. Toman, is there anything that you don't do well? You're like Wonder Woman!" This vote of confidence meant so much to me. Frank disdainfully referred to my work at school as my "hobby". I was actually building a resume and when a friend who worked for the School District of Philadelphia told me about a professional position that had opened up, I jumped at the chance. I accepted the job as a teacher of reading for disadvantaged children in a junior high school with the provision that I return to school and become certified.

I applied for my unused educational benefits under the G.I. Bill and enrolled in the Chestnut Hill College Teacher Certification Program. Chestnut Hill College was one of the schools in the Catholic university consortium in Philadelphia. I felt comfortable in that environment and found that I still possessed the capabilities of a high achieving student on a predominantly white campus. National College had long ago prepared me for this. The 1970's were still much like the 1950's in some respects so there were the issues of racism to be confronted upon occasion. Nevertheless, despite the added pressures and responsibilities, I had learned good study habits and had a pretty solid educational foundation upon which to build. I was used to performing under pressure and to projecting a cool, calm exterior. Of course, that came at a price.

Along with my tuition payments I was allotted some extra money for books and incidentals as well as a small G.I. Bill allowance. I watched my little savings account grow and I knew that this was the beginning of my escape plan. My prayers were being answered. A new season was dawning at long last.

Frank's intermittent affairs continued. He had never threatened to leave or mentioned divorce before until his affair with a much younger Polish woman at work in our twelfth year of marriage. He said he would never give this woman up. I talked with one of the parish priests who was compassionate, unlike so many others I had encountered. He recommended that we see a high-ranking monsignor who was a psychologist and marriage counselor. Frank agreed to go, he said, to prove once and for all that I was crazy.

He tried to manipulate the monsignor and soon became hostile when the priest would not be drawn into his web of deception. We had several sessions together then the priest asked to see us separately. When it was my turn to meet with him, the priest told me that God did not require that I put up with this tortuous situation which by then was not a marriage in any sense of the word. Since the monsignor was involved with the marriage tribunal, he felt almost certain that the Church would grant me an annulment; then I could pursue a legal divorce and be free to remarry in the Church should I so choose. He told me what I had suspected for a long time; that Frank's character flaws were pathological, that he possessed a sociopathic personality and was not likely to ever be able to change. No indirect counseling there. He told me to save myself and the children; to leave the marriage before the children and I were damaged any further.

I knew the priest was right but how would I manage with three children on my own with no network of support? I did not want to be another Black woman, a single mother, struggling on welfare. How could I do that to my children? I needed more time to get my teacher certification and a permanent appointment. I was surprised when Frank revealed that his Polish sweetheart had suddenly up and moved to Florida. He now found it expedient to remain with me. Fine! This would give me the additional planning time that I needed. Some part of me hoped against hope, that by some miracle, my family could still be saved.

In the interim, both of my parents died within a year of each other. Frank was cold and remote even as I attempted to deal with the overwhelming loss of first my mother who succumbed to cancer, then my father whose drinking doomed him to death from cirrhosis of the liver. I loved my parents very much despite the tragic conditions that left them unable to parent in a more effective way. I could not process my grief until years later when I had to deal with multiple losses. I was holding onto my sanity and struggling for the survival of my children and myself with all that I had within. The death of my parents made me truly realize how alone I was in the world and the word orphan fully resonated with me. Whatever was going to be was up to me. My fate was in my hands and only God could see me through.

I attended classes at night and during the summer and managed to become a star pupil despite the racist attitudes of a couple of the professors. On the whole, the professors were very supportive of me and of other mature, continuing education students. Holding down a full time job, taking care of a family and being a student all at the same time was difficult but exhilarating because I was working toward my goal of liberation.

After I did my student teaching, I passed the test and got my permanent certification from the state of Pennsylvania. My first appointment was at an inner city, junior/senior high school where I taught English and Reading for three years, earning tenure. This meant health insurance and other benefits for me and the children and a measure of job security.

Working conditions were less than ideal and safety was an issue. I suffered a concussion when a burly sixteen-year-old learning disabled boy decided to practice karate with a blow to the back of my head as I walked between classes. I was taken to a hospital emergency room by ambulance. After my release, I suffered post-concussion syndrome for weeks before finally returning to school.

MARCHING THROUGH HELL

Frank and I kept an uneasy truce most of the time but his violent outbursts were becoming more frequent. My independence was becoming a threat to him and his mental and emotional abuse was turning physical. He threw me across the kitchen dislocating my shoulder. Neighbors called the police and I was taken to the emergency room. I got a court order defining actions that would be taken against him upon any repeated violence. Frank slept under the dining room table after I asked him to leave our bed. The children felt unsafe and kept out of his way. Even so, when Dino accidentally spilled a can of soda on the kitchen floor, Frank grabbed him by the throat leaving marks on his neck. My neighbors witnessed this incident in horror. Frank was afraid they would testify against him in court and this was enough to curb his violent tirades for a while. In his cowardice, he only victimized helpless women and children.

Dino joined the Air Force immediately after he graduated from Cardinal Dougherty High School. He could not wait to get away from his dad. Dino was an honor student and I knew he would do well in the Air Force. I hoped he would use the G.I. Bill to pursue higher education but he chose to remain in the military, making it a career. He and Cindy were in the same high school graduating class since they were only eleven months apart in age. Mario was entering high school the following fall and Cindy was anticipating starting classes at the community college.

I had saved a few thousand dollars and planned to leave Frank when the school year ended. I had already started annulment and divorce proceedings but did not want him served with the papers until I had moved out of the house. Cindy and I went house hunting and found a nice little affordable three-bedroom row house. My G.I. mortgage had been approved and I was scheduled to make settlement in July. When a lay-off notice arrived in late June, I felt as though the world had caved in. The Philadelphia Teacher's Union fought hard and finally settled on condition that the Board agreed to rehire, by February, the laid-off teachers who had tenure. In the meantime, we were eligible for unemployment benefits and food stamps. My calculations told me that I could still move and get by for six months until February, with the help of food stamps and the unemployment checks, if we lived frugally and budgeted wisely.

I went for a few job interviews but employers suspected that I would most likely return to my teaching job so they were not interested in hiring me into what would very likely be a temporary position. That turned out to be a good thing. I really needed the time to get the children and me physically and emotionally settled in our new home. There were all those post-traumatic stress issues to be dealt with by all of us.

Settlement on the house had to be postponed, but the realtor, knowing my situation, agreed to allow me to rent the house for a little less than what my mortgage payments would be and we would make settlement in February when I returned to work.

I moved out of our family home in July. Mario's leg was still in a cast. He had broken it six weeks prior to that while playing touch football with neighborhood friends. It was a very nasty, compound fracture that required orthopedic surgery with the insertion of pins and screws. When I called Frank from the emergency room, his response was, "Why are you calling me? I'm not a doctor." If I had not fully realized before, I knew then with certainty that the kids and I were totally on our own. Their father was detached, sadistic and cruel, even concerning his own children. It was a sad and scary acknowledgment but I figured God had not brought me this far to abandon me.

Frank overslept the morning that the children and I were scheduled to move surreptitiously. We wondered if somehow he had uncovered our plan and was deliberately staying home that day. I woke Mario up and told him to walk across his bedroom floor and make a racket with his crutches over the dining room where Frank slept. That did the trick and Frank jumped up from his pallet on the dining room floor and raced around like a bat out of hell. In no time at all, he sped off to work in the car, and Mario, Cindy and I had time to dress hurriedly and finish packing the remaining bags and boxes before the movers arrived.

My friend Irene took Mario for his appointment to have the cast removed from his leg. Cindy's friend Hortense came over to help with last minute packing. It felt good to have their help and support. We had moved most of the bags and boxes gradually days before.

The movers were finished loading the van and I was ready to drive to meet them at our new little home on Sharpnack Street, just a few blocks away. We discovered that Frank had very few belongings left in the family home on Ardleigh Street. Apparently, he had been secretly removing his stuff bit by bit and taking it to the place that he shared with his mistress. It became clear that his plan was to abandon us without warning. He had been gone emotionally for a very long time, and during the brief periods that he was at home we were like two ships passing in the night.

He had stopped wearing his gold wedding band and had placed it in his bureau drawer. I took off my matching wedding band and ceremoniously placed it beside his on the windowsill of our bedroom and had the movers come back and take the bureau. Frank and his mistress could afford to buy new furniture. We needed this more than they did.

A neighbor later told me how Frank stormed out of the house raging and cursing that he had been outsmarted when he came home to an empty house that evening after work. We had spoiled his final act of cruelty. I will never know just how he intended to make his exit but it had obviously been carefully planned to shock and pain me had I not been a step ahead of him.

After a final look around the virtually empty house, I closed the door literally and figuratively on this long and painful chapter of my life. Only God knew what lay ahead. I turned the key and heard the tumbler click into place as I locked the "door of no return".

The man in charge of the other burly movers sensed that we were running for our lives. Apparently, they had encountered desperate women and children fleeing their abusers before. He assured us that they would keep us safe should Frank happen to return during our escape. They took extra care with our belongings and put everything in place in the new house so that I would not have to worry about lifting and moving heavy objects. Of all the moving teams that could have come, surely God must have designated this particular muscular band of angels to be our rescuers.

Some might say what they would or would not have done had they been in my shoes for the preceding twenty years. Hindsight is often 20/20. So is criticizing or evaluating someone else's mistakes or errors in judgment. When I knew better and could do better, I did better. I was frightened but I had faith that I would get through whatever lay ahead. Strength for today would have to suffice and tomorrow's burdens would have to wait until tomorrow.

THIS FAR BY FAITH

It is indeed a blessing that we cannot see into the future. We might not have the courage to go on if we could see what trials lay ahead. Cindy was doing so well and making me proud at the community college. Dino, my beloved first born, came home from the Air Force on leave a couple of weeks after we moved. He looked healthy and mature after Basic Training and I was so proud of him. He was eager to help out and assembled some furniture for me and helped us get settled in our new home. He seemed relieved that we were free at last. It was indeed good to have my three children with me once again sans the tension and discord that had overshadowed our family whenever their father was present. Our time together passed much too quickly and it was difficult to give Dino his wings and let him fly from the nest.

I did not see it coming when the next avalanche came crashing down upon us. I discovered that Cindy had become a victim of teen pregnancy and was too far along to even consider abortion. Either she had hidden the pregnancy well or I had been too preoccupied with our survival to notice. Even if we could have gotten past the fact that the Church forbade abortion, it was too late and the decision was out of our hands. It was probably better not to have to go through that struggle with conscience and morality. We would have to see her through the pregnancy and delivery. This meant she would have to apply for public assistance and Medicaid since the father of her baby disappeared. Decisions would have to be made regarding the adoption option.

There are no words to describe the overwhelming panic, sadness, fear and worry that I felt or the amount of courage it took for me to look these looming problems in the face and say, "I can do all things through Him who strengthens me." I had to stay strong for my daughter whom I loved with all my heart. I had to see her through. Cindy blossomed and seemed serene, calm and assured that Mom was in charge and in control and that all would be well.

I had to find it within myself to stand tall and ignore the raised eyebrows, judgmental glances and wagging tongues of the neighbors and acquaintances. I was fighting for our lives and in order to survive, I had to rise above the gossip of those who would revile and malign. Some whispered that those interracial marriages never work anyway and that I got what I deserved; just some more mixed-up, mixed race kids. Who did I think I was anyway, they murmured, with my degrees and "seddity" manners. Urban dictionaries define *seddity* as pretentious or aristocratic. I always treated people with dignity and respect so this accusation, though undeserved, hurt nevertheless.

RATS FLEEING A SINKING SHIP

Erstwhile friends, like rats deserting a sinking ship, shunned us. All but a few behaved as though they never knew us. I did not impose on the few friends who remained faithful for fear of losing them also. Thanks be to God, we never had to ask any of them for anything. We always paid our bills on time and avoided debt. That meant careful shopping at thrift stores and watching for sales. We managed economically but it would certainly have been nice to have someone in whom to confide, someone to offer encouragement or someone to show support and lighten our spirits a bit. I suspect most were carrying burdens enough of their own so I held no malice toward them and had no expectations.

Providence kept us afloat on a stormy sea. The gales were fierce but succumbing to the undertow was not an option. It is said that when God is all you have, you discover that God is all you need. The six-month lay-off from the school district proved to be a Godsend even though it was a financial strain. It gave me time to make the life transitions with a bit more ease than I would have had trying to work full time.

When school resumed, I was assigned to one elementary grade school, then to another as the school district worked out its placement problems. I went to work every day displaying a persona that belied my breaking heart. Teaching in the inner city is a difficult and challenging job under the best of circumstances. As hard as I tried to take one day at a time, I felt like a struggling, broken down mule with too heavy a burden on its sagging back. Silent tears soaked my pillow at night but with each new dawn, my weary body rose from fitful sleep and my spirit somehow carried on.

I was finally transferred to Logan Elementary School. Some of the children in my regular classroom were severely emotionally disturbed but mainstreamed anyway. The district lacked special education resources enough to accommodate all those who needed them. A fourth grade girl urinated in a pail in the coatroom one day and poured the contents on the head of a boy who was harassing her. Another boy regularly crawled around on the floor of the classroom barking like a dog, while another sat in his seat and growled at me, "Kill Toman; die Toman," periodically throughout the day. I was both verbally and physically assaulted by out of control students. Fortunately, most of them were smaller than I so the physical damage was relatively minor.

My principal was a middle-aged Black woman who marveled and praised my job performance under difficult circumstances. We were all doing the best that we could in a dilapidated building with insufficient books, supplies and resources. Our persons and property were always at risk. One never knew when one's car would be stolen or damaged. Once, my older Plymouth was spray painted with graffiti. Another time, the battery was stolen. Finally, a window was broken and the steering column ripped apart in an effort to hot wire and steal my new, hard-earned Chevy Cavalier. The thieves got away with some tapes and a few other possessions before someone interrupted the burglary in progress.

I wondered how long I could function under these circumstances without experiencing total burnout. We had a series of principals, male and female, Black, White and Hispanic. Some were supportive and some were not. I received excellent evaluation ratings from all of them.

When I felt sure that things could not get any worse, I discovered that Mario was skipping school and using drugs. With the aid of a local minister and a psychologist at a mental health clinic, I thought we were making some progress. But Mario got worse and dropped out of school. By the time Cindy was ready to deliver her baby, Mario had overdosed on drugs. I ran back and forth that night between the maternity ward where Cindy was in false labor and the emergency room where Mario was hallucinating and having the drugs removed from his system. I thought I was in the middle of a nightmare struggling to wake up from the terror but unable to.

During the ensuing weeks and months I had to remember that it was the drugs talking and acting when Mario's behavior became bizarre or when he made hostile threats or empty promises to do better. My loving, talented, affectionate son had turned into someone whom I no longer recognized.

I was too stressed out and worried to anticipate my grandson's arrival with joy. Anxiety was overwhelming but I was determined to be strong for my daughter. I was worried about her health and about the health of the baby, though we anticipated a safe delivery. I would have to deal with taking time off from school, figure out how to handle the added responsibilities long term while finding help for my son who was in the throes of addiction to drugs and alcohol.

When Cindy went into actual labor, she delivered a beautiful, healthy baby boy who looked almost identical to my eldest son, Dino, when he was a newborn. She named him Jason Dimitri. One look at him and I loved him fiercely. Every child deserved to be loved, nurtured and cared for, regardless of the circumstances of his birth. Cindy decided to keep her baby. We would raise him and love him but I had to work and could not afford to jeopardize my job. We all depended on my income. Cindy would have to take primary responsibility for her son and for his care.

I learned to ignore the continued curious queries of neighbors. I could not afford to add that to my list of real worries. Of course, that did nothing to assuage my feelings of failure as a single parent. I struggled with guilt and shame and wondered how I could have juggled things differently and perhaps seen earlier and more clearly the signs that Cindy and Mario were in trouble. Teaching only abstinence as the good Catholics demanded was not sufficient and Mario's situation proved that "Just say no to drugs" was a cruel joke.

The psychological implications of being abused and abandoned by their own father are manifold. We were reaping the bitter harvest of those cruel seeds. The scars were enduring and the damage manifested itself in various ways for years to come. The emotional wounds that my children suffered in our dysfunctional family took their toll. I could not protect them sufficiently from their domineering, controlling, violent and abusive father no matter how hard I tried. The decisions I made to stay with him were in an effort to spare my children worse suffering. Had I left unprepared, they would have been subjected to having a sick single mom, unable to work and take care of them and having to resort to living on welfare in public housing without access to decent schools.

I loved my children and agonized over how best to defend and help them. It was no simple task to try and undo or minimize the harm Frank left in his wake. We took advantage of counseling resources and eventually, Mario was placed in a rehabilitation facility in Doylestown, Pennsylvania. When he was allowed visitors, I visited as often as I could to support him in his recovery.

After he became drug free and functioning, Mario was tested and became eligible to enroll in a private academy for youths with learning disabilities. The state paid his tuition after a finding that the School District of Philadelphia had failed to properly evaluate and provide for his special needs. Mario graduated from high school at Wordsworth Academy with honors at age twenty-one.

He then entered an independent living program in Doylestown where he was taught life skills and how to function on the job. Through on the job training, he learned baking skills at a local baking company. When he found a job in Philadelphia, he decided that he wanted to move back to the city and live on his own. He was of age so even though I felt uneasy with his decision and advised against it, there was nothing else that I could do. I felt he might feel more grounded in the smaller town and that there might be less chance of recidivism.

Sure enough, Mario needed my financial assistance as well as other support when he moved back to Philadelphia. Before long, I was paying his rent and buying his groceries. I avoided giving him cash when I suspected he was using drugs again. He became very thin and I discovered he had sold the nice color television set that I had gotten him for his birthday. He finally confessed that he was back on drugs. The devastation that I felt is indescribable. I wondered if my son would ever be drug free and able to lead a normal life.

His landlord told us about a treatment facility in Williamsport, Pennsylvania. Mario decided to go to Williamsport and give it a try. I supported his decision as we knew of nowhere else to turn. My heart broke as he boarded the bus to Williamsport but I allowed myself to feel hopeful. After he was clean and sober again, Mario wrote to me that he was living in a facility provided by The Salvation Army and working for them in their thrift store.

FORGIVING AND MOVING ON

My legal divorce became final about a year before the annulment was finalized in 1978. The annulment process was by far the more difficult of the two. I had to secure the written testimony of four witnesses who knew Frank and me and were familiar with at least some of the problems in our marriage. Fortunately, I had revealed some of the secrets to each of four friends who were willing to fill out the lengthy documents and give sworn testimony as to their truthfulness. I had to fill out what seemed like reams of documents that asked the most personal and embarrassing questions. I had to undergo the rigorous questioning and cross examination of a tribunal of judges who finally handed down their decision with the blessings of the Vatican.

While going through the emotional divorce and annulment process, I was dealing with the multiple crises of Cindy's pregnancy, the arrival of my grandchild, Mario's addiction, the hardship of being a single parent, the stress of teaching in the inner city of Philadelphia and the financial strain created by teachers' strikes and lay-offs for three years in a row. How or why I did not succumb to a complete nervous breakdown at this point is beyond me. I prayed without ceasing. I read spiritual and self-help books and tried to remain as positive and as hopeful as possible. There were many sleepless nights on a tear-stained pillow but I had become an expert at keeping up a controlled and calm appearance. I seemed to inspire envy in others rather than pity or sympathy because I appeared to outsiders to have it all together and to be doing so well. There is a heavy psychological price to pay for concealing that much emotional pain.

Nevertheless, I had survived my two greatest fears, fear of abandonment and fear of divorce, and I was still alive. When one is wronged, they say that the greatest revenge is to survive and to live successfully and move forward rather than looking back with bitterness and anger. This is possible through God's grace. I wasted no energy in a quest for revenge. God and the universe pass judgment and settle the scores. Retribution is not my job. Whether Frank's behavior was due to some form of psychological disorder or mental illness or to pure evil is not for me to judge. I forgave him and prayed for his repentance and redemption. Forgiveness was the gift I gave myself to free my spirit. It was harder to forgive what he had done to my children than to forgive his trespasses against me.

Frank never asked me or his children for forgiveness. He did eventually relinquish our mortgaged family home to me. If that was out of remorse, it is the only sign of remorse that he ever showed. I am more inclined to believe that he simply wanted to unload it and get on with his life. The house, which was once a nice twin on Ardleigh Street in the middle class neighborhood of Mount Airy, was in disrepair and suffering from gross neglect. This greatly reduced its market value, practically to that of a handyman special. I managed to sell the house and invest the modest proceeds in an IRA account.

YOU CAN NEVER GO HOME AGAIN

After the death of my parents, I began trying to rebuild relationships with my siblings. Too many years had passed for immediate intimacy to happen. There was still great love between my siblings and me but our divergent paths, experiences, time and distance had diminished the opportunities and possibilities for creating the real closeness for which I had hoped. Gradually, we established some new bonds and it felt good to have at least some family connection. Perhaps we remind each other too much of the past and of all we have had to overcome. I am reconciled to accepting my siblings for who they are and have become, expecting or demanding nothing and loving them unconditionally. We turned out remarkably well, all things considered.

My siblings and I have each made peace with the past in our own way. Whenever we speak of the past in each others' presence, it is usually with humor and laughter at the irony and incredulity of our individual and collective experiences. We share moments of recognition of the courage and discipline that it took to survive and to carry on. We rarely dwell on the painful details which today often seem far removed, almost like telling someone else's story.

I am sure that some measure of protective denial and detachment prevents old wounds from breaking open in the still fragile parts of our psyches. On the other hand, perhaps we have indeed grown stronger in the broken places.

Thomas C. Wolfe, author of "Look Homeward Angel", may have been right when he said, "You can't go home again." Going back to Savannah for a few funerals and a family reunion felt to me like being sucked into a dark hole of inter-generational trauma and pain. The moments of joy and reconciliation could not compensate for the memories and ghosts of the past that I thought were better left undisturbed. I kept my ambivalent thoughts to myself but no, I could not "celebrate me home".

SINGLES AND LIFESPRING

I had little social life during the turbulent years immediately following the divorce. There was not time or energy for socializing as all my resources were directed toward helping my family land on its feet. Yet I felt the need for some diversion and decided to go to a social evening for adult singles at a predominantly Black Unitarian Church. I actually had fun chatting and dancing. It reminded me of my college years and the dances at the YMCA. At first, I felt almost as awkward as I did initially as a student but it seemed like harmless fun and I enjoyed forgetting all the problems for a couple of hours. I discovered that I was still a good dancer though I had not danced since college. The discussion groups were interesting and the refreshments were good.

Hearing the stories of some of the other single women made me realize how well I was dealing with situations in my own life by comparison. Other stories inspired, encouraged and empowered me. I enjoyed talking with the women of various ages, various levels of education and attractiveness and I wanted to be seen as a friend, not as a competitor or as a threat. On the whole, the men were courteous, gentlemanly and even fun but I soon began to understand why they were single. They did not seem to be going anywhere. Some were living at home with their mothers. Others had dead end jobs and few had real career ambitions; in other words, losers. Some were nice and kind but losers nevertheless. Those with any spark did not come to the singles group week after week. I accepted a few dates after a while, trying to be open minded. I learned what I did not want.

One man was very persistent and would not take a hint that I was not interested, making a pest of himself. I finally told him that I had sworn off of men for the next five or ten years. "He must have really hurt you!" he said. "He did," I answered. "That's why I shot him!" The poor man looked so stunned, I had to laugh. "Just kidding!" I said. I'm not sure he believed me, but he backed off and stopped being a pest.

A woman friend told me about another group that met at the integrated Unitarian Church not far away. It was a multi-cultural group but the clientele was much the same. One Sunday evening, three handsome young firemen, not regulars, attended the gathering. They were cute but too far out of my age range to take seriously. They were witty, fun and good dancers though. I was surprised when one of them asked me for a date. With a straight face, I thanked him and told him that I was sorry I could not accept because I was a plainclothes, undercover nun and that I was just in town for the Pope's visit. That was in 1979 when Pope John Paul II was visiting Philadelphia. The young fireman was flabbergasted and went into a huddle with his two buddies. They were not quite sure what to make of my story. I finally let them off the hook and we enjoyed a good laugh together. We also enjoyed a few more dances before we went our separate ways. Some matches were made among the singles and a few couples even made it to the altar. I realized that swimming in this pool was not a promising place for me to be beyond enjoying the music, exercise, dancing and socializing. These benefits helped me to become more comfortable and confident socially but I needed something more productive and more growth-inducing.

A teacher at work invited me to a Lifespring guest event. Lifespring was an organization similar to Werner Ehrhard's EST with a gentler touch. The seminars and trainings were all about self-actualization and personal growth. The programs resonated with me and I signed up for the basic training that led me to proceed through the advanced seminars and trainings. I found such value in them that I encouraged Cindy to do two of the trainings. Paying for the cost of the trainings took sacrifice but I felt we could not afford not to do it. I am sure that years of therapy would have cost a lot more and Lifespring turned out to be a fast track to resolving some crucial issues.

Cindy and her fiancé were living in an apartment near me and had a second child by this time but the relationship was troubled. Lifespring seemed to give her the courage to leave the relationship which was beyond repair. She did not make the mistake of staying in a hopelessly dysfunctional relationship as I had done. I was able to offer her the kind of support that I wish I had had available to me.

The courses seemed to cut to the chase for me also. I learned to know myself better, to face my fears, to realize my potential, my strengths and weaknesses, to set goals, to articulate my desires and to take charge of my life in new and better ways. I had already explored some of these concerns through self-help resources and through an Adult Children of Alcoholics group that helped me tame some of the turbulence of the past. I was committed to becoming healed and whole. I knew that I could not be right for anyone else until I became right for me.

For a long time, I was afraid to acknowledge the depth of the hurt that a lifetime of suffering, pain, abuse and grief had caused. I feared that admitting it would either drive me mad or kill me. I didn't know whether or not I could handle it without losing control and falling to pieces. Yet, I knew enough to realize that I would have to deal with it bit by bit, piece by piece, if I was ever to heal and enjoy the fullness of life. The supportive Lifespring experience opened the doors to start that process in earnest. I discovered strength and courage that I didn't know I had within me.

After Lifespring, my decision to return to graduate school and finish my master's degree plus at least thirty credits became a priority. I still had unused G.I. educational benefits that would cover most of the cost. The master's degree would increase my earning potential by putting me automatically into a higher income bracket once I graduated. The plus thirty would give me an additional boost in pay. I reached my goal and the struggle was worth it. Cindy brought me a dozen roses at my graduation and I think she was as proud of me as I was of myself.

I considered going on for a doctorate just to prove that I could but I was tired. I needed to live a little and enjoy the hard-earned fruits of my labor. Also, Mother Nature and Father Time were nipping at my heels. I was no longer a young woman and the arrival of middle age urged me to look deeper at priorities and consider all the ramifications. I decided that I did not have that many career years left before retirement to make the rigors and sacrifices, financial and otherwise, of doctoral studies worthwhile. My children, though young adults, were still not out of the woods yet and needed my support and parental guidance. I knew that I would always study and continue to value lifelong learning, with or without a doctorate.

THE CRUCIBLE

About the same time, I was having a crisis of faith, not of my faith in God but of my faith in Catholicism. I could no longer cling to the Church that had brought me suffering and feelings of guilt when I needed comfort and understanding. I felt betrayed by the Church that I had served with all my heart and soul. I began looking for a spiritual place where I could heal and grow. I had been singing at a Black United Methodist Church as a soloist and as a member of the choir for several years but my reason for being there was for the music. I did not feel spiritually connected.

Next, I joined the choir of an integrated Lutheran Church. Again, this was for reasons of music and I followed the esteemed choir director who relocated after so skillfully directing the choir at the Black United Methodist Church. I continued to grow musically and to some extent that satisfied my spirit, but deep within, there was a soul hunger and a longing for something more.

I had recently graduated with my masters degree plus thirty credits when I happened to pick up a newspaper one day and I read about First United Methodist Church of Germantown. This was a racially integrated, multi-cultural church with a strong social justice emphasis. Its mission statement read as follows: "The First United Methodist Church of Germantown (FUMCOG) is a diverse, urban community of faith that seeks to experience and worship God through Jesus' message of love and inclusion and the mystery of grace expressed through his life. We affirm our commitment by working together, taking risks for social justice and peace in our community, our city, our nation and our world." Among other things, the article mentioned a notable choir and a Commission on Religion and Race. I decided to visit and investigate further.

I was ready to continue the self-actualization that I had so courageously begun in Lifespring. I had learned not to sit around waiting for good things to happen to me but rather to take steps to make good things happen. I was working hard at becoming the kind of person who would attract good things and good people into my life. I was a giving person and I felt I had gifts and talents to share. I felt that I was also learning to receive gracefully and ready to open my heart and my life to wonderful possibilities, including love.

I decided to join FUMCOG after a few visits and became active, especially in the choir and in the Religion and Race Commission. There were very few eligible men in the congregation but I made some enduring friendships among the women and enjoyed socializing with them. I participated in personal and spiritual growth groups and again realized that I had a lot going for me and a lot to offer as well as much enrichment to gain.

Once, while I was participating in a growth workshop for women, a minister's wife who was co-facilitating the group felt the need to continually remind me that I was a Black woman. She repeatedly said, "You do realize that you are a Black woman," as though she thought I could forget as the only woman of color in a room full of white women. I was quite comfortable but apparently, this supposedly well educated, professional woman was not. She seemed to have great difficulty seeing me as anyone other than a Black woman.

I wondered why she was unable to acknowledge any of the many other facets of my personhood. Although she mentioned occupations, marital status and other demographic facts about the other participants, she never once referred to their race or ethnicity. I was tempted to shock her with a soliloquy in Ebonics or to flat out ask her to please state her agenda.

I'm sure that, had I made an issue of her puzzling behavior, she would have said I was being too sensitive or that I was misinterpreting her intentions. She may have even called me an angry Black woman. I have to pick my battles. If I tried to respond to every racially motivated encounter, I would quickly succumb to combat fatigue and post-traumatic stress disorder.

We cannot hold on to the anger or to all the hurt that is beneath the anger and remain healthy. We have to learn ways of coping and letting it go or it would destroy us. We learn to channel that energy into positive anti-racist activism. That too can become draining and one has to learn methods of avoiding burn-out and activist fatigue from resisting the resisters. Since it is a lifetime struggle, one has to become adept at choosing which battles merit engagement. Sometimes, it is wiser to walk away. Sometimes, it is wiser still to run.

It certainly helps to have a strong spiritual grounding. Without the comfort and strength given me by the Creator, I would not know how to survive the slings and arrows of racism without becoming consumed by rage or despair. My spiritual base, while helping me to respond with love, has kept me centered, strong and assertive when I need to be but protects me from bitterness and defeat.

There were valuable lessons in the crucible, a purification of sorts in the Refiner's fire. I had been single long enough by this time to grow and to become strong, confident and self-sufficient. I felt bold and daring enough to join a couple of different multi-cultural singles clubs that claimed to find suitable and compatible matches for members. The pool seemed more lucrative than the ones at the singles groups of the local Unitarian Churches. I accepted dates with some college professors, teachers, a medical doctor, a couple of lawyers, a minister, a retired army major and an interesting assortment of men.

I decided not to focus on trying to find a husband but rather to enjoy dating and to explore the possibilities. I had reached a point of taking care of myself and my responsibilities and was reasonably happy with my life. I was not desperate and certainly wanted to take my time and not jump into another dysfunctional relationship.

I felt proud of the person I had become in almost twelve years as a single woman and a single parent. I had gone through many growing pains and come through the crucible of life strong and resilient. I had endured the storms of life and learned to bend like the willow and not break. My time, I felt, had finally come. My God and I had walked and talked together through so many dark valleys and scaled so many rugged mountains that I could trust Him and the Universe to make manifest the blessings that were in store for me.

I did not know what these manifestations would look like, but I felt sure I would recognize them when they presented themselves.

AFTER GOOD FRIDAY COMES THE RESURRECTION

The Lenten Season of 1988 was drawing to a close. Signs of spring were apparent everywhere and new life was beginning to burst forth in glorious profusion. The songs of the birds sounded especially brilliant. Fresh green buds dotted the trees and the spirit of newness and promise seemed ready to effuse the earth with miracles as each fragrant flower opened and as each new leaf unfurled.

I sat quietly leafing through a brand new copy of *Philadelphia Magazine* in my primary care doctor's office after school. I was amused by the fact that the magazine was new, unlike the old, dog-eared outdated magazines that usually litter medical offices. "Maybe it's a sign," I mused as I flipped to the classified ads to entertain myself with the outrageous postings of people looking for matches or relationships of one kind or another.

I had scanned old issues of the magazine upon occasion and could not help but wonder what kinds of people placed or responded to these ads. Initially, I thought they must be desperate people who could not find dates through the normal channels of their lives. I wondered if some were con men or axe murderers looking for victims. It had not yet occurred to me that most were probably normal people like myself who led busy, productive lives and did not have the time or the inclination to hang out in clubs or bars dealing with the frivolous and mundane chatter of air-heads. Perhaps they were frustrated and weary of cramming useless dates into their limited spare time only to realize that they were not meeting quality people with whom they could form healthy relationships. Perhaps they were seeking the company of others who shared deeper values.

Suddenly, I realized that surely I was not the only single person out there desirous of living purposefully instead of playing the meaningless games that so many adult singles seemed wont to play. Perhaps it was time to shed some of my self-imposed limitations, broaden my horizons and increase my options, with circumspection of course. I had no interest in and quickly passed over ads in which such things as bust measurements or blond hair were listed as requirements. I wondered about the seeming popularity and appeal of large breasted, anorexic blonds but figured to each his own.

Then, my eyes fell upon a classy ad that spoke to my sensibilities. I was considering it when the nurse indicated that the doctor would see me in a few minutes. I carefully detached the page and tucked it in my purse. I could always reconsider at my leisure. Later that evening, after grading papers and listening to the evening news, I remembered the ad. I took it from my purse and reread it, endeavoring to read what was said and what was not said. Perhaps I imagined the flush of an inexplicable current that I felt as I held the page in my hands and tried to read between the lines and interpret with wisdom any clues that might guide my inner knowing. "An ad, is an ad, is an ad," I murmured aloud to myself, trying to shake off the vibrations that I felt. It was as though the spirit of this man beckoned from wherever he was.

Thinking that I was overly tired and had allowed my imagination to take flight, I put the ad away and went to bed. I said my prayers, then lay awake staring into the darkness. The beckoning feeling would not leave me. After a few minutes, I knew that I needed to let go of these obsessive thoughts and get some sleep. Thinking that I had nothing to lose and that he probably would not respond anyway, I got up, quickly found some tasteful stationery and penned a brief note to Mr. X. I included my phone number but no other identifying information except my first name and ethnicity which would either make a difference to him or not. I needed to know up front.

Being inexperienced with this process, I wondered if I had taken sufficient precaution and decided that if I took to answering other ads, I would rent a post office box. That settled, I fell promptly to sleep.

Once I mailed my response the following morning, I forgot about it and became preoccupied with work activities leading up to Easter vacation and a much needed break from teaching at Logan Elementary School.

When I came home from a community organizing meeting a few nights later, the light on my answering machine alerted me that I had new messages. The first message that I played was from a man who spoke in the most beautiful, resonant, baritone voice that I had ever heard. It was HIM! His name was Gene. I replayed the message many times, listening to every inflection and nuance. I soon found myself literally dancing with excitement around my bedroom.

Nine o'clock seemed a bit too late to call without appearing overly eager. I returned his call the following day and left a cheerful message on his answering machine thanking him for his call and telling him when he could reach me live. He called back promptly, and we talked with the ease of old friends for several minutes. Gene must have felt good vibes also because he asked if we could arrange to meet and if it would be all right to call me again in the meantime. He gave me his home telephone number in New Jersey and invited me to call him also.

We talked several times and were enjoying becoming better acquainted. I was comfortable with agreeing to go for a morning walk in Tyler Park with him, which evolved into an all day outing as we moved easily and naturally from one activity to another. The late March weather was beautiful and Gene's sensitivity to the beauties of nature and the courtesy and respect with which he treated me touched my heart.

I learned that Gene was Jewish, not particularly religious but clearly spiritual. He told me about his family and exhibited an openness and honesty about his life that I found quite remarkable and refreshing. He was so intelligently conversant on any topic and we must have touched on them all, at least the important ones. Honesty was very important to me. My youthful looks in those days were deceptive so I reluctantly revealed that I was three and a half years older than he. He seemed no more fazed by that revelation than by my race.

Twelve hours passed quickly from listening to the birds singing on our three mile walk around the park to a scenic drive to the Pine Barrens, a wonderful seafood dinner at the Sweetwater Casino and enjoyment of the early spring sea breezes at Ocean City. Gene's finely chiseled nose and bearded face looked so handsome as we stood on the jetty at Ocean City with the sunlight in his still golden hair and his sparkling blue eyes reflecting the sky and the sea. I really believed before that day that love at first sight was a myth. This big, gentle, sensitive, intelligent man was special indeed.

The day was fast coming to a close and it was time to head back to Philadelphia. I was a bit surprised when Gene suggested that we stop briefly by his house on the way. I wondered for a moment if he might have ulterior motives but those concerns were quickly allayed. It turned out that he wanted me to know where and how he lived. He had seen my little house and this was part of showing his transparency. A striking pencil drawing of an elderly Chinese man hung on a wall in Gene's living room. His sister had done the drawing in art school years before and I found it intriguing. I mistook the bearded man with smiling eyes for Gene's father wearing a yarmulke. To this day, he teases me about his secret Chinese father!

I had never enjoyed a day more or the company of a gentleman more. When we arrived back at my house, Gene stayed just long enough to say goodnight. I thanked him for a wonderful day. He said he would call and he was quickly on his way home across the

Tacony-Palmyra Bridge. The promise of the Resurrection after Good Friday seemed very real indeed.

THE COURSE OF TRUE LOVE

We had some wonderful dates after that and spent more and more quality time together. We met each others young adult children and friends but were not rushing into commitment. Gene and his former wife must have done something right in order to raise such extraordinary children, three sons and a daughter. When I complimented Gene on raising such beautiful children, he modestly resorted to humor and told me that he had rented them from an agency in order to impress me.

In addition to being good, caring young people, all were academically gifted, independent and self-sufficient. I was impressed and deeply touched by the respect and acceptance with which they welcomed me. I thought that some hostility might eventually surface but with the passing years, that never happened. I grew to love them and to embrace them as my own. They were all grown and already had a mother but I was pleased to be their friend, and eventually, Grandma Poco to their children.

They say the course of true love never runs smoothly. Gene's divorce became final several months into our relationship. I had been divorced for twelve years and had adjusted to and dealt with issues that were just beginning to surface for him. I was very conscious of this and knew that he needed time to sort things out. I wrestled with doubts of my own at the prospect of looking to the future and making a major life change. Both of us, being analytical types, had to feel confident that our relationship could endure the challenges that were certain to come if we made a lifetime commitment.

As much in love as we were, we could not allow emotion and romance to blind us to the fact that this was a serious endeavor on many levels. In addition to all the issues and considerations that any couple has to deal with before remarriage, we were challenging society's racial norms, even in the late 1980's. There was so much to think about that could not be done in haste.

Meantime, I decided to enjoy the relationship that we had without pressure or too many expectations. The relationship would unfold in its own time if it was meant to be. This was not an easy decision for me, which came after much soul searching and some very upsetting times, but we weathered the fears and doubts and worked them through during our two-year courtship.

We traveled and shared many wonderful experiences together. We made a marvelous road trip to Nova Scotia that first summer and proved to be good travel companions. Another trip took us by airplane to the West Coast to explore Washington and Oregon. We seemed so compatible and right for each other despite the fact that our backgrounds were so different. We had much to teach and to learn from each other and were both enriched by the exchange. Life was fun and exciting and it became difficult to imagine life without each other.

We tested the waters and did reality checks on functioning as an interracial couple in twentieth century America. I had married a Polish Catholic man in 1957 and was hopeful that some things had changed for the better in the intervening thirty years. Gene had not experienced a great deal of interracial interaction and social contact. I was amazed and pleased with how well he handled it.

In addition to our relationship concerns, Gene faced two major life events. He mourned the death of his beloved father and also made the decision to undertake a major career change at this relatively late juncture in life. Faithfully, I stood by his side to support and encourage him. He had gravitated toward the legal field since his youth and I recognized his need to give it a try so that there would be no future regrets about the road not taken.

Gene decided to enroll in law school, which was a long held dream, but dropped out shortly thereafter. He felt it was not his calling after all. I supported him in each decision to do what he felt was best. I knew that I could not bear to be in a relationship that was coerced. I wanted a love that was willingly given by someone who would love and appreciate me as much as I loved and appreciated him.

I did not want to make the mistake of staying too long at the fair but by the same token, I did not want to cut my losses too soon and miss out on what a little more patience might have brought. I loved Gene with all my heart and I knew he loved me. I trusted his goodness and integrity to not string me along under false pretenses. Most of all, I trusted myself enough to know that ultimately I would make the choices that were right for me should that become necessary, no matter how hard that might be. I had already gone through the Refiner's fire in the crucible of life. My failed marriage to Frank had made me cautious but not too mistrusting to be open to loving again.

The last time I saw Frank was in the spring of 1989. He and his new wife were visiting Cindy and her family one rainy Saturday afternoon when I made an unscheduled stop at their apartment. I had come straight from checking in on Gene who was bedridden with influenza in Riverton. I had baked a chicken and purchased an apple pie for him so that he would have something to nibble on without having to cook.

Gene was much sicker than I expected but he insisted that I make my visit brief in order to minimize my exposure to the flu germs. Reluctantly, I drove back to Philadelphia taking the apple pie for which Gene said he had no appetite. I decided to drop it off at Cindy's. I was shocked when I walked into her living room and saw her father and his wife sitting there. I kept my composure and cheerfully greeted everyone. I had been rained on but did not look too unkempt. I explained that I just dropped by to deliver the pie and that I was expecting company to arrive at my house shortly and needed to get home.

When I got home, I felt the emptiness of the house acutely and I collapsed on a dining room chair in tears. The realization that Frank had married the younger woman with whom he was involved during the final years of our marriage and had moved on with his life while I had nothing was more than I could bear. Gene and I had been dating for over a year but there was no expressed commitment or real plans for the future in spite of the fact that we seemed so right for each other and cared so deeply for each other.

I had vowed to myself that I would not live with a man to whom I was not married. "Why buy the cow when you can get the milk for free?" That was not the example I wanted to set for my children or for Gene's. I valued myself enough that I did not want to be taken for granted. I felt I deserved to be a wife and not someone's live-in girlfriend who could be discarded on a whim.

Realistically, I knew I would be judged by many as a loose woman and a stereotypical African American slut if I had consented to moving in with Gene. We had both taken turns commuting back and forth across the Tacony-Palmyra Bridge for more than a year but at my age and with the demands and fatigue of my teaching job, I was beginning to feel the strain of schlepping to Riverton regularly, especially since I found driving tedious and stressful.

I was beginning to feel that the relationship might be headed toward a dead end and I needed more. I called Gene, as was our habit to let each other know when we arrived home safely. I broke down on the phone and told him about the brief encounter with Frank and his wife. I told him that at that very moment, they were probably eating my apple pie and laughing at me. I told him how Frank had moved on with his life and of the emptiness I felt having no one in my life and no sense of a future in sight.

At first, Gene thought my sadness and upset were about losing Frank. I quickly explained that the loss of Frank was good riddance and that my upset was about the emptiness in my own life and my uncertain prospects for the future. I confessed that I struggled with the question of whether or not it might be time for me to cut my losses and move on.

That was a lot to lay on a guy with the flu and Gene seemed surprised, even stunned. "You have me, and you really feel you have nothing?" he asked, out of his feverish fog. "But you're not mine, I don't have you," I answered. "We have no commitment. What we have is very special but where is it leading?"

There was a pause on the other end of the line that seemed interminable. I thought, "You couldn't have chosen a worse time to break down, Poco." Then, Gene said so gently, "I'm too weak and woozy to come to you and I know you just left here in this bad weather...but can you please come back?"

The drive back to Riverton was treacherous as the downpour became so heavy that poor visibility forced me to pull off the road a couple of times. Nightfall was approaching and I barely managed to pull into Gene's driveway by daylight.

I used my key to let myself in and Gene grabbed me in his arms. "Flu be damned!" I thought. At that moment, I didn't care if I caught the flu and died in his embrace. We were both glad I had come back and we talked far into the night. At times, I wondered if it was Gene's fever talking but the honesty went far beyond what either of us had ever dared. It stopped short of a proposal but Gene assured me that I meant too much to him and that we shared too much to ever be "dead-end".

Gene was much better the next day when I returned home to prepare for the workweek ahead. Within a few days, I came down with the flu. It was Gene's turn to come over with chicken soup and flowers and nurse me back to health. The relationship had shifted in a magical and beautiful way. We were truly taking care of each other and it felt so natural and so good. Soon, statements that Gene formerly prefaced with "If we get married..." became "When we get married..."

After Gene decided in 1990 to buy the Voice-Tel franchise, a high-risk venture with a new and unproven franchisor in a pioneer field, his focus was sure and he never wavered. It was not easy to risk all and start a new business, but together, we decided we could do this. We became engaged in April of 1990. On bended knee with a dozen roses in hand, as coached by his daughter Brie, Gene asked me to become Mrs. Eugene Gertler. We eloped three months later and were married in Elkton, Maryland on June 29, 1990. From our first kiss to the "I do's" we knew that we had something very unique and special which has grown even deeper and stronger with each passing year.

After I moved to Riverton, New Jersey, I settled easily into housekeeping and the wonderful role of wife with the man I loved. We were happy! We were busy with work and getting the new business running, almost too busy to notice that we didn't have any local social connections. We maintained some ties with long-time friends and got together with them occasionally. In an effort to reach out and make friends, I joined the Cinnaminson Community Chorus and we explored the local Friend's Meeting house and a synagogue in Willingboro. Neither felt quite right so I continued to commute to FUMCOG in Philadelphia but with less frequency as time passed. Gene joined me on some occasions. I remained actively involved in the Cinnaminson Community

Chorus for several years as a valued soprano with solo opportunities.

No one was openly hostile to us in Riverton. Gene had raised his first family there. In fact, some folks were quite courteous. To others, I was invisible. There simply was no interaction beyond the walls of the buildings where services or chorus rehearsals and performances took place. I was finally able to make friends with Molly, a mixed race woman of color who was originally from Surinam. She told me that the races stayed to themselves socially and that the white people preferred it that way. Molly and I began walking together for exercise and continued to socialize for as long as I remained in Riverton.

In summer I helped Gene in the Voice-Tel office daily until we had sufficient hired staff. During the school year, I commuted to my still stressful teaching job in Philadelphia until I took early retirement in 1993 when injuries from an assault by a student triggered disabling fibromyalgia. I have experienced chronic pain and fatigue since that time.

OF JOYS AND SORROWS

Life always has its share of both joys and sorrows. That's the price of being human and the cost we pay for being in the world. Burdens shared with those we love are always lighter because we're stronger when we raise each other up during the difficult times. Time passed and my biological children seemed to have landed on their feet at long last. Dino was gaining rank quickly and appeared happy in his Air Force career. Cindy was married and Mario was clean and sober.

Mario had fallen off the wagon a number of times but at last, Narcotics Anonymous and Alcoholics Anonymous along with other counseling seemed to be effective and he was faithfully working the programs. Gene and I explored ways to help Mario toward economic independence. School seemed the best route to this goal. Our hope was that art school would harness his talents and enable him to earn a living doing what he loved. Mario graduated with honors from the two-year program but had become addicted to food and was so morbidly obese that no one would hire him in any commercial art position despite his talents and skills.

We don't understand what caused Mario to have an addictive personality. It seems that it is common for addicts to exchange one addiction for another. We can speculate that his neurological problems beginning in infancy may have caused some minimal brain damage or that the emotional stresses of childhood abuse contributed, but there is no way to ever know for sure. Mario remained grossly obese and eventually wound up on Social Security Disability. We feared for his life and sought out every possible intervention that we could. He never lost his cheerful, optimistic outlook or his loving, charming manner. He also never lost the excess weight. It was painful to witness my once lean, fit, muscular son's physique turn morbidly obese.

Gene was by my side as we helped Cindy through a divorce and as we later celebrated her remarriage. We were family and were there for each other always. It was hard for me to accept that Gene did not consider me and my troubled children too burdensome. I felt truly blessed and thankful that he was steadfast and faithful far beyond what most men would have undertaken.

Dino married a young woman in the Air Force and he and Susan came for a visit with us when they returned from a tour of duty in Japan in the early 1990's. We enjoyed good fellowship and feasting as our combined families got better acquainted. Times like these eased the sting of the difficulties of the past and we hoped they could last forever. Would that life were that simple!

Dino was always quiet and introverted. He gained rank rapidly in the Air Force. I was aware that he was sensitive and introverted and that he held his feelings too much inside. He, like Cindy and Mario, had been traumatized in childhood by their father's cruelty. I wondered if he too had suffered permanent or lingering effects from those early years. In conversation, he refused to revisit those memories or to acknowledge any possible negative effects. Since he was so uncomfortable approaching the topic in a direct manner, I tried talking in generalities about the value of psychotherapy at any point in one's life when one felt the need for support in dealing with various life issues. I told him about the value that Cindy and I had received from the Lifespring personal growth experience.

My heart knew that Dino was stuffing down and possibly repressing an enormous amount of emotional baggage. I did not know how to get through his resistance, defensiveness and silence without alienating him. He was a grown man now and I tried to respect his privacy while encouraging him to talk. I gently assured him that there were benefits to therapy that he might want to explore.

His wife Susan was a vivacious, cheerful brunette who taught serious Dino to play more. She seemed to add lightness and joy to his life and that made me glad. Her family supported their interracial marriage and they seemed very much in love. We were shocked when we learned that he and Susan were getting a divorce sometime after their visit. I tried to be as supportive as I could from afar as they said the divorce was amicable though painful and that they remained friends. Susan came out, living openly as a lesbian soon after that.

My beloved sister Bunny died on December 20, 1994. We were having Thanksgiving dinner at our house with Gene's children and mine when we were informed that Bunny had suffered a stroke and was hospitalized near her home in North Carolina. The news was upsetting but we were hopeful that her recovery would be swift. We later learned that she never fully regained consciousness. Cancer was discovered and it was terminal.

Gene had to hold down the fort at Voice-Tel so I flew to North Carolina alone to visit Bunny and to be with the rest of the family. Bunny's husband George, her son Michael, my other siblings and I made the dreadful trip to the hospital. Bunny looked as beautiful as ever and it was inconceivable to me that she was dying. She opened her eyes briefly as I talked to her and stroked her face and arms but I could not tell whether or not she was aware of our presence. It all seemed so unfair, but who ever said that life was fair. We play with the hand we're dealt.

Our hearts were broken but each of us struggled to hold in our grief and be strong for the others. My sister Gloria, who is very emotional, fell apart and wept inconsolably when the doctors told us that there was no hope. George asked us to help him make prearranged plans for my sister's funeral, which would be held at St. Mary's Church, the parish church of our childhood in Savannah, Georgia. I had no fondness for George because he treated Bunny so badly and caused her such pain throughout the marriage with his repeated philandering. However, this was no time for bitterness and we all gathered at the funeral home and made the final arrangements for my precious sister.

The following day, I flew home to wait either for a miracle or for news of Bunny's death. No miracle happened. I found myself on a train alone on Christmas Day bound for Bunny's funeral. All flights to Savannah were booked so bus or train were my only options. It was a long, wearisome trip. The sad, lonely wail of the nocturnal train whistle and the sound of the wheels on the tracks intensified the surges and waves of pain, both physical and mental, that morphed into numbness and back into pain again and again and again.

As we sat in the highly polished pews at St. Mary's Church during Bunny's funeral, the past and the present seemed to fuse and morph. One moment, I was a six-year-old, gripped by fear of my scolding first grade nun. The next moment, I was the troubled pre-teen struggling with an identity crisis and wondering why God would not answer my prayers and give me lighter skin so that my life would be easier in a world obsessed with whiteness. Memories of kneeling in those pews until my knees were numb praying for my father's sobriety flooded my mind. Reality repeatedly drew me back into my sixty-two-year-old self, struggling to keep my composure as the eldest sibling and to be there for the support of the others, especially Gloria who sobbed hysterically throughout the Requiem Mass. Bunny died a practicing Catholic in good standing.

I wanted Gene. I needed him at my side. I needed his strength and comfort. Again, I reminded myself that "When God is all you have; God is all you need." My faith told me that I would get through this travail leaning on the Everlasting Arms.

Each of us siblings dealt with Bunny's death in our own way. We all loved her dearly. Grief brought out the worst in my younger sister Gloria. Her outbursts before, during and after the funeral were volatile and difficult to endure. Her uncontrollable sobbing and screaming reverberated throughout the packed and quiet little church of our childhood and filled every corner of its sacred spaces. She was hostile and angry with everyone while the rest of us tried to be as supportive of each other as we could. My brothers, Samuel and Richard, were stoic and controlled in their restraint. My efforts to comfort Gloria were ineffective. She was inconsolable. I dared not allow myself to fully feel the loss until I returned home to New Jersey.

First, I was numb. Then, the surges of pain almost drowned me and I wondered if they would ever stop. For the next three months, I put one foot ahead of the other as I moved around in a thick fog. Gradually, the fog began to lift and allow some sunlight to filter through for brief periods. I prayed, meditated and read books on the grieving process and wrote letters of consolation to my siblings. The first year was the hardest and the grief came in waves. At times, it felt as though I was grieving a lifetime of sorrows and losses and perhaps I was; those past and present as well as those to come.

So much had been repressed over the years, including the deaths of my parents who had died more than two decades before. I finally felt safe enough to grieve their loss and allow myself to break through the numbness, then the pain.

I had experienced enough of life to know that we each encounter our share of both joys and sorrows. Some of us seem to get a greater share of one or the other but I suppose for most of us, the scales generally balance out. I had also learned that change is constant and inevitable and that nothing stays the same. The sharper edges of the grief would eventually subside.

In hindsight, I know that hiding the depth of my grief from Gene made the healing process more difficult and more prolonged. I felt I had to protect him since he had enough on his shoulders with keeping the new, fledgling business afloat. I needed him so desperately with me in North Carolina and in Georgia during those difficult days when Bunny died but it was not possible for him to leave the business. We would surely have lost it if he had. When he came home from the office, I did not have the heart to burden him with my pain and sorrow. I tried to hide it as best I could. At some level, I'm sure I felt anger that Gene could not read my mind and know how much I needed him. I suppose I felt that our young marriage had borne so much already that I was afraid to put any more weight on it lest it break.

Healing and reconciling the losses began to happen over time. Though difficult, I could accept the death of my parents more easily than I could that of my sister, although my parents died at relatively young ages. I will always love and miss them.

The death of a sibling changes one's way of being in the world. Everything is seen from a different perspective. Bunny's death put me in touch with my own mortality in a more conscious way and I recognized more passionately the importance of living fully and appreciating the gift of life each day. I thought it impossible to love and appreciate my husband any more than I already did but everything meant more to me now. Acknowledging death eventually led me to somehow feeling more alive and living with renewed purpose and intention. I gained an empathy that has made me a more compassionate person, better able to comfort others who have experienced profound losses.

JOY COMES IN THE MORNING

Remarkably, the world just keeps on turning when we take some time out to grieve and to heal. It does not stop or slip off its axis simply because we feel that perhaps it should or will. It moves right along, orderly as usual, until we are ready to resume our lives. Perhaps that is the Divine signal that we are not supposed to dwell too long in sorrow but to re-enter the sphere of the living. "Weeping may endure for a night, but joy cometh in the morning." (Psalm 30:5)

Indeed, Gene and I have found great joy in our marriage and in the great love that we share. Our lives have been continually enriched by family visits, weddings, the arrival of new grandchildren, celebrations and rituals and many happy events and experiences shared with both immediate family and extended family.

Gene's only sister Joan and I have enjoyed a long and amiable relationship, primarily by e-mail since we have seen each other in person only a handful of times. We have been able to compare notes, encourage and commiserate with each other concerning fibromyalgia. Joan has suffered from fibromyalgia since the tender age of twenty-three. I was diagnosed at age sixty though I had not recognized the gradual onset of symptoms that began years before but flared fully after the assault by one of my students.

Other members of Gene's extended family have welcomed me warmly to family events and gatherings and many have kept in touch periodically despite their advancing age and declining health. I have returned the mutual respect, admiration, acceptance and affection that the family has shown me. We are richly blessed for such is not the case with many interfaith and interracial families.

As with any blended family, a few rough places have surfaced but have been smoothed with civility, respect and dignity. At the weddings of Gene's children, I was mindful of and sensitive to the presence of their mother and her role and I was determined always to be low key, dignified and to take the higher ground. Likewise, at the Bar Mitzvah and Bat Mitzvah of the grandchildren, I never in any way tried to usurp the role of their genetic grandmother. The grandchildren were taught by their parents to call me Grandma Poco and I have always found that delightful, as I have embraced them as my own.

Cindy and Tony were married at our home in Riverton, New Jersey. Gene gave the bride away and two of his sons, J.J. and Dave, participated in the small but lovely wedding ceremony on our spacious lawn. When Cindy became Mrs. Tony Brown, she acquired the nickname "Sunshine", his name for her because she brought such warmth and light into his life.

To see my beautiful daughter happy at last filled my heart with gladness and I prayed that she and Tony would enjoy a bright future together. My then teen-aged grandsons Jason and Julian needed a father figure in their lives. Cindy had managed quite remarkably as a young, single mother. The absence of the boys' father had its negative effects to be sure but things could have turned out a lot worse.

Tony's radio show on WDAS in Philadelphia has continued its thirty year plus popularity and Sunshine eventually became an integral part of that success.

Misfortune struck again in March of 2006 when Tony suffered a stroke. Gene steadfastly supported Sunshine and me through the difficult and uncertain days and weeks that followed. As the weeks passed, by the grace of God, Tony made a miraculous recovery and was able to resume his radio career.

Jason and Julian finished high school in Phoenixville, Pennsylvania, their new hometown, before the family moved to Collegeville, Pennsylvania. Jason joined the United States Army but decided after one tour of duty that the Army was not to be his chosen career. He returned to Collegeville and as time passed, he and Julian eventually started families of their own.

I love my grandsons and worried about their futures. It had been a tremendous struggle for Sunshine, raising them as a single mother though I, and later Gene, pitched in wherever we could. Adversity is often overrated as a builder of character. Sometimes, it makes us stronger and sometimes it leaves scars and wounds that are not easily healed. Julian, though the younger of the two, landed on his feet first and hit the ground running. Jason got a slower start, but both are strong, bright, capable young men and will surely do well in life.

Grandchildren and great-grandchildren have begun to enrich both sides of the family. Gene and I love them all dearly and his and mine have become "ours". As we celebrate the various rites of passage, we look forward to seeing them all come into their own. We feel profoundly blessed to reach this stage of life enjoying reasonably good health and prosperity and a devotion to each other that grows deeper and richer with each passing year.

Business travels and travels for pleasure started Gene and me thinking about what we would do after retirement and where we would live. We wanted a fresh beginning in a home that we created together. After we married, I sold my house in Philadelphia and moved to Riverton, into the house where Gene's children had been raised. I think we both realized that there were far too many reminders of another time and another life in that house... too many ghosts of seasons past.

We fell in love with the Southwest as we traveled around New Mexico and Arizona. We researched best places to retire on the Internet and in retirement magazines. Prescott, Arizona caught our attention as a location with four-season climate in a small town of some thirty-five thousand souls, equidistant from Phoenix and Flagstaff. Phoenix was too hot for most of the year and Flagstaff was too cold and snowy in winter. Prescott seemed just right and worth investigating.

PRESCOTT - EVERYBODY'S HOMETOWN

I remember the late August afternoon in 1998 when we drove over scenic Mingus Mountain and into Prescott, Arizona after the long trip across the country from New Jersey. At the start of our trek, we had planned a few detours along the way, including a trip to Cherokee, North Carolina, the land of my maternal ancestors. Qualla Boundary is the name of the Cherokee Indian Reservation there and is the home of the Native American Eastern Band of Cherokee Indians. The exceptionally beautiful and lush flora and fauna, the virgin forests and the clear running streams of the Great Smoky Mountains brought back childhood memories as we traveled the local roads, visited the museum and other sites while munching on a local favorite, boiled peanuts, purchased at a roadside stand.

As we traveled on, Gene was eager to set foot in Mississippi just to be able to say that he had been there. It was one of the only two states that he had never visited. Remembering the violent history of the state, especially that of the Civil Rights Era, I was much less eager to visit Mississippi. In fact, I was downright apprehensive. After seeing my clenched knuckles and trembling hands, Gene turned around soon after we touched soil on the Mississippi side of the border.

Another detour took us to Cherokee country in Oklahoma where we did some sightseeing and visited a few historic sites. We could not tarry for long because we had to beat the moving van to Prescott. I wish we could have spent more time learning about what the Cherokee People call "The Trail of Tears". This refers to that dark period in United States history, in the 1830's, when President Andrew Jackson ordered the forced removal and genocidal relocation of the Cherokees and other tribes from their homelands in the southeast to Oklahoma Territory.

The Indian Removal Act of 1830 also forced the relocation of other members of the so-called Five Civilized Tribes, the Chickasaw, Choctaw, Creek and Seminole. The Black and Red connection is a legacy that preceded the Trail of Tears. African Americans who were either slaves or who were intermarried with the Indians made the trek westward and endured the same indignities and suffering that befell the Indians. All suffered the brutal scourges of starvation, disease, exposure and exhaustion with many deaths along the way.

Some of the Indians escaped and remained in or near their ancient homelands in the southeastern United States. A goodly number of Cherokees hid in the Great Smoky Mountains and escaped relocation. They and their descendants are now called the Eastern Band Cherokee while those who were removed to Oklahoma and their descendants are called the Western Band Cherokee.

Making our way west, Gene and I drove all day from dawn until after dusk, making rest and meal stops and crashing in a motel each night. As we traveled over the highways and byways, beholding the vastness and varied beauty of the country, the song "America The Beautiful" took on deeper significance and meaning. The irony of our country's tragedies and triumphs filled me with awe and wonder as I considered where we as a nation have been and pondered over our future direction.

It was an incredible trip through some amazing territory and Gene drove all those miles in record time. I regretted that I could not be a relief driver. I learned to drive later in life, shortly before I divorced the father of my children. Unlike some late beginning drivers, I never became a comfortable driver and never learned the skills of highway driving. I was a safe local driver who knew my limitations.

As we drove into Prescott, signs of welcome read "Prescott - Everybody's Hometown". We did not yet know that the welcome applied to white, political and religious conservatives, leaving people of color and many others marginalized. The exclusion was not blatant and obvious at first and we felt that as newcomers, we would be welcome. We assumed that we would make friends in time and become active participants in the community. I tend to look for the best in people and Gene does also.

We certainly were not naive enough as an interracial couple to think that everyone in Prescott would embrace us with open arms. We hoped, and I dare say even presumed, that there would be a liberal element in the area to which we could relate. We had done our homework regarding the weather, climate, geographic wonders, nearby Indian cultures and almost everything environmentally but had neglected miserably to learn more about the people, the politics and the Southern attitudes and culture of Arizona. We were not social butterflies so we took for granted that we would be able to make the minimal social contacts to which we were accustomed.

We signed on as members of the local synagogue shortly before our move and made a couple of preliminary visits to Prescott. People seemed courteous and friendly enough. On one visit, a couple from the temple invited us to dinner at their lovely home where we met the rabbi and two other couples. One of the couples took us out to breakfast the following morning and we met the other couple for a Dutch treat dinner before our return trip back East. We were delighted to meet the three couples and the rabbi and prematurely assumed that they might be a core circle of friends once we moved to Prescott.

We also met our prospective neighbors when we came back to Prescott a second time to inspect the house that was to become our home. They too were friendly and courteous so we had no real misgivings about moving into the community. I try not to be overly sensitive so I tried to shrug off the Black Mammy door stop that the homeowners prominently displayed near their kitchen door. It reminded me of the coal black, red-lipped, Topsy doll that so traumatized me as a child. I suppose what mattered more to the homeowners was the color of our money rather than the color of my skin, as we made an agreement on the house. They seemed quite satisfied when we offered them their asking price.

I did have some second thoughts later when we went to visit one of the couples we had met from the temple. As we drove into their development, the first house that we saw had a coal black lawn jockey in the front yard. It held a lantern and grinned broadly with its grotesque red lips. I tried not to feel paranoid but the mocking grin seemed to say, "Welcome to Prescott, everybody's hometown except yours and people who look like you!"

I had dealt with racism all my life but I had not seen these blatant racist symbols so openly and prominently displayed for decades. Most civilized people, I thought, had come to realize that such symbols expressed racism and that they were at the very least in extremely poor taste. I have always been an adaptable person accustomed to dealing with difficult situations, so I told myself that as long as I felt no physical threat, I could overlook the inconsiderate and often mean attitudes of the dominant society. I even told myself that perhaps I was being overly sensitive and making too much of some Prescottonians' warped and tasteless choices in home and yard decorations. The dull ache inside stayed with me even as I looked around at the environmental beauty and asked myself, "What's not to love about this charming town with its moderate climate, clear blue skies, high desert breezes, fragrant pine forests and the ever present grandeur of the mountains and the San Francisco Peaks?"

Gene was excited and enchanted by it all which made me even more hesitant to voice my misgivings. He had worked so hard to bring us to this point in life and we were both looking forward to spending our retirement years happily together in a beautiful place. I loved our prospective neighborhood and the lovely house on the cul-de-sac was truly my dream house with a nice layout and it was just the right size for an easy to maintain retirement house.

Soon after we put a deposit down on the house and returned to New Jersey, the homeowners had a change of heart and accused us of trying to force them to sell their house to us. The dispute was supposedly over their dining room set that we were negotiating to buy with the house. We don't know for sure whether that was the issue, whether they received a better offer or whether someone opposed to having a neighbor of color had managed to influence them. We had offered them their asking price and we were not about to back out of the contract. We liked the house and the neighborhood and especially the scenery with the view of the San Francisco Peaks from the redwood deck.

It took a few more months to sell the Riverton, New Jersey house which we had put up for sale, but it did sell soon after we made settlement on the house in Prescott. We were ready to begin the next new and exciting chapter of our lives.

Over Mingus Mountain we came, two days ahead of the movers. We waited anxiously at The Prescott Resorts Hotel for the arrival of the moving van. When the call came, we met the van at our new home on Dell View Lane in the Horizon Hills Development.

Moving day was a bright, clear, happy one. None of our property got damaged. Even the fragile items arrived intact for Gene had packed them so well. We did some minimal furniture shopping and very soon, the house looked and felt like home. The immediate neighbors all brought housewarming gifts of baked goods, fruit from their trees and such and we invited them all over for a social get-together one evening.

Soon after that, we invited the rabbi over to bless the house and to install mezuzahs at our front and rear doors. We served a nice luncheon to him and to our other guests. These included the three couples whom we originally met at the temple and Fred Brown, an African American builder and business man, who had taken time out of his busy schedule to show us around Prescott on our first visit. The realtor told us about Fred and his family when we inquired about other people of color in town. He said there were a few.

We were surprised at how few African Americans there really were in the area. We were invited by the one African American City Councilman, Dick Cooper, and his wife, Lula, to join a social group called Potluckers. The Coopers had helped to form the organization so that African Americans and other people of color moving to the area could feel some connection while becoming acclimated to a very white Prescott which was not always welcoming to minorities.

We met fifteen or twenty people and attended the meetings off and on for several years. They were nice people but somehow, deep connections did not develop with most of the people in the group.

Common color does not always mean common backgrounds, interests or compatibility. It's nice to know that there are African Americans here and we see each other from time to time. Friendships cannot be forced or based solely on ethnicity any more than can other relationships.

Relationships at Temple B'rith Shalom too were cordial but superficial. We came to the conclusion that demographically, most people here are too old to be really comfortable with interracial relationships or with forming close friendships with us as an interracial couple. I suspect that many of the temple folks had never related to African Americans as other than maids, janitors or in other subservient roles. In addition to age, ethnicity and race, the class factor was also no doubt in play.

We tried to be as outgoing and friendly as we knew how to be, attending services, joining Sisterhood, inviting people to our home or out for meals, participating in classes and activities and volunteering. I was asked to address congregants twice and to share about my journey as an African American-Native American Woman. My carefully prepared programs were warmly received with positive feedback and seemingly appreciated by those who attended.

I thought this might lead to wider acceptance; that getting to know me as a person, not as a representative of my race, might make me seem more approachable. I hoped that showing that we had things in common would create a rapport. I endeavored to make my talks relevant, emphasizing ways in which we were all alike as human beings, highlighting our shared values, similarities between certain aspects of our cultures, common heroes, ideologies and the many things that would make my "otherness" seem less strange or threatening to them. This brought back memories of my days on the speaking and singing circuit at National College.

THE CHURCH PEOPLE

I thought the local, almost all white Granite Peak Unitarian Universalist Congregation, with its reputation as a liberal spiritual group might be more receptive and accepting than the town in general. Again, most folk were friendly and courteous. After visiting services for a while, I decided to join the congregation. I did not expect Gene to join but he attended regularly with me. I thought that if I became a member, the other members would be more likely to see me as "one of them" over time, not just as a flash in the pan, exotic visitor. We simultaneously continued as regular members of Temple B'rith Shalom.

I became a visible participant, serving on a couple of committees and joining the newly organized choir of the Unitarian Universalist Congregation. We were mostly older singers who had a history of choir and other choral singing. We found joy in singing and I was certainly happy to be able to sing again. I was pleased to do some solos, duets and trios. Eventually, I was asked to speak during several of the Sunday services and share about my life and experiences. People seemed receptive and some expressed the desire to learn more about racism and diversity.

As a result of my talks, a retired professor from the congregation decided to lead a series of classes called "Weaving the Fabric of Diversity: An Anti-Bias Program For Adults". This program was formulated by people at the Unitarian Universalist Association Headquarters in Boston and was the predecessor of "Journey Toward Wholeness" (JTW), their more developed diversity and anti-racism program which the leadership and members of the congregation later decided to undertake. I volunteered to serve as leader or co-leader for some of the sessions and to work with the JTW Committee. The group dwindled with each of the eight sessions of the former program and "Journey Toward Wholeness" barely got off the ground.

I can only assume that participants found it too difficult to acknowledge and talk about racism openly and honestly. Most seemed to see racism as a problem of and for people of color and were unable to understand or acknowledge the concept of White Privilege or how racism negatively affected white people. Rather than stick with the sessions and learn from them, some found it easier to blame the victims of racism and accuse them of inciting guilt and of dragging white people over the coals. Learning about and confronting racism was met with resistance and anger. Soon it became personal and I felt under attack. I was given the cold shoulder, frozen out of conversations and told to "Just get over it!"

Some of the more open minded folk attended the diversity films sponsored by JTW, including "The Color of Fear" by Lee Mun Wah, and the follow-up discussions. As other members of the committee began to feel the heat, their commitment wavered. After a while, the hostility became so palpable and personal that we began to feel disrespected and overwhelmed. I had been an active member of the Granite Peak Unitarian Universalist Congregation for five years at that point. As long as I and others on the committee said what the majority of the congregation wanted to hear, things were fine but when challenged to grow and to examine other points of view, people felt threatened and became hostile. Others felt racism didn't concern them so they became disinterested. Some felt they knew all that they needed to know. After all, they said, they were not racists so what was the point.

I left the congregation to preserve and protect my own mental and spiritual health. I had given so much to the congregation that I felt drained and exhausted. Some would never be able to "get it". Again, demographically, these were predominately older white people, many of whom felt they had "been there and done that" during the Civil Rights Movement. They were not interested and seemed to feel that the problems of racism were solved back then and were no longer relevant.

A few misguided persons sought to convince me that racism was neither as prevalent nor as serious as I perceived it to be. They tried to persuade me that I was just too sensitive. Trapped in their parallel universes, their reality bore no resemblance to my existence in the real world. It was like having someone try to convince you that it's raining when in actuality, they are urinating on your shoe. I clearly know the difference between rain and pee. I have danced in the rain and it did not smell anything like the foul atmosphere of denial, indifference and complicity that permeated that congregation.

The silence of the so called good people is what allows the evil of racism to flourish. Dr. Martin Luther King, Jr. reminded us that "In the end, we will remember not the words of our enemies, but the silence of our friends." Truer words were never spoken. We expect assaults from our enemies but we trust our friends to advocate for us and work with us.

I found it very difficult to understand how so called liberal, highly educated, religious people could be so clueless and in such denial. Some of those who voiced support and smiled most broadly in my face were the very ones who knifed me in the back when they grew afraid of losing the approval of their peers or afraid of being perceived as a "nigger lover". At the risk of sounding judgmental, the word "hypocrisy" comes to mind. The devastating betrayal of trust by so called friends was extremely painful and has taken years to heal.

Of course, the betrayal made me angry but underneath the anger was the enormous amount of hurt. Nevertheless, forgiving and letting go was the gift I had to give to myself in order to heal. I suppose many of the people of a certain age are victims of their own racist history and upbringing and victims of the history of racism and bigotry in our country. Younger people are often infected by the disease of racism as it is passed down from generation to generation but some seem able to transform themselves and to rise above it to become allies and anti-racist activists. Therein lies our hope for the future.

Prescott has been a precarious balancing act as Gene and I have experimented with various ways of coping and carving out a happy life for ourselves. Like the brave souls who have gone before us, Richard and Virginia Loving and others who challenged the bans on interracial marriages, our love has kept us strong. We certainly were not seeking heroism or notoriety. We were and are simply two people who love each other much too deeply not to exercise our right to be married and live out our lives together in happiness and peace.

Acts of intimidation like the large Confederate Battle Flag that our next door neighbor flew facing our house for at least a year have been disturbing. Finding a noose hanging from a tree in our front yard in 2007 was very disconcerting. Glares and rude behavior and treatment occur in public places from time to time but each hurdle that we overcome makes us stronger. I try not to become too perturbed when I am profiled while shopping or challenged about what country I am really from. I wonder if I should carry my birth certificate around since it seems the Tea Baggers and Birthers are not only after President Obama but ready to harass others as well. As a sensitive person, it has taken patience and skill in order to develop a thicker skin and to minimize the psychological and emotional damage that racism inflicts.

I have grown much stronger spiritually and intellectually and have developed a richer interior life as a result of the non-inclusive nature of life in Prescott. Since my social life is limited, I spend more time reading, writing, enjoying music, doing research on the Internet, engaging in meaningful communication via computer, watching good movies, exercising and benefiting from personal growth and enrichment. However, since God created us as social beings, I do hunger from time to time for local friendships and for the satisfaction that such relationships can bring. Gene and I find much contentment with each other but we know that it is also healthy to interact with others from time to time and that compatible friends can add a positive dimension to life. Until that is possible, we are thankful for all that we share and for the unwavering support that we give each other.

Gene is a "show me" more than a "tell me" kind of guy. He demonstrates his loyalty and feelings rather than talking a lot about them. Talk is cheap but on the other hand, there are times when there is no substitute for words. There are also times when no words are sufficient. The generous measure of both words and actions make up the close knit loving relationship that defines our marriage in the face of all that we have encountered. We continue to explore ways of inviting people into our lives. New people move to Prescott each year and the population has reached about forty-five thousand to date. As the area continues to grow, we have not given up on developing a circle of friends.

In 2010, the Miller Valley School mural incident went viral worldwide when a Prescott City Councilman, Steve Blair, made racist remarks about the painting of a bi-racial Mexican American-African American child that appeared on the mural. The outrageous demand that the child be painted with a lighter skin color caused some citizens to stage a large, peaceful anti-racist demonstration at the mural. Most of the participants were younger people of a more liberal bent.

A recall petition to have Steve Blair either issue an apology and undergo tolerance and diversity training or be removed from City Council was started by Barbara Braswell, a younger Unitarian Universalist woman. Too few people remained committed and the movement lost its steam. The vitriol of the good old boys and other conservatives in town dissuaded those who spoke up at the City Council town meeting advocating for an end to the racist practices in the town. The bigots seemed to outnumber those who desire to dismantle racism and see the town become more inclusive of all its citizens.

A while after we left the Unitarian Congregation, we decided to visit a few other more liberal area churches. We visited Unity Church and the United Methodist Church and eventually The Church of Spiritual Living, now The Center For Spiritual Living, which is a Science of Mind organization. I have not yet found another church that resonates with me but I did have an opportunity to sing at The Church of Spiritual Living. In looking for someone to accompany me on piano, a woman who joined the Unitarian Congregation after I left was recommended. Joan, too, was a retired school teacher. We enjoyed practicing and performing together at the church.

I was paid twenty-five dollars for each performance, fifteen of which I gave to Joan, keeping just ten for myself. Rather than splitting the stipend in half, I wanted to make sure that Joan did not feel treated unfairly or imposed upon. We did some performances at area nursing homes also and Joan seemed to enjoy the opportunities as much as I did. Gene was our agent, making contacts and arranging for our volunteer performances. Joan was hired for some other gigs as a result and she was happy for the exposure and experience.

We had lunch together a couple of times; once, I treated her. The topic of our mutual teaching experiences came up and Joan told me about a racial incident that happened at her school in Minnesota. She became quite emotional and animated as she told about a situation in which she was apparently trying to help some African American parents get a school-related benefit for their children. She felt that the parents had somehow turned on her or been ungrateful to her after she felt that she had gone out of her way to be helpful to them, unlike some of her colleagues.

She sounded resentful after all that time and was still not able to understand their anger. I knew too little about the situation to understand where the anger of the parents came from or why? Joan felt angry, hurt and insulted by their apparent ingratitude "after all she did for them". What I did realize once again is how difficult it is for most white people to deal with anything that sounds remotely like anger from Black people. Any expression of dissatisfaction or anger on the part of Black people, no matter how justifiable, seems so upsetting and puzzling to many whites. Many seem to need to feel heroic and want to be showered with the praise and thanks that they feel is owed to them.

I remember that years ago, tennis champion Arthur Ashe was asked who he would choose to be if he could be someone else. He said he would be John McEnroe. When asked why, he said because John McEnroe, as a white man, was allowed to express his anger and that as a Black man, he himself did not have that luxury. That story speaks volumes about the self-control that people of color have to exhibit in order not to scare white people or become further maligned by them.

Until we can have those honest conversations and come to a deeper understanding about the differences between the black and the white experience in America, it will be difficult to build trust and to relate on more meaningful levels. Until that happens, relationships will be superficial and lack the level of trust necessary for the nurturing of intimacy and true friendship. This is not just a black and white issue of course but an issue that we all must confront in order to break through the things that divide and separate races, religions and cultures and keep us in an attitude of "us" and "them".

Gene and I both realize that we cannot cure the world of racism but we have worked diligently to try and make a difference in our own small ways.

THE STUFF OF LIFE

Generally, we are ones who see the glass half full rather than half empty. We have, therefore, enjoyed the geographic beauty of the

Southwest and have tried to live as fully and productively as possible.

Despite aging and some health challenges, we consider ourselves very fortunate. We have worked out a division of labor between us that enables us to keep up with the housework, shopping and other chores and have hired assistance with housecleaning, gardening and incidentals that prove difficult to handle.

Family visits from our children and their families have been especially enjoyable. We had hoped to travel East to visit them more often but since air travel has become more of an ordeal since 9/11, we have not done as much traveling as we thought we would. Neuropathy has affected Gene's mobility somewhat and fibromyalgia and chronic fatigue have made travel more difficult for me also. Even so, we have made a few trips back East to visit family and friends and for the Bar and Bat Mitzvahs of the grandchildren.

We have made any number of road trips exploring places and things of interest in Arizona, New Mexico and other parts of the Southwest, including visits to Las Vegas to visit son Dino and for a reunion there with my siblings. Once, we rented a motor home to try out the concept of RV-ing. We concluded that it probably would not work too well for us since we had already bought and sold two motor homes after becoming disillusioned.

We have driven to the San Francisco area a few times to see my brother, Samuel, who has health issues and to southern California to visit Gene's son Nat and family. We always try to extend these travels with side trips and tours. We took a fantastic Alaska cruise for our tenth anniversary in July of 2000. That was a memorable follow-up to our renewal of vows ceremony at Temple B'rith Shalom. Most of our children and local friends attended the ceremony followed by a lovely reception.

The tragic events of 9/11 dampened our enthusiasm for foreign travel but we decided to treat ourselves to a ten day romantic get-away and went to Jamaica in the West Indies for Valentine's Day in 2007.

THE REZ WAGON

Before we came to Arizona, we knew that we would like to learn more about the various Indian tribes in the area. We knew of some of the difficulties of living on the reservation and thought we might be able to assist in some way. Gene had no delusions about becoming the Great White Father of Manifest Destiny and even with my Cherokee/Tuscarora heritage, I did not want to be perceived as an Indian Wannabe coming in arrogance to help save the tribes.

Gene and I talked it over and decided that through the organization called Futures For Children, we could sponsor a Native American child for a few hundred dollars a year and correspond with the child and his family. We chose a boy from the Hopi Reservation whom we could travel to visit and establish a relationship with the family. The family turned out to be troubled and struggling with many of the dysfunctions that plague families and individuals on the reservations: problems of poverty, alcohol and drug abuse, domestic abuse, suicide, high dropout rates for students, diabetes and other health issues and general feelings of hopelessness.

Seeing the conditions, we decided that some corporal works would mean a great deal to our sisters and brothers on the Rez so we sent out to friends and associates a solicitation for used clean clothing and household goods. We wound up with over six hundred pounds of clean, usable clothing and other items.

We bought a bright red flat-bed trailer and called it The Rez Wagon. We loaded it up, tied it down and delivered the goods to the reservation just before Christmas. The little children there thought Gene was Santa Claus as he unloaded the trailer, hoisting large garbage bags filled with clothing on his back. His white beard and whiskers made him a very convincing Santa. In fact, one shy little fellow who had remained on the edge of the crowd crept up behind Gene and swatted him on the backside. "I know where you live," he said, "The North Pole!"

When we returned home, our phone was still ringing with offers to contribute more clothing and household goods for the Indians. We rented a storage facility and bought a bigger trailer and we sorted, hauled and schlepped usable goods first to the Hopi and then to the Navajo Reservation for several years.

This mission probably did more for us than it did for the recipients. It took a while to earn their trust but in time, we created a network of friends and contacts with churches, Chapter Houses and social agencies throughout both reservations. We brought our little Hopi friend whom we sponsored home for a few visits with us. His first trip off the Rez was an adventure. He had never seen traffic lights or eaten in restaurants. He could not believe that we actually bought rocks for landscaping our yard when there were so many free rocks of many colors and sizes on the reservation. He asked where we got the rocks and when we told him that we bought them, he asked incredulously, "You *bought* rocks?"

We began to learn about the Indian cultures and even picked up a few words of the difficult Navajo and Hopi languages. We became involved with several schools and with the two tribal colleges, becoming mentors to some of the students and offering some nominal scholarship aid to several of them. We see education as the way to a better life for the youth on the reservations. Teaching them to fish rather than just feeding them for a day seems like the wisest approach.

The economic downturn of the last few years has had a tremendous impact on us as it has on most Americans and regretfully, we have had to curtail some of our charitable giving. We have also not been physically able to do as much collecting, hauling and schlepping of goods to the Rez. We hope to do as much as we can for as long as we can. We are grateful for the generosity of all the people who donated clothing, household goods and even a couple of wood stoves to heat homes in remote areas of the Rez. Homes frequently burn down and families lose everything when homemade stoves fashioned from oil drums burn through or malfunction. I suspect that carbon monoxide poisoning is a serious concern also.

WHEN YOU HAVE REACHED THE END OF YOUR ROPE, TIE A KNOT AND HANG ON

God has been good to us and we feel bountifully blessed. Some rain falls into every life. Instead of waiting for all the storms to pass, we are learning to dance in the rain. As the seasons roll, great is the faithfulness of God who sustains us. Joys and sorrows come and go but these words of St. Francis de Sales, posted on my desk blotter remind me daily to "Have no fear for what tomorrow will bring. The same loving God who cares for you today will take care of you tomorrow and every day. He will either shield you from suffering or give you unfailing strength to bear it. Be at peace, then, and put aside all anxious thoughts and imaginations." May I remain ever mindful of this promise, especially in moments of weakness and grief.

In the natural order of things, and certainly in a fair world, parents expect to die before their children. Life, however, is not fair. No one ever said that it was. In our desire and hopefulness, we sometimes expect it to be until experience teaches us that our assumptions are false. We work hard and play by the rules and still, bad things happen. We see people who appear less deserving prosper all around us and we question the fairness of it. We see innocent children and good people suffer and we ask why. Sometimes, we tend to think that we ourselves deserve more than our lot.

Some of the gurus tell us that we attract misfortune into our lives through The Law of Attraction and that it is our own fault if we are not as happy, prosperous, healthy and successful as we wish to be. So then, on top of the misfortune, we heap self-blame and guilt upon our already burdened souls.

To think positively and to maintain an attitude of gratitude is by all means desirable and has its own merits, but can these measures protect us from life's tragedies and the misfortunes that befall so many of those who with all their hearts endeavor to live righteously? Will justice ultimately prevail? Will they like Job of the Bible be rewarded many times over for having remained faithful?

On a cool spring day, in Yarnell, Arizona, I sat before the shrine of St. Joseph the Worker. I shivered in the shadow of the Cross, my prayers trying to find their way to Heaven. My questions found no answers, only more questions. Four years had passed since that day when my life was forever changed.

He was young, my son, Joseph Mario, only forty-four when he lay dying as Gene and I kept vigil beside his hospital bed. Mario had been born in this very hospital at Albert Einstein Medical Center. I held him then, soon after he took his first breath, and I held him as he took his last breath and transcended the agonies of illness and suffering; his spirit at last set free. No more pain and no more sorrow for my child, who through no fault of his own arrived on the planet with birth defects that would make life for him a difficult journey.

A flood of memories washed over me as I sat before the shrine on this fourth anniversary of Mario's death. Who knew that the feelings would still be so fresh and raw? In a flash, I took an instant trip back in time. The years passed vividly before my eyes. I could smell the antiseptic cleanliness of the delivery room. I could hear the words, "It's a boy!" as my beautiful child was placed in my arms. I could feel him move. I could hear him cry. I could see his eyes squint under the bright lights as I whispered, "Welcome to the world!" And I loved him fiercely.

Mario was born with a blood incompatibility that required a complete exchange transfusion. A couple of days after he was born, he became jaundiced. His skin and eyes took on a yellow hue and I noticed that the shape of his head seemed slightly irregular. The doctor reassured me that his head would round out and explained that the positional crowding in the womb sometimes caused this to happen. Of more immediate concern was the life-saving exchange transfusion.

When I questioned the doctor about the risks of this procedure, I was told that it was absolutely necessary and he did not discourage me, but rather helped me to arrange for Mario to receive emergency Baptism. A priest came to the hospital from Holy Child Catholic Church just a few blocks away.

It had been a difficult pregnancy and delivery. I was weak and fragile but my concern was for my baby. As is customary in

Catholic tradition, boy babies who receive the Sacrament of Baptism under emergency circumstances are given the name Joseph in honor of St. Joseph, the husband of Mary. In such instances baby girls are given the name Mary or Maria in honor of Mary, the Mother of Jesus. I therefore chose Mario as my baby's middle name for extra protection. I was also an avid fan of Mario Lanza, famed tenor, and I always loved the name Mario, though that was not uppermost in my mind that day.

Mario had to remain in the hospital for several days after my release. It felt odd to return home with empty arms and it was awkward to explain to three and four-year old Cindy and Dino that their new baby brother was sick and had to remain in the hospital for a while. With my duties of caring for a newborn postponed for a while, I used the time to recover and to reestablish my bond with Dino and Cindy and prepare them for the baby's homecoming.

My marriage had reached an all time low during the pregnancy. Frank was having an affair with a woman at work, though he denied it, and actually claimed to be unable to understand why I would not permit the other woman to be Mario's godmother when the official Baptismal ceremony took place at St. Benedict's, our parish church. I stood my ground and chose the twelve and thirteen-year-old children of my friends, the Vitali and Craig families, to be Mario's god-parents. The other woman boldly showed up for Mario's Baptism. I was naive enough to believe that seeing our family together in this setting would give her pangs of conscience. Perhaps it did because she relocated to another state shortly thereafter. I should have known by then not to be too relieved as there would be a series of others to replace her.

Mario seemed to thrive physically but I continued to question the doctors about his slow development. His head had not rounded out. I groomed his thick, curly hair in such a way as to compensate for the lopsidedness of his head. He was a beautiful child sharing the same gorgeous, lightly tanned hue of his siblings' complexion. His eyes, which started out hazel, developed into a deep brown, fringed by lush, long eyelashes fit for a mascara commercial.

When Mario was finally diagnosed with a premature closure of the sutures or fontanel, I was devastated. The neurosurgeon would have to open his skull in two places and line the openings with a material that would eventually dissolve. This would keep the skull open and able to expand normally as his brain grew and developed.

By the grace of God, after the surgery and recovery, Mario began to catch up and tested well within normal I.Q. range by the time he entered school. He excelled in music and art and got on well with his peers. He was an affectionate, cheerful, loving, funny and demonstrative child who was well liked and made friends easily. These traits characterized him throughout his life.

After all the testing that was known by the child guidance people at that time, no one seemed able to name specifically the condition that caused the hyperactivity and lack of impulse control that characterized Mario's behavior at times. There were apparent learning disabilities that were labeled dyslexia by the psychologists. Today, Mario would probably be diagnosed as having ADHD (Attention Deficit Hyperactivity Disorder).

When at last I was healthy enough to pursue my teaching career, the stresses of urban school teaching, being in a dysfunctional marriage and parenting a special needs child was more than challenging. Somehow, one day at a time, I got up each morning, clothed myself in faith and prayer and did what had to be done. Will and determination more than strength and stamina kept me going. Quitting was not an option. I had to work and free my children and me from the cruel circumstances of our lives. I finally filed for divorce and began the annulment process.

SEASONS OF GRIEF AND SORROW

Some years later, I could look back and see how far the children and I had come, how much we had undergone and how much we had overcome. Mario had courageously worked his twelve-step programs for alcohol and drug abuse. We did not yet realize that a food addiction had replaced the addictions to drugs and alcohol. Mario seemed on the road to recovery having earned his associates degree with top honors. He looked forward to a career in computer graphic arts and related fields.

Dino and Cindy (Sunshine) had settled into their respective lifestyles. I was in a loving marriage with Gene and he was all that I could wish for in a husband and more than I could wish for as a step-father to my now adult children. A man among men, Gene stepped up to the plate and showed me how a real husband and father behaves. Always there for me and for my adult children, grandchildren and extended family, he has my deepest love, highest respect and greatest admiration.

Gene supported me with his love at all times. At the same time, he did all that he could to support and encourage Mario, to give firm guidance and financial support and whatever would help Mario to become self-supporting, independent and established in a career. It was not to be. Mario succumbed to his food addiction, became grossly and morbidly obese and his health failed rapidly.

First came the usual health problems associated with obesity, problems of hypertension and high cholesterol, sleep apnea and eventually hospitalization with congestive heart failure. I tried not to think of the average five year survival rate in cases of congestive heart failure. I almost succeeded in convincing myself that Mario would be an exception. I could not yet wrap my mind around the fact that my youngest child's life would be shortened. I survived by functioning in a state of denial emotionally, though intellectually I knew what the statistics said. I even began to prepare Dino and Cindy (Sunshine) for the eventuality by sharing the statistical data. Like me, I think they protected themselves by not allowing the reality to penetrate on an emotional level.

Mario experienced breathing problems and chest pains which took him to the hospital emergency room in early March of 2007. He underwent many medical tests before exploratory surgery revealed an inoperable, malignant mass in his chest. When Gene and I arrived at the hospital in Philadelphia, we were shocked by Mario's condition and by all the tubes and medical paraphernalia that surrounded him.

He was conscious and lucid when we arrived and remained so throughout our brief visit with him. He was tired and his speech was slurred, we assumed from sedation. He said that he was not experiencing much pain. I fed him Cheerios with sliced peaches for breakfast. I don't remember what other items were on his tray along with a can of Canada Dry Ginger Ale. After he ate the cereal and fruit, he asked for some ginger ale but his fluid intake was being carefully monitored and he was not permitted to drink anything for another hour. I promised to give him the ginger ale as soon as we returned from talking with his doctors in a nearby conference room.

We were still thinking that Mario would recover and that we needed to make arrangements for his convalescence after his release from the hospital. We met with a team of very grave-looking doctors and were unprepared for the devastating information they imparted. We were told that Mario's condition was terminal. He had hours, perhaps days at most to live. I convinced myself that it would be days at least. To think otherwise was unbearable.

Numbness and disbelief gave way to feelings of horror and inner pain like I have never felt before. My baby was dying! This child that I carried under my heart and loved and felt move within me; this cheerful child who needed me and whom I had protected throughout his difficult childhood, was dying. This child, my child, who had endured so much suffering on this earth was dying, never having fully realized his dreams or my dreams for him.

I remember wanting to howl and rage at the unfairness of it. I held the screams inside as I clung to Gene and let the silent tears fall down my face. The doctors quietly disappeared, these angels of mercy and bearers of bad news who could do no more for Mario or for us. They needed to move on and save the saveable. They could only keep Mario comfortable.

Mario was sedated and asleep when we returned to his room. We sat for a long time thinking he would awaken and have his ginger ale. He did not awaken. I never saw my son conscious again.

A kind, gentle, woman resident doctor, Indian I think, came to talk with me about signing a DNR (Do Not Resuscitate order). I knew I did not want to prolong Mario's suffering of drowning in his own fluids, but I could not bring myself to sign at that moment. I wanted Mario to wake up just once more. I wanted him to have his ginger ale.

After praying and thinking aloud with Gene, I knew what I had to do and it was my decision and my duty to let nature take its course and grant Mario the dignity of a peaceful death. I owed him that and I loved him too much to do otherwise. I signed the DNR, and the next phase of the painful process of letting go began. Mario slept into the evening and we decided to take our weary souls and bodies back to the hotel for some nourishment and sleep in order to be functional the next day.

Each time the phone rang that evening, we dreaded answering it. Phil, one of Mario's best friends, called to let us know that he, Mario's deacon from his church and three other friends had visited Mario soon after we left. They spent some time with him and prayed with him. They had all been friends since their grade school days. Phil said that Mario gave them a thumbs-up as they left.

We called Cindy (Sunshine) and her husband, Tony to alert them. They planned to meet us at the hospital the following morning and to bring Jason, Julian and his family. I talked with Dino who began checking the airlines for flights to Philadelphia. I did not have contact information with me for old friends in Philadelphia nor the inclination or energy to try and locate them. It took all my strength just to cope moment by moment.

When Gene and I arrived at the hospital the following morning, Mario lay motionless on a bed of fresh white linens, all quiet and still but for the sound of his labored breathing and the rise and fall of his chest. He did not respond as we softly called his name and tenderly stroked him. As he lay peacefully dying, off the ventilator and the array of life support equipment removed from the room, he looked so serene with only a small apparatus over his mouth and nose to ease his breathing. He looked so much like the sweet, helpless babe that I held in my arms forty-four years before with no clue about all that lay ahead. I could not fathom then that my child would precede me in death, breaking my heart wide open.

I prayed silently as I held my son and released him into the arms of God. I said the Twenty-third Psalm and the Lord's Prayer aloud and I told Mario that it was okay for him to leave, that I would be alright and that I would meet him in Heaven when my time came.

Gene had gone out of the room to call Cindy and Tony, who were enroute to the hospital, to let them know that time was running out. Jason was delayed enroute. Soon after Gene returned and just before Cindy (Sunshine), Tony and Julian and family arrived, Mario took a deep breath and then seemed to stop breathing. This happened a second time and then a third. The third time, breathing did not resume. He was gone to a better place.

I the mournful mother wept, feeling close to Mary who held her crucified Son, Jesus, in her arms after He was taken down from the cross on Calvary. My son would not rise in three days. I could only trust in God's promise and blessed assurance that the soul is immortal and everlasting and that eternal life will be made manifest. That faith enabled me to remain sane and to traverse the thickets on the road through mourning and unimaginable grief without being totally destroyed. Even so, I could not wish my precious son back to earth to suffer such pain again. He had beat the odds again and again. He had fought a good fight. He had run a brave and grueling race. He had won the victor's cup.

TO HEAL THE GRIEVING HEART

The process of letting go is not linear in its stages. The journey toward healing and reconciliation has continued by the grace of God. Perhaps the journey never truly ends until it has gone full circle and our own work on earth is done.

And so, I sat before the shrine of St. Joseph realizing why the loved ones left behind are called "survivors". The word took on new meaning. I had survived for four years since Mario's death and it had forever changed me. I would always be a mother who had lost a son, but I had to realize that I was other things too and I had to learn to fully embrace all those other parts of myself and to run my own race, giving it my personal best.

Next to me at the shrine and tenderly holding my hand, sat the most loving man in all the world, my husband, my hero, my beloved Gene. My mind flashed back to that hospital room when I kissed my son, my grown-up baby boy good-bye, trying to memorize every feature of his sweet face. I walked away from his lifeless body, lying in silent repose, motionless, quiet and still.

Supported by Gene, my tower of strength, my legs felt too heavy and too weak to ambulate.

Gene calmly assembled the family in the chapel of the hospital. We eventually proceeded to notify extended family and friends by cell phone as we comforted each other and those whose voices came to us over the miles.

At some point, I talked to my friends Rev. Dick Cox and Terri McNamara, who were members of First United Methodist Church of Germantown (FUMCOG) dating back to the 1980's when I was a member. The congregation at FUMCOG had embraced me as a divorced single mother and the church became a place of growth and healing for me. I treasure my spiritual family of which Dick, his wife Julie, my friend Terri and others are a part. They offered their condolences and any assistance that they could render. Dick contacted the current pastor of FUMCOG, Rev. Michele Wright Bartlow, who happened to be out of town.

A few months before his death, in casual conversation, Mario had expressed to me that he wished to be cremated after his death, whenever that occurred. Who knew it would occur so soon?

Together, Gene and I went to the funeral home to make the final arrangements after the rest of the family had dispersed. The first funeral homes that we had called left us feeling less than confident. From my days in Philadelphia, I remembered the family owned and operated Emmanuel Johnson's Funeral Home, an African American establishment, as having a good reputation, so we chose them. They were very professional and were most reassuring and accommodating.

Rev. Michele Wright Bartlow returned from her trip and graciously organized a tasteful, comforting, dignified and lovely memorial service for Mario. The eulogy, prayers, hymns and organ music were all so fitting. The personal reflections shared by Mario's closest friends touched my heart and comforted me. Mario was a very spiritual person and I think he was pleased with the small but beautiful tribute. I think his spirit felt honored by the presence of family and friends who loved him for his goodness of heart and the courage with which he faced adversity. He looked for the best in people and dealt bravely with hardship and trials without bitterness. "Be of good cheer" seemed to be his mantra.

My step-son, David, drove all the way up from Wilmington, Delaware to attend the memorial service. His son Aaron, our grandson, was making his acting debut in a high school play that evening which meant that David would have to fight rush hour traffic in order to get back home in time for the curtain call. I was deeply touched that Dave would make this huge sacrifice in order to be with us. Nat was far away in California but my other step-children, Jerry and Brie, were at Dave and Sue's home when we arrived in Wilmington the following day. Just to be able to exchange hugs was a great comfort. I have little recollection of Aaron's matinee performance. Through the brain fog of grief, I could not focus or concentrate clearly enough to remember. Everything still seemed unreal as I struggled to keep my composure and not make others uncomfortable.

We brought Mario's ashes back with us to Prescott. Gene and I made plans for an intimate family memorial service to be held in May, at the Shrine of St. Joseph, a place that was special to Mario and to us. Joseph Mario's ashes were dispersed near the shrine of the saint for whom he was named.

Sunshine and Tony each wrote lovely poems to honor Mario and they shared them during the service. Dino and Lori, his girlfriend, drove over from Las Vegas to participate. Through some horrible breakdown in communication right after Mario's death, they had decided not to come to Philadelphia. Had my mind not been so muddled by grief, I'm sure I would have detected and corrected the mix-up sooner.

Gene and I were occupied and preoccupied, hurriedly and busily running around in a haze trying to make final arrangements for Mario. We were in a state of sleep deprivation and exhaustion, having kept vigil at the hospital for the preceding days. Between age, my fibromyalgia and Gene's neuropathy, we were both pushed beyond our physical and emotional limits.

True to habit, my protective instincts kicked in. My main concern was to help my surviving children cope with the loss of their brother as well as possible. Grief sometimes brings out the worst in families. Behaviors are sometimes irrational and misunderstood and things are sometimes said and done that are difficult to undo. Some misunderstandings happen because of omission rather than commission. It is difficult to know or to remember just the right thing to say and do at every moment.

I endeavored to support my children rather than rely on them to support me. I wanted to spare them as much pain as possible. I guess I still have not learned to let go of the need to be strong for everyone else, even to my own detriment. Only later did I come to realize that putting my own grieving on hold had later repercussions and delayed my grieving process. But I was not my own first priority; my children were. I also felt a strong need to shield Gene. Deep down, I think I had fears of losing control and of being abandoned because of it. Old stories of marriages that went down the tubes after the death of a child haunted me. I was too eager to recover quickly before I caused worry or trouble for anyone, including Gene. I wanted to make sure that my surviving children did not feel neglected while I was wrapped up in my own grief.

I am slowly learning that I cannot take care of others unless I also take care of myself. I am learning that Wonder Woman is a myth and that I am not she. My history has been one of taking care of others and remaining the calm and controlled one in times of crisis. In some instances, trying to maintain that role is unreasonable. The death of a child is indeed one of those instances.

The appearance of eagles became a common phenomenon following Mario's death. The first incident occurred in April, soon after we returned from Philadelphia. Gene and I went to the shrine for some quiet time and reflection. We were half way up the hill following The Stations of the Cross when we heard the call of what looked like a golden eagle circling overhead. In fascination, we watched its graceful gliding for a long time and its presence was comforting and peaceful. We later confided in each other that the feeling had seemed mystical and supernatural.

The second incident occurred about a week later while Gene was at the market. I sat in the kitchen talking to Sunshine on the phone. As I told her about the eagle at the shrine, a huge shadow came over the kitchen window like a cloud obscuring the sun. I looked up to see what again looked like a golden eagle swoop past the window and stare at me. I was not frightened but quite stunned and awestruck and nearly speechless as I described the experience to Sunshine over the phone.

When Gene came home, we decided to hang a painting that Mario had done of a Native American man playing a flute as an eagle loomed over his right shoulder. Several times after that, I inadvertently turned on the radio just in time to hear a rendition of the song "On Eagle's Wings", an adaptation of Psalm 91. The beauty of the song and the Psalm always made me cry with its description of God's loving protection. The song was one of my favorite solos to sing in church. It was written by Michael Joncas, a Catholic priest, and it ends with these inspiring words:

> *And He will raise you up on eagle's wings,*
> *Bear you on the breath of dawn,*
> *Make you to shine like the sun,*
> *And hold you in the palm of His Hand.*
> *For to His angels He's given a command*
> *To guard you in all of your ways;*
> *Upon their hands they will bear you up,*
> *Lest you dash your foot against a stone.*
>
> *And He will raise you up on eagle's wings,*
> *Bear you on the breath of dawn,*
> *Make you to shine like the sun,*
> *And hold you in the palm of His Hand.*
> *And hold you in the palm of His Hand.*

The third incident happened at the close of the family memorial service at the shrine after we dispersed Mario's ashes. Several of the majestic raptors flew over in formation. It was a breathtaking sight and a fitting send off for my son, the artist who painted eagles.

And yes, on this fourth anniversary of Mario's death, a golden eagle appeared on the crest of the hill overlooking the shrine and the Stations of the Cross as Gene and I stood on the craggy pathway just below the image of the Crucifixion. "They that wait upon the Lord shall renew their strength; they shall mount up with wings as eagles; they shall run and not be weary; and they shall walk and not faint." (Isaiah 40:31)

In American Indian cultures, the eagle is a strong, spiritual symbol, a sacred messenger who carries our prayers to the Creator on its powerful wings. Perhaps some would say that the repeated appearances of eagles following Mario's death was all coincidence and wishful thinking. I choose to believe that they had a much deeper meaning.

On March 15, 2008, almost a year to the date of Mario's death, the slowly healing wounds are reopened. We were notified of the sudden death of our seventeen-year-old step-grandson, Joshua. Josh was the youngest son of Sunshine's husband, Tony. Josh became a part of the family when Tony and Sunshine got married. He was only five-years-old at the time.

Josh collapsed on the basketball court after making the winning shot for his high school team in Pottstown, Pennsylvania. He was rushed to the hospital where he was pronounced dead. The autopsy showed that Josh died of an undetected enlarged heart. Josh was a beautiful boy whom everyone loved and we were all shocked and pained by his sudden death.

God, in His mercy, does give us respite and times of joy down the road but the place that a deceased child leaves in the heart of a parent cannot be filled. We try to honor our departed children with our lives by living them as fully as possible going forward and doing good things in their names. We make the road map as we go and faith lights the way. Ever so tenderly, time brings healing to the sorrow and ever so gently, peace replaces the heartache.

From the day we arrive on this beautiful planet called Mother Earth, Life presents us with many paths and we have a multitude of choices about which path we will take. In faith, we may choose the Road Less Traveled not knowing where it might lead or what the journey might be like. We might be more cautious and look for a smoother appearing, flower-strewn path but as we journey onward, there are no guarantees as to road conditions ahead. There might be mud, hurdles, washed out bridges, stumbling blocks, ruts and detours ahead. Whatever our lot, we must complete the journey. We cannot tell whether the journey will be a slow trek or a swift race.

I decided long ago to ask God to "Guide my feet, while I run this race." I learned early on that faith is the premium fuel for high performance. I also learned that I could throw in the towel or I could use it to wipe the sweat from my face and keep on running. I learned that losers quit when they are tired but that winners keep going.

THE SERENITY OF ACCEPTANCE

Nothing can undo the painful experiences of the past but love has the power to heal. My husband Gene's tenderness, nurturing, love and understanding have caused the memories to fade into the distant mist and lose their power. Therefore, when I am gone from this earth, I hope that those who might weep for me will not weep for long, knowing that my years with Gene have been gloriously happy and fulfilling. Ours has been the kind of passion, love, contentment and spiritual connection that many dream of but find beyond their reach; the substance of dreams and wishes; a great love story of the immortal kind.

Before Gene came into my life, the love of my three children and my deep love for them was the driving force that kept me alive. Even when times were dark and it would have been easy to give up, I knew that for my children, I had to find the will, the courage and the strength to push on. They deserved so much more than the legacy of abuse and neglect left by their father.

When Dino went into the Air Force, he stopped communicating with his father altogether. His father never reached out to him to try and mend the breach in any way. Mario also gave up on trying to maintain a relationship with Frank and considered his father dead.

My grandson, Jason, conducted an Internet search and contacted Frank as Mario lay dying in the hospital. He also told him of the memorial service at FUMCOG when Mario died. Frank told Jason that it would be better if he did not show up. It probably was better for most likely, Frank would have done something inappropriate and hurtful had he shown up. He had failed to show up for his family on so many occasions over so many years that a death was probably not the best time to finally show up.

Sunshine tried for years to maintain a relationship with her father and to have him in her life. She eventually concluded that his meanness, sarcasm, narcissism and bitterness were too toxic and hurtful to her and she refused to have her children exposed to his unpredictable and volatile pathology.

Reconciliation between my children and their father seems remote at this point. Time alone does nothing to heal and to mend if responsibility is not taken and if efforts are not made to right wrongs, make amends, earn trust and ask forgiveness. None of this has ever happened. As I have learned to forgive and let go, I have encouraged my beloved children to do the same, as a gift to themselves for their own freedom and well-being. It has been difficult for Dino and I still worry about how the anger negatively affects his life. Sunshine seems to be more able to let go and to move on without as much burdensome baggage.

It is neither simple nor easy to heal those wounds but it is necessary in order to free the soul and to enjoy the fullness of life. Thus we pray in the words of the Serenity Prayer: "God, grant me the serenity to accept the things I cannot change; courage to change the things I can; and wisdom to know the difference."

Although we have been wounded by life, mentally, emotionally and physically, healing is a conscious process and we are not defined by our wounds. What matters is how we have responded and moved forward, becoming stronger in the broken places.

THE COURAGE AND THE WILL TO HEAL

When quitting is not an option, courage is what keeps me going. I love the quote by Mary Anne Radmacher which says, "Courage doesn't always roar. Sometimes courage is the quiet voice at the end of the day saying, 'I will try again tomorrow.'"

Life, by any measure, is an unpredictable mix of joys and sorrows. The dimension of race and ethnicity added to this mixture adds exponentially to its complexity. I am humbly grateful for those principles that have guided and emboldened me and enabled me to live through both the trials and the triumphs of my life. I do not fear being labeled a non-conformist, a rule-breaker or a free-spirited pioneer. I think I was born hardwired to help change the world in my own small way. As a woman of color, it has not always been easy.

Those who have not experienced the wear and tear caused by chronic racial battering sometimes find it difficult to understand why we cannot "just get over it". We are certainly told to often enough and the absence of empathy in itself is more injurious than some of the more open and direct assaults. The gross lack of understanding and humanity add insult to injury.

Often, added to these is the ultimate insult of the people who self-righteously lecture people of color on how they should feel, think, act and respond to these attacks on our personhood. "If only you people would do this (or that), you wouldn't have these problems", they pontificate. Then comes the sermonizing about working harder, speaking differently, styling the hair differently and an endless list of things to change, falling just short of a suggestion to bleach the skin and modify the features with plastic surgery. In other words, "Be white like me", they are saying. "Being yourself is not good enough."

This relentless devaluing of a person's color, culture and heritage is injurious on many levels and it begins at birth. Consider the impossible role models and standards of beauty which society urges us to aspire to and to emulate. It takes work, courage and chutzpah to resist and to minimize the psychological damage inflicted by the dominant culture. It takes daring just to be ME!

Not everyone is strong enough to avoid an identity crisis. Some people comply and conform so much that they lose themselves, their individuality, their unique and special qualities, their very souls. The stress may become too formidable, the cost too great, leading to dysfunction or rage.

To maintain one's integrity and to remain true to one's self is an exercise in valor, fortitude, faith and mindfulness. The miracle is that so many people of color do manage to overcome the many obstacles and limitations imposed and do achieve far beyond expectation. The remarkable strength of the human spirit and the amazing grace of a Higher Power cause extraordinary things to happen and cannot be denied or underestimated.

The hopes and dreams of those visionaries who have worked for peace, justice, liberty and equality have power and possibility. They dared to dream a different world. Let them be our motivation and our inspiration to continue the struggle, "Until justice rolls down like water and righteousness like a mighty stream." —Martin Luther King, Jr.

We need one another as friends, neighbors, sisters and brothers to tear down the walls of hate and indifference that separate and divide and to build bridges of love and understanding that unite and heal. Our profound hope is that our white sisters and brothers will come out of denial and recognize and acknowledge that they enjoy a host of advantages and unearned privileges. These privileges of white skin color come as a result of slavery, Jim Crow and other egregious, systemic practices that are part of our national history. The bitter legacy continues today. It keeps us locked in our separate prisons of fear and dishonesty and in the unequal roles of oppressor and oppressed.

The oppressor blames the victim and the victim gets stuck in victimhood. All become prisoners and no one is really free. No one wins. The oppressor becomes angry and defensive to justify the continuation of oppression and the victim becomes angry and tired of the foot on his neck.

We have made progress to be sure. That is undeniably true. Still, the playing field is not level and there are those who continue to fan the flames of fear and intolerance. Racism has morphed into an insidious neo-racism that is covert, institutional and systemic. A few minorities are allowed to rise high enough to give the illusion of equality and a level playing field, but the glass ceiling is all too real as is the invisible quota and few are permitted to go beyond these restrictive covenants.

As people of color, we must think like survivors, not victims. We have come far and we must not lose the gains for which we have fought and died. We must take advantage of the doors that open and push them wider for our children. We must not use the oppressions of the past or the covert racism of the present as excuses not to live up to our fullest potential. We must lift each other up and work for the good of all. This is our country and we are worthy citizens with the rights and responsibilities of every other citizen. In our pluralistic society, we must allow our better angels to prevail and we must keep the dream alive until there is liberty and justice for all. Our country's strength is in our diversity.

Take my hand, sisters and brothers of all hues. Let us lift each other up and make a rainbow circle. I open my circle to take you in. Close not your circle to keep me out. We can run this race of life together, no winners or losers. We can cross the finish line together, triumphant and free: free from anger, hurt and pain; free from fear and hostility; free from xenophobia and thoughts of oppression; free to create a new and different paradigm based on solidarity and mutual respect.

Our destinies are intertwined and we are forever linked. As John Donne said, "No man is an island, entire of itself; every man is a piece of the continent, a part of the main." Our most basic moral principles tell us that we are equal and connected in the heart and mind of the Creator. We human beings win or lose together. We make false starts; we stumble and fall; we get up and brush ourselves off and begin again, striving toward the harmony, peace and justice for which we yearn. Let us run together with hopeful hearts and clear intention toward these attainable goals.

With our faces turned toward tomorrow, let us join hands today. Let us lift up our voices until the heavens ring with the melody and words of an old African American spiritual.

> *"Guide my feet while I run this race.*
> *Guide my feet while I run this race.*
> *Guide my feet, Lord, while I run this race,*
> *For I don't want to run this race in vain."*

PHOTOS
&
UPDATES

POCAHONTAS (POCO) GERTLER

**HIGH SCHOOL
VALEDICTORIAN 1950**

COLLEGE CO-ED 1952

AIR FORCE 1956

AIR FORCE 1957

POCAHONTAS (POCO) GERTLER

WIFE & MOTHER 1975

SCHOOL TEACHER 1985

GENE & POCO 1990

POCO & GENE 2011

GENE AND POCO GERTLER

HON. BOB STUMP

OF ARIZONA
IN THE HOUSE OF REPRESENTATIVES
Thursday, October 3, 2002

Mr. STUMP. Mr. Speaker, I rise today to pay tribute to the spirit of charity and two very good people in my district.

Gene and Poco Gertler joined us in Prescott just a few years ago, but they have made quite a difference for our community. While they came to enjoy retirement in Arizona, they ended up working harder than they ever imagined—not for themselves, but to improve the lives of other Arizonans.

One day, while cleaning out closets for the winter, they decided to donate their surplus clothes to the citizens of the Hopi reservation 250 miles north of Prescott. And, since there was extra room in the pickup truck, Gene sent an e-mail to 21 neighbors and friends, giving them the opportunity to add their contributions.

Well, instead of the few bags of clothing Gene and Poco expected, neighbors showed up with over 600 pounds of donations—enough that they had to rent a trailer. Many of the donations came from families the Gertlers didn't know, but who had heard about the trip by word of mouth.

Word continued to spread, and the Gertlers' one-time visit to the reservation became a regular shuttle. Furniture and other household items joined the clothes, and soon there was too much for the pickup and trailer. It seemed like every load was bigger than the last. Many people would be overwhelmed, or say, "I've done my part." Gene and Poco bought a bigger truck and a bigger trailer and kept on hauling.

The years bring new challenges to all of us, and sadly, Gene and Poco have found that they are no longer able to carry on their work. But that wasn't until they had rounded up and personally delivered over 25,000 pounds—yes, over twelve tons—of clothing, furniture, and other assistance for Arizona's Native Americans. All for no remuneration other than knowing they'd helped keep other people warm.

The Bible says, "By their works shall ye know them." We sure know about Gene and Poco. And we are proud to call them our neighbors.

SOCIAL AND RACIAL JUSTICE

AWARD

PRESENTED TO

POCAHONTAS AND GENE GERTLER

BY THE

FIRST UNITED METHODIST CHURCH

OF GERMANTOWN

PHILADELPHIA, PA

MARTIN LUTHER KING SUNDAY

JANUARY 20, 2008

In June 2012, the author became **Dr.** Pocahontas Gertler when Northcentral University bestowed upon her an honorary LHD degree (Doctor of Humane Letters). This honor was in recognition of her lifetime of achievement and service to the community.

Pocahontas had, in her fifties with a teaching career and a family, gone to graduate school evenings and summers, and had received the Master of Education degree. She continued beyond the Masters degree, with the idea of someday achieving her doctorate. Tending to her family and continuing to teach full-time made that impractical, merely deferring her dream, which has now materialized.

A NOTE FROM THE AUTHOR

I hope that reading my book was a positive experience for you, that you learned something about what life was like for a woman of color starting when and where I did, and that I have demonstrated to you what determination, perseverance and faith can overcome. Writing this book, dredging up all of the details of my life, was at times difficult and even gut-wrenching, but I wrote it in honesty for my descendants and for you.

I invite your questions and comments. Please write to me at:

Poco@Gertler.com

Pocahontas Gertler M.Ed., LHD

Made in the USA
San Bernardino, CA
20 March 2019